Teachers
as Allies

Carollyn James

Butterflies are a symbol used in the DREAM Movement to represent migration. They appear fragile but can travel great distances. Butterflies, like DREAMers, thrive in secure and nourishing environments.

Teachers *as* Allies

Transformative Practices for Teaching DREAMers & Undocumented Students

Shelley Wong
Elaisa Sánchez Gosnell
Anne Marie Foerster Luu
Lori Dodson
EDITORS

Foreword by Aviva Chomsky

TEACHERS COLLEGE PRESS

TEACHERS COLLEGE | COLUMBIA UNIVERSITY

NEW YORK AND LONDON

Published by Teachers College Press, 1234 Amsterdam Avenue, New York, NY 10027

Cover design by Rebecca Lown Design. Cover photo by Maryia Ihnatovich / Shutterstock.

This book features artwork by Carollyn James (carollynjames.com).

Library of Congress Cataloging-in-Publication Data is available at loc.gov

ISBN 978-0-8077-5886-1 (paper)
ISBN 978-0-8077-5887-8 (hardcover)
ISBN 978-0-8077-7677-3 (ebook)

Printed on acid-free paper
Manufactured in the United States of America

25   24   23   22   21   20   19   18   8   7   6   5   4   3   2   1

Contents

PART III: ACCESSING, SURVIVING, AND THRIVING: DREAMErs GO TO COLLEGE

PART IV: FINDING, SHARING, AND TRANSFORMING IDENTITY THROUGH ART: DREAMErs PERFORM

PART V: BECOMING AN ALLY

Foreword

In one of the best immigrant films made in the United States, *El Norte*, two young Guatemalan siblings flee to the United States alone after their father is murdered for trying to organize workers on a coffee plantation and their village is occupied by the army. Though the film was released in 1983, it still feels startlingly relevant.

After enduring a harrowing border crossing and mistreatment or scorn from virtually every representative of U.S. government and society they encounter, the young woman, Rosa, meets an older Mexican immigrant, Nacha, who suggests that she sign up for ESL classes. The classes are free; they're run by the government, Nacha explains. Rosa recoils, worrying that she'll be deported. No, Nacha tells her, to Rosa's bewilderment, the *migra* never goes to the public schools. "Look Rosa. If you try to understand the gringos, you're just going to get a terrible headache," Nacha scolds. Indeed, the English teacher offers Rosa and her brother a completely different vision of America than the condescension and exploitation they encounter on the border, in their apartment complex, and in the labor market.

Little has improved for undocumented immigrants in the United States since the 1980s, and much has gotten worse. Under the Trump administration, even Nacha's promise that the *migra* hesitates to track down students in their schools may no longer be tenable. But the essential role that teachers play in opening doors in young lives remains the same.

Although the U.S. Congress has failed to agree on a comprehensive immigration reform since the Immigration Reform and Control Act of 1986, piecemeal legislation at the national, state, and local levels and memos, actions, and orders by the executive branch have accumulated to cobble together a dysfunctional, punitive, and arbitrary system that governs the lives of some 11 million people who currently live in the United States without official documents.

One thing that has been consistent is an increasing trend of criminalizing immigrants. From Bill Clinton's 1996 Illegal Immigration Reform and Immigrant Responsibility Act to George W. Bush's workplace raids and programs like Secure Communities and 287(g) to Barack Obama's promise to deport "felons, not families" and protect young people who entered the United States "through no fault of their own," there has been a steady accretion of language and policy from above that reinforces popular perceptions that many immigrants are in fact criminals and that immigration is a crime. When anti-immigrant bigots resort to the query "What part of 'illegal' don't you understand?" they are only echoing the overwhelming message they receive from our media and our political class about illegality and criminality.

But let's pause for just a moment to examine what it means to illegalize and criminalize people who have crossed a border. The laws do this in two ways. One, the laws punish crimes differently depending on who commits them. If an immigrant is convicted of a crime, they may be punished not only by their sentence, but also by deportation. Thus a conviction magnifies into a permanent and immutable criminalization. Two, the laws turn freedom of movement—that is, crossing a border—into a crime for some people but not for others. Criminality becomes a vicious circle: Noncitizens are legally defined as lacking rights and are therefore criminalized by virtue of their status.

The last 4 decades have seen the cancerous growth of the carceral state, as prisons, militarized police, longer sentences, and postrelease punishment and ostracism have all proliferated. Criminalization and the carceral state have particularly targeted African Americans, to the extent that many have followed Michelle Alexander in terming mass incarceration "the New Jim Crow."

The criminalization of immigrants has followed its own special logic in addition to sharing characteristics with the criminalization of others who are poor and who are people of color. Of course many immigrants are both, which compounds their vulnerability. But since the last half of the 20th century, law, institutions, and opinion leaders have collaborated to exponentially expand the criminalization of immigrants based on their status. While the Trump administration may be taking this to new rhetorical and enforcement heights, Trump is only building on a foundation long under construction.

Teachers are uniquely placed to support undocumented students facing adverse circumstances and to challenge the narrative of immigrant criminality in the public sphere. This book should help enable them to do both.

—Aviva Chomsky

References

Alexander, M. (2010). *The new Jim Crow: Mass incarceration in the age of colorblindness.* New York, NY: The New Press.

Nava, G. (director). (1983). *El Norte.* United States/United Kingdom: American Playhouse/ Channel Four Films.

Acknowledgments

This book is a heartfelt collaboration between DREAMers and teacher allies that grew organically from the experience of hearing the *testimonios* of youth and allies involved in the DREAM movement. The personal testimonios of Hareth Andrade, Ben Merlos, and K–16+ educators Anne Marie Foerster Luu, Nasim Khawaja, Rachna Rikhye, and Shelley Wong were shared with an audience of K–12, higher education, and adult education ESL and bilingual education teachers at a Washington Area Teachers of English to Speakers of Other Languages (WATESOL) conference in 2013. One elementary ESOL teacher, Lori Dodson, was in the audience and joined our project. Elaisa Sánchez Gosnell, Sylvia Y. Sánchez, and Eva K. Thorp joined the editorial team as we envisioned and crafted our first book proposal. As we wrote and presented at educational conferences and in online discussion groups, still more teacher-authors joined our efforts and inspired further dedication to our goal.

There have been countless people and organizations—our students of all ages, colleagues, family members, DREAMers, DREAM student organizations, immigrant and civil rights groups, legal and community organizations, teachers unions and professional associations—involved in this book. A special thank you is due to Aviva Chomsky for her pathbreaking and insightful historical analysis. We are grateful for her foreword to this book. We salute the courage and creativity of Tam Tran and Cinthya Felix and UCLA IDEAS, Kent Wong and the UCLA Labor Center, United We DREAM, Mason DREAMers, the Dream Project, CASA de Maryland, the National Education Association and American Federation of Teachers (teacher unions), Teachers of English to Speakers of Other Languages International Association (TESOL), WATESOL, the Electronic Village Online (EVO), and other organizations and professional associations. There were those who listened intently to our passionate discussions and shared their perspectives. We would like to acknowledge the inspiring work of Renata Aldaz, Jennifer Binkes Lee, Virginia Collier, Dulce Elias Martinez, Susanna Eng, Candace Kattar, Ricardo Sánchez and countless leaders in the immigrant rights movement. Some people, like Comfort Davis Mangot, came to our planning meetings and read our drafts, and others, like Janna Mattson, our managing editor, and Doug Hernandez, our technical support specialist, helped us organize the detailed logistics of getting a book proposal to a publisher and a manuscript to the publisher's desk. We would also like to acknowledge the dedication of our graduate research assistant Maryam Saroughi and our work-study students Sancia Celestine, Khoa (Kenny) Le, and Charlina Mansara.

At Teachers College Press, we want to thank senior acquisitions editor Brian Ellerbeck, who has guided us and kept us grounded with feedback, advice, and support. We want to thank John Bylander, our production editor, for his understanding of our mission and for making himself available to answer technical questions. Thanks also to Jamie Rasmussen and Nancy Power for their promotional support and expertise. Our anonymous reviewers provided valuable feedback that served to encourage and guide us.

Shelley Wong would like to acknowledge institutional support from the College of Education and Human Development at George Mason University; recognize the inspiring example of Ignacia Rodriguez and Marilyn Corrales from UCLA IDEAS, who were recognized by TESOL International with the President's Award in 2009; and express her gratitude to Rev. Dr. Tyrone Pitts, Kent and Marshall Wong, and Suhanthie Motha for their spiritual support, advice, love, and wisdom.

Elaisa Sánchez Gosnell would like to thank her husband for his patience and support while she secluded herself to work on the manuscript. Also, she greatly appreciates her family's encouragement and humor, which helped her to stay on task.

Lori Dodson would like to acknowledge her sister and mother for their love and support. Thank you, Claire Johnson and Becky Dodson, for volunteering your time and expertise.

Anne Marie Foerster Luu would like to thank her family for their consistent support in words and deeds. Her husband continues to be an inspiration. Her parents have supported this effort with conversation, artwork, and pride. Her daughters and son have been especially helpful with their insights into youth perspectives on social justice and politics.

Prologue

Hareth Andrade-Ayala and Natalia

Para mi familia—Mami, Papi, Hazi, y Claudia: Immigrating to the United States could have been my deepest sorrow, but it was our struggles at home and school that taught me to speak up against injustice and to follow my mission in life. I appreciate most of all your encouragement to write and share my story. As I dedicate my work in the creation of this book to you, my family, I've come to realize that perhaps none of my personal achievements alone will change the world; however, who I become moving forward will.

In my journey through college I grew alongside the DREAM and immigrant rights movement. Among the movement leaders I shared space with, I met the educators who became the team that published this book! When you read the stories of the people featured in this book, I know you'll recall similar uncertainties that we shared as a family. The following pages honor your sacrifice and that of millions of other families.

Papi, when we fought to stop your deportation, I presented this poem to the AFL–CIO (American Federation of Labor and Congress of Industrial Organizations). This is an example of how my love for you and my understanding of justice come together to make a difference in our new country. I asked people to stand for you as a strong member of the community who has contributed so much. And stand they did.

America

America,
We need to talk.
Don't be afraid and stand
Because we believe that this is the year,
The year that the dreams of my parents will be realized
And the dreams of millions
Who came and crossed borders unimaginable
to reach the land of opportunities.

A story comes to mind
Of a little girl's dream
to become a spokesperson
And she did not mean to take anything,
Let alone make a scene.

She
Was just trying to fit in
yet by the age of 15
Treated like she was sin
Illegal—
Placed in a category,
A shelf
A cell
Incarcerated in the words
Sentenced without conviction

Alone

She would crumble—yet the dream kept her humble
And she built a suit of armor to join the fight.
Empowered by the liberation
We the people must build a suit.
Let's go on and tell them
While they who have the power sit
Separating us as they see fit.

While my father's hands blister from work all day
And he doesn't feel like he has a say?

As this nation dedicated to the proposition
That all people are created equal rises with 11 million dreams

America,
We are liberated
By the pain
So let's talk,
Because America is home,
a land of dreams
for all dreamers.

Con mucho amor,

—Hareth

Watch a video of the poem being performed by Hareth at the AFL–CIO
convention: www.youtube.com/watch?v=wZztYukJlwQ&t=108s

Hope

This painting was created by an undocumented student who completed her K–12 education in the United States and whose family had to leave the country. The support of one of her teachers empowered her to join a DREAM Act student advocacy group called the Dream Project. Her painting is described here in her own words:

> Doves are universally recognized as a symbol of peace, hope, and grace. In this painting the dove also represents DREAMers. The weight attached to its leg represents the weight that not having citizenship, along with such issues as racism and financial need, has on us. The dove is unable to fly with the weight attached to its leg and would certainly hit the ground if the cupped hands at the bottom weren't there ready to catch it. These hands are the mentors of the Dream Project and all who are supporting the DREAMers in our pursuit of a brighter future. They are the hands of those willing to help take the weight off of us.
>
> —Natalia

Part I

WORKING WITH UNDOCUMENTED STUDENTS AND THEIR FAMILIES
UNDERSTANDING THE ISSUES AND STRATEGIES

Carollyn James

CHAPTER 1

Undocumented Students, Families, and Communities in Our Schools

What Every Teacher Should Know

Shelley Wong and Jennifer Crewalk with Rodrigo Velasquez-Soto

Teachers are often the first adults outside the immediate family whom undocumented children and youth trust enough to turn to for help. Jose Antonio Vargas, who came from the Philippines to the United States at age 12, remembers that he first revealed his undocumented status to his high school music teacher, Jill Denny (Vargas, 2011). The teacher had announced that they would raise money for the choir to perform in Japan. When Jose shared with his teacher that he could not go on the trip because he didn't have a passport—that he would be able to leave the country but he wouldn't be able to come back—his music teacher faced a dilemma. Should the group go without him?

Jill Denny was a first-year teacher. The decision to change the venue of the trip for an individual student was not an easy one. Fundraising for a high school group to travel requires teamwork, energy, organization, and *heart*. It is never a small undertaking—whether for a music group, sports team, or debate team. For the trip to be successful it would require approval from her principal and active support from parents.

Ms. Denny took the unusual position that if Jose couldn't go with the others to Japan, she needed to rethink her plan. She researched and found that, though the competition was based in Japan, one of the venues for the competition would be in Hawaii. The entire choir, including Jose, came together as a team and successfully participated in the competition, traveling to Hawaii instead of Japan to perform. At Jose's graduation from high school he wore a lei. Today, as a Pulitzer Prize–winning journalist and advocate for immigrant rights, Jose Antonio Vargas credits his music teacher with being his first ally (Vargas 2011, 2012).

It is not easy to become an ally of an undocumented student. Some teachers don't want to get involved out of fear that they may be breaking the law, which they are not. Others take the attitude that they don't want to know a student's or parent's immigration status—that the less they know, the better. And some teachers are concerned and want to help but, lacking information, don't know where to begin.

This book was written for educators who want to be effective advocates for undocumented students but are in need of information, analysis, and strategies. It was also written to encourage teachers who are not currently engaged with supporting immigrant students to become involved. Becoming aware of the issues that affect undocumented students and their families is the first step to becoming an ally. In the current political climate there is so much misinformation and disinformation concerning undocumented students and their families. It is imperative that pre-K–12 teachers, counselors, and principals be aware of the laws and court cases that establish the right to public education for all students, irrespective of immigration status (National Education Association, 2015). It is also increasingly important for educational leaders to address school bullying and to nurture and strengthen cultures of peace in schools and on the playground (Wong & Grant, 2009). Finally, we must counter common myths, stereotypes, and misconceptions about immigrant communities (Chomsky, 2007).

The true measure of educational success is reaching the student who is the *hardest* to teach. Some students, like Jose Antonio Vargas, are very easy to reach. Others may provide clues, but it is up to us, their teachers, to dig deeper, to look closely at the clues provided by the students in our classes, and to address the systemic barriers a student may encounter that interfere with learning. We need to engage in dialogue with our students to ask questions as we attend to our students' (un)documented realities. Is a student falling asleep in class or frequently absent from school because he or she is lazy, or is there something else going on? Why is it difficult to reach a parent for a parent–teacher conference? Too often, parents and students may be fearful of reporting a problem such as abuse, injury, or wage theft because of their status or fear of endangering a family member.

The problem-posing or dilemmas approach introduced in Chapter 2 asks educational leaders in pre-K–16 institutions to begin by attending to the clues that students may provide to better reach them. Becoming an ally involves not only learning about our students' lives, but also *un*learning and challenging the dominant stereotypes concerning the lives of undocumented students and their families (Freire, 1970; Wong, 2011).

Sociopolitical Context of Immigrant Education in the United States

In the United States, political candidates for public office will often speak with pride of their immigrant roots, signifying that their ancestor who came from humble beginnings worked hard to achieve the American dream of success. The phrase "a nation of immigrants" and the Latin phrase found on the dollar bill *E pluribus unum*—out of many one—are employed in public discourse to forge a national identity, emblematic of an inclusive, diverse, and pluralistic society.

However, by referring to the United States as "a nation of immigrants," at least two significant groups are excluded: Native American peoples who were indigenous to the land at the time of Christopher Columbus' voyage in 1492 (Bigelow & Peterson 2003; Dunbar-Ortiz, 2015) and Africans who were brought to the Americas in chains through forced migration and worked as slaves on the plantations in the early 17th century under brutal and inhumane conditions (Bennett, 1993; Marable, 2015). Enslaved Africans spoke a variety of languages and came from many ethnic groups and cultures, but their languages were forbidden and suppressed, and it was against the law to teach slaves to read (Baugh, 1999; Delpit, 2012). Even after the United States gained its independence, Indigenous people and people of African descent were denied education and basic human rights under the Constitution.

When Christopher Columbus landed on Ayiti (what would later be called Haiti), the Caribbean island was populated by the Taino, a peaceful, communal people without weapons of war (Robinson, 2007). Randall Robinson (2007) reports:

> Although the Tainos had never before *seen* a European, Columbus, warped by the widespread social prejudice that marked fifteenth century European civilization, ridiculed virtually everything he saw about them, including their inability to speak *his* language. . . . In December 1492, an estimated 8 million Tainos were living on the island. Within twenty years there were fewer than 28,000. Thirty years on, by 1542, only two hundred Tainos remained alive. (p. 3)

The omission from the historical record of genocide and enslavement committed against Native American Indians and American Africans, and the exploitation of other non-White people such as Chinese, Filipinos, and Mexicans, has serious implications for school textbooks, school curriculum, and determining who may study in pre-K–12 and beyond. It also has implications for current heated and polarizing debates over immigrant policy, practice, and the treatment of undocumented students.

Some of the xenophobic, racist, and anti-immigrant discourses concerning undocumented students and families that are broadcast today over television, social media, radio talk shows, and newspaper tabloids are really not new. In times of economic crisis, when many people are unemployed or lose their homes, immigrants to the United States have often been blamed as the source of the problem. Current campaigns against Asian, Latinx, Arab, and Muslim American immigrants have historic antecedents in organized movements such as the Chinese Must Go campaign over 100 years ago. Historian Ron Takagi (1989), who chronicled the history of Asian American immigration, pointed out that in the racial imagination of White society one can see the blurring of racial stereotypes between various darker-skinned peoples, such as between Chinese and Native Americans and Chinese and American Africans. After the Civil War, the *New York Times* warned that the newly freed slaves and the newly arrived Chinese workers would be a threat:

> We have four millions of degraded negroes in the South . . . and if there were to be a flood-tide of Chinese population—a population befouled with all the social vices, with no knowledge or appreciation of free institutions or constitutional liberty, with heathenish souls and heathenish propensities . . . we should be prepared to bid farewell to republicanism. (quoted in Takagi, 1989, p. 101)

Under free market economic cycles of boom and bust, immigrants have always been blamed for taking away jobs from *real* (European) Americans (Wong, 2000). Historically, immigrants from China, Japan, and the Philippines have been the target of anti-immigrant legislation—from the Chinese Exclusion Act of 1882 to the Johnson-Reed Immigration Act of 1924 marking the end of open immigration from Europe and the establishment of restrictive quotas based on national origin. According to historian May Ngai, from 1924 to 1965 numerical quotas for immigration restriction were set based on a "global racial and national hierarchy that favored some immigrants over others" (Ngai, 2004, p. 3). Their shifting status as "illegal aliens," "alien" citizens, colonial subjects, and foreign contract workers set their immigrant journey apart from the normal pathway to U.S. citizenship for (white) European Americans.

Historically, discrimination and attacks on immigrant communities rise dramatically during times of war (Zinn, 2003). Before World War I, there were many German heritage language schools, but they were closed due to anti-German sentiment during the war. During World War II, German Americans, Italian Americans, and Japanese Americans saw their businesses and homes attacked. But while the United States was at war with Germany, Italy, and Japan, only Japanese Americans were given emergency notice to evacuate their homes and were interned in concentration camps surrounded by military guards.

After the attacks on the World Trade Center and the Pentagon on September 11th, South Asians and Middle Easterners became the newest target of anti-immigrant rage. Anti-Arab and anti-Muslim discrimination has reached alarming proportions (Nguyen, 2005). The contemporary Muslim bans must be understood as a way of creating an "us vs. them" mentality that is detrimental to all (Sokolower, 2013; American-Arab Anti-Discrimination Committee, 2017).

No Human Being Is "Illegal"

The labeling of immigrants as "illegal" is a distortion and violation of their personhood and shared humanity. The discursive processes of representation into "us" and "them" serve to divide newer immigrants from people born in the United States and to divide working people who have the most to gain by uniting. Through the process of "othering," dehumanization occurs, so that some lives are considered to be worth more than others (Hall, Evans, & Nixon, 2013; Milofsky Mojito, 2009; hooks, 1994). DREAMers, activists, and teacher allies in this book present examples of transformative work that can help to abolish the I-word and the "othering" that occurs when the label "illegal" is used by naming the micro- and macro-mechanisms, processes, and structures that serve to sort, label, and dehumanize immigrants. In our book we use *undocumented* or *without papers* because the term "illegal immigrants" implies that the 11 million undocumented immigrants who reside in the United States are criminals. In fact, most undocumented immigrants have never committed a crime (Chomsky, 2007; Waters & Pineau, 2015). Labeling people—instead of actions—as "illegal" dehumanizes individuals and is thus a form of symbolic violence that provides justification for brutal, inhumane, and demeaning treatment (Bourdieu, 1991;

Chomsky, 2014). Even worse is the term "illegal alien," used in some rhetorical contexts to connote a *thing* that is loathsome or frightening. With the intersectionality of racism and an anti-Muslim and anti-immigrant mentality, counternarratives of DREAMers and teacher allies are needed more than ever to unite divided communities and to develop interest convergence among many disparate communities under attack (Patel, 2013; Pérez Huber, 2009, 2010).

Liminal Status of Undocumented Youth

The concept of liminality, or the quality of indeterminacy being "betwixt and between," as developed by the anthropologist Victor Turner (1987), provides a window onto the passage from youth to adulthood, when a youth has not been granted all the rights, status, and responsibilities of an adult—but is also no longer a child. Undocumented children have the right to attend K–12 schools just like their U.S.-born siblings and peers, but as they move from being adolescents to becoming adults, they face a seemingly insurmountable number of arduous obstacles in their passage to independence and adulthood as they learn to drive and attempt to get a driver's license, find a job, and consider applying for college.

In the transition from adolescence to adulthood, the liminal status of undocumented youth has been characterized as a period of ambiguity and uncertainty—a kind of permanent temporariness (Bailey, Wright, Mountz, & Miyares, 2002)—as they are caught between two worlds. There are many reasons people leave their homeland; they may leave hoping for a better education and future for their children and better economic opportunities, or they may flee their home as a result of war, natural disaster, or persecution based on political, religious, social or sexual orientation (Gonzalez, 2011). The situation of being undocumented affects their health and safety, including their ability to combat domestic violence, their vulnerability in the streets, and their chances in the labor market (Menjivar, 2006). Lesbian, gay, bisexual, transgender, and queer (LGBTQ) immigrants may experience "double exile" (see Ríos Vega & Franeta, Chapter 9 of this volume) or multiple levels of marginalization.

Liminality has also been seen as a potentially hopeful or transformative space through which to transcend rigid either/or categories. Overcoming rigid binaries is important for immigrant youth identity formation and belonging in anti-immigrant times (Massey & Sánchez R., 2009). In Cantonese there is an idiomatic expression, "not 3, not 4," denoting something that is strange or queer. Queer theory enables one to go beyond binaries to embrace formerly stigmatized identities (Nicholls, 2013; Terriquez, 2015). Dual liminality, as in the case of undocu/DACAmented Asian American and Pacific Islander youth, may involve resisting both model minority and yellow peril stereotypes (Dao, 2017). Coming of age means trying to find one's place—"to fit in" within the gendered prescriptions and complex social maps of racially and linguistically segregated schoolyards (Olsen, 1997). As a "betwixt and between" space (Turner, 1987), liminality also affords a site for the emergence of new cultural identities (Bhabha, 1994) and ways of knowing or new critical epistemological resources under empire (Motha, 2014).

Mixed Status and *Under*documented Families

A mixed-status family is a family in which one or more family members are U.S. citizens and one or more are unauthorized, undocumented, or "without papers." According to a report by the Tomas Rivera Policy Institute at the University of Southern California (USC) and the Institute for Immigration, Globalization, and Education at UCLA, about 7% of all school-age children live in mixed-status families. In fact, the total number of U.S.-born children living with at least one undocumented parent doubled between 2000 and 2012, from 2.2 million to 4.5 million (Suro, Suárez-Orozco, & Canizales, 2015, p. 6). *Under*documented is a term meant to describe a family member who entered the country under a student visa or work permit, but due to barriers, was unable to renew his or her visa or work permit and became undocumented.

Research in child development has long shown that parents are powerful determinants of children's well-being all the way into adulthood. Children from mixed-status families face an uncertain present and future as a result of the actions, policies, and practices of the Department of Homeland Security (DHS), Immigration and Customs Enforcement (ICE), and Customs and Border Protection (CBP). The incarceration and deportation of parents following raids by ICE and the limited involvement of child welfare services in these cases has led to widespread economic hardship (Capps Castaneda, Chaudry, & Santos, 2007). The resulting separation has long-lasting effects on the emotional, physical, and mental health within family units.

Understanding how immigration policies, ICE enforcement, and societal attitudes affect undocumented students and their families is critical to helping teachers recognize how they can ensure that all students, irrespective of their immigration status or that of a family member, are provided with a safe learning environment and the opportunity to live to their current and future potential.

Who Are the DREAMers?

The term *DREAMers* refers to the undocumented youth who would have qualified for the federal DREAM Act (Development, Relief and Education for Alien Minors Act), which was originally introduced in Congress in 2001. Despite many efforts to introduce a version of the DREAM Act in Congress, it has never passed. If it had passed, it would have granted undocumented youth who came to the United States as minors the right to stay in the country without fear of deportation and to work and continue their education with possible routes to citizenship (Tran & Lal, 2009). The DREAM Act never proposed "amnesty" or immediate citizenship. Students in the DREAM movement have testified before Congress, lobbied, marched, demonstrated, and mobilized for a pathway to citizenship since 2001, and this movement continues today.

DREAMers are united in their pursuit of key goals. First, like many of their fellow classmates who are citizens and who graduated from the same neighborhood high schools, DREAMers want the option to pursue a better life for themselves and their families. For DREAMers, this pursuit of a better life might entail various personal visions, such as enrolling in higher education or a training program, getting a job, applying for a driver's license, obtaining a social security card, and/or applying for a college loan. Undocumented students must pay out-of-state or international student tuition rates in 35 out of 50 states. While U.S.-born students can obtain scholarships and federal loans to pay tuition, DREAMers do not qualify for federal loans nor for most scholarships that require permanent residency or citizenship. This creates a tremendous hardship for the student and family members, who often work two or three jobs to make ends meet. In the 2015 UndocuScholars Report, a survey of 909 undocumented college students, 61.3% had an annual household income below $30,000, 29.0% had an annual household income of $30,000 to $50,000, and 9.7% had an annual household income above $50,000 (Suárez-Orozco, Teranishi, & Suárez-Orozco, 2015).

Second, these students want a pathway that takes them toward the dream of citizenship for themselves and their families—a path that can give them the right to vote on leaders and policies that impact their families. Contrary to the public stereotype that undocumented students are all Latinx or Mexican, undocumented students actually come from diverse countries with a multitude of linguistic and cultural backgrounds. Results from the 2015 UndocuScholars report showed that the 909 undocumented college students surveyed had emigrated from 55 different countries of origin and reported 33 different primary languages spoken at home (Suárez-Orozco, Teranishi, & Suárez-Orozco, 2015). Many DREAMers consider themselves to be what William Pérez calls "Americans by heart" (Pérez, 2012) because the United States is the only country they have known. Third, they want to unite their families, stop the deportations, and not live in constant fear of losing a parent or family member to deportation. The reunification of families and the end to deportations, combined with a just immigration policy, are central to DREAMers' goals (Madera et al., 2008; see also unitedwedream.org).

While we focus broadly on DREAMers, the authors of this book recognize that there are fluid lines that delineate the immigrant community. Thus, we focus on the educational implications for the many children and youth affected by current U.S. immigration policy. For our children and youth, their status identifies them as a societal problem, and as they become aware of this, their dreams may seem to be impossible to achieve. W. E. B. Du Bois (1903) identified the origins of this conscious awareness, which he called "double-consciousness" in his book *The Souls of Black Folk*, by posing the question, "How does it feel to be a problem?" (p. 213). Artists and writers are coming up with new language, images, and self-definitions that challenge labels and stereotypes that criminalize and dehumanize. For example, activists with the DREAM movement have successfully fought to have the Associated Press eliminate the dehumanizing term of "illegal" in the AP's references to undocumented people (Colford, 2013).

Deferred Action for Childhood Arrivals (DACA)

After the defeat of the federal DREAM Act in 2012, President Barack Obama issued an executive order, Deferred Action for Childhood Arrivals (DACA), that offered a temporary stay of deportations and a social security number or work permit. In some states, DACA recipients were provided access to a drivers license and eligibility for in-state tuition (National Immigration Law Center, 2015; United States Citizenship and Immigration Services, 2015). Approximately 800,000 undocumented immigrants were granted DACA (Shear & Hirschfeld Davis, 2017). DACA only applied to those who were 30 years old or younger and who came to the United States before the age of 16 and had resided in the United States continuously since June 15, 2007. In addition, DACA applicants needed to show that they were in the United States on June 15, 2012, and that they were in school, had earned a high school diploma or a GED, or were an honorably discharged veteran. Furthermore, to be eligible, an applicant could not have been convicted of a felony or of multiple or significant misdemeanors. Toward the end of his term, President Obama issued another executive order that expanded DACA, known as Deferred Action for Parents of Americans (DAPA), which would protect from deportation undocumented parents of children born in the United States (USCIS, 2015). While both executive orders offered promise to the immigrant community, neither provided a pathway to citizenship—only temporary protection from deportation. DAPA was stopped by the courts before it went into effect. DACA did go into effect under President Obama.

In the summer of 2017, a group of attorneys general threatened to file a lawsuit if DACA was not rescinded by September 5, 2017 ("10 Republican attorneys general," 2017). On September 5, 2017, Attorney General Jefferson Beauregard Sessions announced that DACA would be rescinded. No new applications for DACA would be accepted, and only those whose DACA status expired before March 5, 2018, could apply for one last renewal. United We Dream, the largest undocumented immigrant youth organization in the United States, immediately issued a statement of support for DACA recipients and advocated for federal legislation that would protect the human rights of all 11 million undocumented people (United We Dream, 2017).

Federal Immigration Legislation

Sadly, although the DREAM Act was presented to Congress in 2001 and DREAMer youth activists have continued to gather support (through petitions, legislation, and lobbying) for its passage, to this day, there is no pathway to citizenship for the DREAM students. Contrary to public opinion, undocumented students cannot pay a fine, take a citizenship test, and be sworn in as citizens. There is no "line" to stand in (Chomsky 2007, 2014). The 2017 version of the DREAM Act introduced in the U.S. Senate with bipartisan support includes a pathway to citizenship; however, this iteration required an extended period of conditional permanent resident status (DREAM Act, 2017). There is also movement in the House of Representatives to support DREAMers through the American Hope Act of 2017. On the flip side, the public rhetoric has become even more heated with the RAISE Act in the Senate. If passed, this law would reverse many of the gains made on immigration reform (Nakamura, 2017). Regardless of the final outcome of these legislative efforts, the rhetoric is divisive, leaving DREAMers and undocumented youth and families in the middle of the storm.

Anti-Immigrant Policies and Legislation

Although there are many policies and micro- and macroaggressions aimed at immigrants that could be included in this section, the anti-immigrant policies imposed in Arizona are representative of the overall national context affecting the lives of immigrant students and their families. In April 2010, Arizona passed SB 1070, a bill requiring local and state police to stop and interrogate anyone they suspected of being an undocumented immigrant (State of Arizona, 2010a). This law has been criticized for racial profiling and anti-Latino discrimination because Latino Americans, including legal permanent residents and U.S. citizens, especially those of Mexican heritage, have been stopped disproportionately. Some local law enforcement officers spoke out against the measure because they saw that if they were responsible for enforcing immigration laws, it would interfere with their efforts to serve local communities and protect them from crime. If people who are undocumented are afraid of deportation or of being held in prison without the right to counsel, they will be afraid to call the police when they witness or are themselves victims of crime. In July 2010, a federal judge issued an injunction to block key provisions of the act, writing, "There is a substantial likelihood that officers will wrongly arrest legal resident aliens. . . . By enforcing this statute, Arizona would impose a 'distinct, unusual and extraordinary' burden on legal resident aliens that only the federal government has the authority to impose" (Gonzalez, 2010). Arizona has been supported with amicus curiae, or friends of the court, briefs filed by Michigan's state attorney general and signed by almost a dozen states: Alabama, Florida, Idaho, Louisiana, Nebraska, Pennsylvania, South Carolina, South Dakota, Texas, and Virginia (Associated Press, 2010). Arizona is not the only state that is determined to enact legislation to penalize undocumented immigrants. Similar bills have also passed in Alabama, Georgia, Indiana, South Carolina, and Utah. Most recently, Texas passed SB 4, a bill with many of the same goals.

Overview of the Book

Part I of this book is entitled "Working with Undocumented Students and Their Families: Understanding the Issues and Strategies." Chapter 2, by Eva K. Thorp, Sylvia Y. Sánchez, and Elaisa Sánchez Gosnell, provides a framework for helping teachers respond to challenges with students, families, and colleagues that present as problems or cultural dilemmas related to immigration status. The process they recommend asks teachers to slow down, consider their own cultural lens, consider all the factors of their dilemma, and collaborate with colleagues to come up with nonjudgmental ways of resolving concerns and supporting students and families.

In Chapter 3, Eva K. Thorp explores the issues of deportation and separation through the stories of three children. She outlines the fears and stressors in the lives of children who can't possibly understand the complex realities of immigration status. Their fears present themselves in ways that can be easily misinterpreted as resulting from poor parenting or bad behavior. She recommends that teachers use the dilemmas approach to find ways to understand and develop practices to support the well-being of undocumented students and citizen children in mixed-status families.

Part II is "Reaching Students from Immigrant Families Through Transformative Culturally Responsive Education." The chapters in this section help us to rethink the intersections of dialogic and critical race pedagogies, including culturally responsive and contextually relevant education from positions of privilege as well as marginality. In Chapter 4, Sandra Duval provides examples of her learning in community and Haitian Creole and French heritage language education, in which everyone knew her name. Teachers can become allies by building strong relationships with their students using pedagogical practices that center the students, their histories, and their ways of understanding the world, making the students feel appreciated and visible. She outlines how important teachers are in ensuring social, emotional, and physical safety in the classroom.

In Chapter 5, Tiffany Mitchell and Brett Burnham with Gaby Pacheco help us to rethink the teaching of controversial topics and to reflect deeply on the meaning of civic engagement. They describe a project-based civics lesson that takes students from text to Capitol Hill. In Chapter 6, Anita Bright and G. Sue Kasun describe inviting Dario Lopez to share his story as a science, technology, engineering, and math (STEM) student with preservice teachers. His *testimonio* in this teacher education classroom is an example of how teachers can come to understand their students' lives and realities in order to support them as they resolve challenges in these unpredictable times.

Part III is "Accessing, Surviving, and Thriving: DREAMers Go to College." This section offers examples of educators and students who come to understand the needs of their students and work with them to make their dream of higher education a reality. In Chapter 7, Samantha Spinney with Danna Chávez Calvi shares her experiences as a high school teacher who refused to accept that her students' achievements in high school would end at graduation. She found ways to help them mitigate the legal, financial, academic, and social-emotional barriers to higher education. In Chapter 8, Emma Violand-Sánchez and Marie Price describe how the community established the Arlington Dream Project as a nonprofit organization that educates the broader public, advocates for and mentors undocumented high school students, and provides scholarships. This program is an inspiring model of what is possible when DREAMers and teachers as allies work together. In Chapter 9, Juan A. Ríos Vega and Sonja Franeta discuss the double exile of LGBTQ students. They address the costs of rejection often felt by DREAMers who have embraced the intersectional character of being not only undocumented and unafraid but also queer. In coming out twice—as undocumented and as queer—they have changed the discource of the immigrant rights movement to be even more inclusive. In Chapter 10, Aurora Chang discusses her relationship with her student Nancy Gutierrez and the way she consciously sets up her class as a safe space through the use of *testimonio*—so that students can understand themselves and others in very personal ways. Her process requires a lot of mutual respect, reflection, and balance.

In *Part IV*, "Finding, Sharing, and Transforming Identity Through Art: DREAMers Perform," the reader will find a combination of personal narratives, explorations of the arts as a vehicle for representing immigrant stories, and descriptions of effective teaching practices. In combination, this section's chapters provide new perspectives that will enable teachers to see how to integrate approaches that respond to the issues that uniquely challenge immigrant children and youth. In Chapter 11, Gertrude Tinker Sachs and Theresa Austin use critical analysis to have their students analyze pro- and anti-immigration messages in music. While they are learning to analyze language, they are learning about a significant issue in their community. In turn, these students come to understand issues of immigration from multiple perspectives and could potentially become allies to undocumented peers. In Chapter 12, Susan Harden and Robin Witt describe a theatre project in which students interview members of the community to better understand the real lives of their friends and neighbors who are undocumented. Then they write and perform a play to share what they have learned with the community in two sold-out performances. This type of community education is a deep learning experience that can also develop peer allies.

The final section of the book, *Part V*, is entitled "Becoming an Ally." Becoming an ally involves speaking out against bullying to create safe schools and "undocufriendly" campuses for K–16+ (Suárez-Orozco et al., 2015) and speaking up for the most vulnerable students, especially those who cannot speak for themselves. Chapter 13 is a call to action from Anne Marie Foerster Luu and Lori Dodson with Hareth Andrade-Ayala and María Verónica Cevallos Rodríguez. The chapter directs the reader back to the larger sociopolitical context of immigration policies and implications addressed throughout this book. For teachers to become allies they must learn their students' realities, respond in nonjudgmental ways, and find ways to weave current issues into the curriculum to make it reflective of and relevant to their students' lives. As a result teachers become politically involved. In Chapter 14, Elaisa Sánchez Gosnell, Janna Mattson, Doug Hernandez, and Maryam Saroughi provide print, video, and web-based resources that can be used by teachers and higher education faculty in their work on behalf of immigrant children, DREAMers, and their families.

Teachers are, without question, well positioned to be that first trusted and caring adult outside the students' families who can partner with them on their journey to success. It is a matter of social justice. Much of the anti-immigrant rhetoric used by those calling for a crackdown on immigration, visa holders, and refugees is not new. Nevertheless, teachers are expected to provide an equitable education to our nation's children regardless of the color of their skin, their immigration status, acculturation level, languages, and income level. "Without an education . . . undocumented children, already disadvantaged as a result of poverty, lack of English-speaking ability, and undeniable racial prejudices, . . . will become permanently locked into the lowest socio-economic class" (Plyler v. Doe of 1982, Page 457 U. S. 208).

A teacher's perspective on the social, economic, and political circumstances of his or her students impacts his or her success as an educator; silence or neutrality becomes part of the problem. Thus teachers are well positioned to become integral to the life of the communities in which they work. Our nation depends on teachers becoming transformative practitioners and allies.

K–16 educators have a key role in supporting young people to grow into their own self-actualization and upward mobility. When making pedagogical choices, teachers often hear two opposing messages. Those who advocate a subtractive approach, saying that it is best for immigrant children to fully assimilate in language and culture, lose sight of the deep-rooted value of the home language and culture. In fact, students' culture is fertile ground for academic success. A sad byproduct of the subtractive approach to schooling is that teachers complain that students do not care about school and students complain that teachers do not care about them (Valenzuela, 1999). By contrast, in supportive school environments, students can build their own social and cultural capital to the benefit of their families and the future of our country. This additive approach to the education of immigrant children maintains home language and culture that keeps family bonds strong and promotes positive identity development.

Between the direct, lived experiences of our immigrant students' educational needs and local/state/national policy, practices, and laws, it is our teachers and administrators who are uniquely positioned to make the greatest difference as advocates and allies. Can educators, in their relationships with students, families, coworkers, and community members, begin to dispel the myths that swirl around our immigrant students? Immigration attorney Isabel Garcia notes,

> "Most of the people [in the United States] do not understand the issues involved in immigration—how it is that we have 11 million undocumented people [here]; what [the United States'] role has been in creating that. . . . We don't believe that we have achieved justice yet, because we have a long road ahead of us to really have true immigration reform [that includes] a reform of our trade policies and a real look at how we're militarizing our border, privatizing it—with unprecedented expenditures—to

the detriment of our real security needs, such as education, healthcare, infrastructure." (quoted in Gonzalez, 2010)

Imagine where Jose Antonio Vargas as a Pulitzer Prize–winning journalist and advocate for immigrant rights, might be today without his teacher-ally, Jill Denny (Vargas 2011, 2012). As Dominican-American writer Junot Díaz states, "From the bottom will the genius come that makes our ability to live with each other possible" (Tippett, 2017).

References

10 Republican attorneys general threaten to sue Trump admin over DACA. (2017, June 30). *Democracy Now!* Retrieved from www.democracynow.org/2017/6/30/headlines/10 _republican_attorneys_general_threaten_to_sue_trump_admin_over_daca

All Things Considered. (2017, July 14). Arizona's ethnic studies ban in public schools goes to trial. Retrieved from www.npr.org/2017/07/14/537291234/arizonas-ethnic-studies -ban-in-public-schools-goes-to-trial

American-Arab Anti-Discrimination Committee. (2017, September 26). The Trump proclamation: Arab and Muslim ban 3.0. Retrieved from www.adc.org/2017/09 /breaking-the-trump administrations-proclamation-is-arab-and-muslim-ban-3-0/

Artiles, A. J. (2011). Toward an interdisciplinary understanding of educational equity and difference: The case of the racialization of ability. *Educational Researcher, 40*(9), 431–445.

Associated Press. (2010). States join legal brief supporting Arizona Immigration Law. Retrieved from www.foxnews.com/politics/2010/09/04/states-join-legal-brief -supporting-ariz-immigration-law-donations-roll-gov

Bailey, A. J., Wright, R. A., Mountz, A., & Miyares, I. M. (2002). (Re)Producing Salvador-an transnational geographies. *Annals of the Association of American Geographers, 92*, 125–144.

Baugh, J. (1999). *Out of the mouths of slaves: African American language and educational malpractices.* Austin: University of Texas Press.

Becerra, X. (2017). June 29, 2017, letter from Ken Paxton re Texas, et al., v. United States, et al., case no. 1:14-Cv-00254 (S.D. Tex.). Retrieved from oag.ca.gov/system/files/attachments /press_releases/7-21-17%20%20Letter%20from%20State%20AGs%20to%20 President%20Trump%20re%20DACA.final_.pdf

Bennett, L., Jr. (1993). *Before the Mayflower: A history of Black America* (6th ed.). Chicago, IL: Johnson Publishing Company.

Bhabha, H. K. (1994). *The location of culture.* London, England: Routledge.

Bigelow, B., & Peterson, B. (2003). *Rethinking Columbus: The next 500 years.* Milwaukee, WI: Rethinking Schools.

Bourdieu, P. (1991). *Language and symbolic power.* Cambridge, MA: Harvard University Press.

Capps, R., Castaneda, R. M., Chaudry, A., & Santos, R. (2007). *Paying the price: The impact of immigration raids on America's children.* Washington, DC: Urban Institute.

Chomsky, A. (2007). *They take our jobs! And 20 other myths about immigration* (Vol. 556). Boston, MA: Beacon Press.

Chomsky, A. (2014). *Undocumented: How immigration became illegal.* Boston, MA: Beacon Press.

Colford, P. (2013, April 2). "Illegal immigrant" no more. Retrieved from blog.ap.org /announcements/illegal-immigrant-no-more

Dao, L. T. (2017). Out and Asian: How undocu/DACAmented Asian Americans and Pacific Islander youth navigate dual liminality in the immigrant rights movement. *Societies, 7*(3), 17.

Delpit, L. (2012). *"Multiplication is for white people:" Raising expectations for other people's children.* New York, NY: New Press.

DREAM Act. (2017). Summary and answers to frequently asked questions. Retrieved August 4, 2017, from www.nilc.org/issues/immigration-reform-and-executive-actions /dreamact/dream-act-2017-summary-and-faq/

Du Bois, W. E. B. (1903). *The souls of Black folk.* New York, NY: Oxford University Press.

Dunbar-Ortiz, R. (2015). *An indigenous peoples' history of the United States.* Boston, MA: Beacon Press.

Freire, P. (1970). *Pedagogy of the oppressed.* New York, NY: Herder and Herder.

Gonzalez, J. (2010, July 29). On eve of major protests, federal judge blocks key provisions of Arizona anti-immigrant law. *Democracy Now.* Retrieved from www.democracynow .org/2010/7/29/on_eve_of_major_protests_federal

Gonzalez, J. (2011). *Harvest of empire: A history of Latinos in America.* New York, NY: Penguin.

Hall, S., Evans, J., & Nixon, S. (Eds.). (2013). *Representation: Cultural representations and signifying practices.* Thousand Oaks, CA: Sage.

hooks, b. (1994). *Teaching to transgress: Education as the practice of freedom.* New York, NY: Routledge.

Jordan, M. (2010, April 30). Arizona grades teachers on fluency: State pushes school districts to reassign instructors with heavy accents or other shortcomings in their English. *Wall Street Journal.* Retrieved from online.wsj.com/article/SB100014240527487 03572504575213883276427528.html

Madera, G., Mathay, A., Najafi, A., Saldivar, H., Solis, S., Titong, A. . . . Monroe, J. (Eds.). (2008). *Underground undergrads.* Los Angeles, CA: UCLA Center for Labor Research and Education.

Marable, M. (2000). *How capitalism underdeveloped black America* (Updated ed.). Cambridge, MA: South End Press.

Martin, M. (2012). Threatened in Tucson: Mexican American studies tell me more. *National Public Radio.* Retrieved from www.npr.org/2012/01/05/144737952/threatened -in-tucson-mexican-american-studies

Massey, D., & Sánchez R., M. (2009, September). *Restrictive immigration policies and Latino immigrant identity in the United States* (Human Development Research Paper 2009/43). United Nations Development Programme. Retrieved from hdr.undp.org /sites/default/files/hdrp_2009_43.pdf

Mauch, A. D. (2012, November 3). HB 1804: Where are we now? Oklahoma's landmark immigration legislation five years later. *Oklahoma Bar Journal, 83*(29), 2351–2354. Retrieved from digitalprairie.ok.gov/cdm/ref/collection/stgovpub/id/135201

Menjivar, C. (2006). Liminal legality: Salvadoran and Guatemalan immigrants' lives in the United States. *American Journal of Sociology, 111*(4), 999–1037.

Milofsky Mojito, A. L. (2009). *Breaking the cycle of hate: A phenomenological study of teachers' lived experiences as both other and otherer.* College Park, MD: University of Maryland. Retrieved from drum.lib.umd.edu/1903/9118/1/Mojto_umd_0117E_10201.pdf

Motha, S. (2014). *Race, empire, and English language teaching: Creating responsible and ethical anti-racist practice.* New York, NY: Teachers College Press.

Nakamura, D. (2017, August 3). Trump, GOP senators introduce bill to slash legal immigration levels. Retrieved from www.washingtonpost.com/news/post-politics/wp/2017/08/02/trump-gop-senators-to-introduce-bill-to-slash-legal-immigration-levels/?utm_term=.e771c572ae9d

National Education Association. (2015). *ALL In! How educators can advocate for English language learners.* Retrieved from http://www.colorincolorado.org/sites/default/files/ELL_AdvocacyGuide2015.pdf

National Immigration Law Center. (2015). Frequently asked questions: The Obama administration's Deferred Action for Childhood Arrivals (DACA). Retrieved from www.nilc.org/issues/daca/faqdeferredactionyouth/

Ngai, M. (2004). *Impossible subjects: Illegal aliens and the making of modern America.* Princeton, NJ: Princeton University Press.

Nguyen, T. (2005). *We are all suspects now: Untold stories from immigrant communities after 9/11.* Boston, MA: Beacon Press.

Nicholls, W. J. (2013). *The DREAMers: How the undocumented youth movement transformed the immigrant rights debate.* Stanford, CA: Stanford University Press.

Norton, B. (1998). Rethinking acculturation in second language acquisition. *Prospect: An Australian Journal of TESOL, 13*(2), 4–19.

Olsen, L. (1997). *Made in America: Immigrant students in our public schools.* New York, NY: The New Press.

Patel, L. (2013). *Youth held at the border: Immigration, education, and the politics of inclusion.* New York, NY: Teachers College Press.

Pérez Huber, L. (2009). Challenging racist nativist framing: Acknowledging the community cultural wealth of undocumented Chicana students to reframe the immigration debate. *Harvard Educational Review, 79*(4), 704–729.

Pérez Huber, L. (2010). Using Latina/o critical race theory (LatCrit) and racist nativism to explore intersectionality in the educational experiences of undocumented Chicana college students. *Journal of Educational Foundations, 24*(1–2), 77–96.

Pérez, W. (2012). *Americans by heart: Undocumented Latino students and the promise of higher education.* New York, NY: Teachers College Press.

Plyler v. Doe, 457 U.S. 202 (1982). Retrieved from supreme.justia.com/cases/federal/us/457/202/case.html

Robinson, R. (2007). An unbroken agony: Haiti, from Revolution to the kidnapping of a president. New York, NY: Basic Civitas Books.

Shear, M. D., & Hirschfeld Davis, J. (2017, September 5). Trump moves to end DACA and calls on Congress to act. *New York Times.* Retrieved from nyti.ms/2x7xOo2

Sokolower, J. (2013). *Teaching about the wars.* Milwaukee, WI: Rethinking Schools.

State of Arizona. (2010a). Senate Bill 1070. Retrieved from www.azleg.gov/legtext/49leg/2r/bills/sb1070s.pdf

State of Arizona. (2010b). House Bill 2281. Retrieved from www.azleg.gov/legtext/49leg/2r/bills/hb2281s.pdf

Suárez-Orozco, C., Katsiaficas, D., Birchall, O., Alcantar, C.M., Hernandez, E., Garcia, Y., Michikyan, M., Cerda, J., & Teranishi, R. T. (2015). Undocumented undergraduates on college campuses: Understanding their challenges and assets and what it takes to make an undocufriendly campus. *Harvard Educational Review, 85*(3), 427–463.

Suárez-Orozco, M. M., Teranishi, R., & Suárez-Orozco, C. E. (2015). *In the shadows of the ivory tower: Undocumented undergraduates and the liminal state of immigration reform.*

The UndocuScholar Project, Institute for Immigration, Globalization, and Education, University of California, Los Angeles.

Suro, R., Suárez-Orozco, M. M., & Canizales, S. (2015). *Removing insecurity: How American children will benefit from President Obama's executive action on immigration*. Los Angeles, CA: Tomás Rivera Policy Institute at University of Southern California and the Institute for Immigration, Globalization, and Education at University of California, Los Angeles.

Takagi, R. (1989). *Strangers from a different shore: A history of Asian Americans*. Boston, MA: Little, Brown & Company.

Terriquez, V. (2015). Intersectional mobilization, social movement spillover, and Queer youth leadership in the immigrant rights movement. *Social Problems, 62*, 343–362.

Tippett, K (Host). (2017, September 14). Junot Díaz—Radical hope is our best weapon. *On Being*. Retrieved from onbeing.org/programsjunot-diaz-radical-hope-is-our-best-weapon-sep2017/

Tran, T., & Lal, P. (2009, September 1). Undocumented but undaunted: Immigrant youth at work in the nonprofit sector. *Nonprofit Quarterly*. Retrieved from nonprofitquarterly.org/2009/09/01/undocumented-but-undaunted-immigrant-youth-at-work-in-the-nonprofit-sector/

Turner, V. (1987). Betwixt and between: The liminal period in rites of passage. In L. C. Mahdi, S. Foster, & M. Little (Eds.), *Betwixt and between: Patterns of masculine and feminine initiation* (pp. 3–19). Chicago, IL: Open Court.

United States Citizenship and Immigration Services (USCIS). (2015). Executive actions on immigration. Retrieved from www.uscis.gov/immigrationaction

United States Department of Education. (2007). *State and local implementation of the No Child Left Behind Act, vol. II: Teacher quality under NCLB, interim report*. Retrieved from 2.ed.gov/rschstat/eval/teaching/nclb/execsum.html

United We Dream. (2017). unitedwedream.org

Valenzuela, A. (1999). *Subtractive schooling: U.S. Mexican youth and the politics of caring*. Albany, NY: State University of New York Press.

Vargas, J. A. (2011, June 29). My life as an undocumented immigrant. *New York Times*. Retrieved from www.nytimes.com/2011/06/26/magazine/my-life-as-an-undocumented-immigrant.html?pagewanted=all&_r=0

Vargas, J. A. (2012, June 25). Not legal, not leaving. *Time*. Retrieved from time.com/2987974/jose-vargas-detained-time-cover-story/

Waters, M. C., & Pineau, M. G. (Eds.). (2015). *The integration of immigrants into American society*. Washington, DC: National Academies Press.

Wong, S. (2011). *Dialogic approaches to TESOL: Where the ginkgo tree grows*. New York, NY: Routledge.

Wong, S. (2000). Transforming the politics of schooling in the U.S.: A model for successful academic achievement for language minority students. In J. K. Hall & W. Eggington (Eds.), *The sociopolitics of English language teaching* (pp. 117–139). Bristol, England: Multilingual Matters.

Wong, S., & Grant, R. (2009). Nurturing cultures of peace with dialogic approaches to language and literacy. *TESOL in Context: Journal of ACTA, Australian Council of TESOL Associations, 19*(2), 4–17.

Zinn, H. (2003). *A people's history of the United States*. New York, NY: HarperCollins.

Zubrzycki, J. (2016, June 23). California bill would create first statewide ethnic studies template. *Edweek*. Retrieved from blogs.edweek.org/edweek/curriculum/2016/06/ethnic_studies.html

CHAPTER 2

Embracing Cultural Dilemmas

A Framework for Teachers Working with Immigrant Students and Their Families

Eva K. Thorp, Sylvia Y. Sánchez, and Elaisa Sánchez Gosnell

A Teacher's Dilemma

Tessa is a 3rd-grade teacher in a school with a high percentage of children of immigrants. Tessa is concerned about Rafael, a boy in her class who is struggling in math. He is required to meet a benchmark on a high-stakes assessment. She wonders whether he might need to be evaluated for specialized math instruction or special education. One day, she checks his book bag for an overdue permission slip and notices that prior notes home are still there, apparently unread. When out of frustration she tells this story to a colleague who taught Rafael's older brother, the colleague says, "What do you expect? This is an immigrant family. The father does yard work all over the place. No one knows exactly how to reach him at any time. His cell phone number is always changing or disconnected, and the mother doesn't speak any English. Rafael's brother just started middle school, so we can't count on him to help with getting things out of the backpack or to explain things to his parents. I think you should refer him to special education."

This teacher is facing a dilemma, and whatever she decides to do will have a tremendous impact on the child's future. It will also affect her professional growth and will influence the direction of future interactions with immigrant families and children. This dilemma is not uncommon for teachers working with immigrants. We see Tessa's perplexity, but we also get a sense of the attitudes and stereotypes about immigrants that are part of the anti-immigrant narrative that has invaded the culture and school environments. Dilemmas such as these have led to our development of the dilemma strategy that we describe in this chapter.

The Power of Cultural Dilemmas

The cultural dilemma approach was developed as part of a graduate-level teacher preparation program designed by two of the authors, Thorp and Sánchez (Thorp & Sánchez, 1998; Sánchez & Thorp, 2008). The program was experiential, with a strong emphasis on culturally responsive and reflective practices (Brookfield, 1995; Delpit, 2002; Kidd, Sánchez, & Thorp, 2005). Grounded in theory and research, it exposed preservice and in-service teachers to the social justice dimensions of issues they faced in their work with immigrant students and their families. The program provided opportunities for them to learn directly from diverse students and families while gaining greater insight into their own cultural perspectives. We developed this approach to help preservice and in-service teachers examine the perplexities they encounter and view them as opportunities, rather than simply as problems.

The approach and strategies presented in this chapter have been tested with teachers at all levels of professional experience and are designed to help you move forward as culturally responsive practitioners working with immigrant students and their families (Thorp & Day, 2012; Thorp & Sánchez, 1998; Sánchez & Thorp, 2008). We use dilemmas that we have collected in our work to demonstrate the dilemma-based approach. The cultural dilemmas that we use in this chapter have been compiled from the real-life challenges and perplexities faced by preservice teachers.

Why Focus on Dilemmas?

Early on we noticed that the student teachers came to our university classes with stories about the interactions they had at their internship or work. Often these stories were presented as problems or challenges that desperately needed to be resolved. It appeared that these perplexing situations were being shared to demonstrate the challenge that working in diverse communities posed for them as teachers. It seemed as though the students were blaming others as the source of the problem. They did not place themselves in the center of the issue in which they had a role. The dilemmas were not viewed as learning opportunities. Most of the students did not see themselves as cultural beings. They did not recognize that they have a cultural lens through which they view and interpret their experiences. They did not recognize how that lens affected their interpretation of the dilemma. To highlight this important feature, we decided to call them *cultural dilemmas*.

Because most of the student teachers had little or no experience working with diverse children and families, particularly those who were immigrants and undocumented, at this point in their work they were relying on preconceived notions about the hopes, dreams, decisions, and intentions of communities they did not know (Delpit, 2002). The dilemmas shared in class often included interactions with students and families in a language other than English, yet limited thought was given to the possibility that some cross-cultural miscommunication was involved in the exchange. Although the dilemmas were filtered and shared from the student teacher's perspective, often little thought was given to the possibility that the dilemma was triggered by the student teacher's own cultural worldview. For these reasons, we chose to use cultural dilemmas as a means to help preservice and in-service teachers to recognize, describe, and address the cultural dimensions of challenging situations. The dilemmas approach helped student teachers reflect on the multiple components of the issues that were troubling to them.

The remainder of this chapter focuses on the strategies we developed and tested with preservice and in-service teachers. We discuss how you can recognize, describe, and address the dimensions of the perplexing situation you encounter in your teaching and integrate the cultural dilemma approach into your routine as a reflective practitioner. We especially emphasize the importance of using the dilemma approach for learning from immigrant students and their mixed-status families.

Fundamental Principles of the Dilemma Approach

Dilemmas Are Everywhere. Defining a situation as a dilemma can be difficult. For the purpose of this chapter, we define a dilemma as a perplexing event that occurs in one's work with students, families, community members, and colleagues. A dilemma has multiple possible responses and involves making challenging decisions. These are cultural dilemmas, because the perplexing interactions that occur with students and families most often have a cultural and social justice dimension (Thorp, 2009). It is important for teachers to acknowledge the role their own culture plays in the dilemma, the cultural perspectives of the students, families, and colleagues involved, and related aspects of social justice. Given the anti-immigrant policies unfolding in the United States, there is a strong social justice element to many dilemmas.

Dilemmas are emotionally challenging. When you and a close colleague view a dilemma in completely different ways, you experience an emotional conflict. Being perplexed and feeling uncertain about appropriate responses can contribute to feelings of incompetence, uncertainty, and frustration. As you work through this approach, we ask you to embrace the possibilities that arise when you recognize a challenge as a dilemma and purposefully spend time considering the meaning of the dilemma for you (Kidd, Sánchez, & Thorp, 2008).

Dilemmas often surface in the daily routines of teachers working with undocumented students or students in mixed-status families. We encourage you to adopt the dilemma approach to better understand the multiple issues that you face in your work with children and their families.

The dilemma approach is process, not product, oriented. When a situation is perplexing, there is a difficult decision to be made. This cannot be made impulsively. Rather, the teacher must analyze and deconstruct the dilemma to reflect on the nature of the dilemma and consider possible responses. Not all situations are equally appropriate for dilemma work. There are times when one must take immediate action; however, often when action precedes reflection, solutions are less than effective.

Dilemma success requires a willingness to slow down the process. In slowing down the process, one is able to reflect on the dimensions of the dilemma, particularly the cultural elements. For example, a child's disruptive behavior may require an immediate response in the service of the greater classroom. However, repeated disruptive behavior, the repeated failure of the teacher's response, or a new pattern of behavior requires thoughtful reflection about the nature of the dilemma the behavior is posing. Consider the case of a classroom teacher who was disturbed by the behavior of one of the immigrant students in her classroom. She was considering referring the student for a special education evaluation when she approached us about her dilemma. It became clear that the behavioral change had occurred suddenly, over a very short period of time. As she discussed her dilemma, we saw the need for more information and suggested she make a home visit. She learned that the child's father had recently been detained, no one in the family knew where he had been taken, and out of fear, the student's mother had left the country. The student was living under the care of her 18-year-old sibling. By slowing down the process and gathering information prior to making a formal referral, the teacher was able to work with her student's older sibling and other school staff to establish an authentic, reciprocal home–school connection and address behavioral concerns without a referral.

Dilemma success requires a willingness to be a risk-taker and to make oneself vulnerable. Having experienced a dilemma, a willing teacher wonders, "Why is this a dilemma for me?" and "Why is this particular issue a hot button for me?" How one views families, their routines and beliefs, varies widely, so it's important to recognize that what one experiences as a source of frustration may not be a dilemma for the parents or another teacher. A willing teacher asks, "Do the various people involved in the dilemma perceive the issues in the same way?" Remember that a dilemma involves difficult choices, so familiar responses may not be the most appropriate. You must be willing to see the dilemma from multiple perspectives, your own and those of others involved in the dilemma, and to wonder how viewing it that way can influence a course of action. Thus, the teacher who embraces dilemmas must be willing to take the risk of trying something new and possibly uncomfortable.

Establishing a Dilemma Routine

We live in a world where we are often expected to make speedy decisions and to do so with confidence. Adopting the dilemma approach requires a new kind of discipline. It will require practice and adopting some new routines. There are several strategies that can help you build a routine.

Start a Dilemma Journal. Set aside time to journal about dilemmas. Select a few minutes a day or a longer period once a week. When we asked teachers to reflect on their classroom experiences by keeping a daily journal, we found that their ability to integrate it into their normal routine affected the quality of the journal, highlighting the need to commit a few minutes a day to writing.

At first, just write down the dilemma. Who was present? What happened? How did you feel? Using sticky notes to jot down a dilemma as you go through your day may help. Perhaps you already spend a few minutes each day noting and recalling some of the events of the day. You may want to use the Cultural Dilemma Story form that we developed (Figure 2.1). Using the form allows you to go back and review each of the elements at a future time.

Find a partner— a dilemma ally. Select someone to be your dilemma ally. You will be more likely to stay on track by committing to work with another person. Engaging in dilemma work with another person provides multiple perspectives. This is especially true with cultural dilemmas. How we experience new situations is reflective of who we are as cultural beings. The child or family one teacher finds challenging may not be viewed as challenging by another teacher. Your dilemma ally, as a trusted friend, offers data and assistance in examining a dilemma through another lens (Costa & Kallick, 1993).

The time that you schedule with your dilemma ally should not turn into a venting or gripe session. There may be times when you need to vent, but you need to be clear that you are venting and not engaging in the problem solving that

Figure 2.1. A Cultural Dilemma Story Form

Setting (no names):

People involved (descriptors or first name only):

The story—description of what happened:

What perplexed me about this:

Something I wonder:

Developed by Thorp & Sánchez

distinguishes dilemma work. Venting before describing the dilemma runs counter to the process. So select a partner with caution. The person you select may not be the friend or colleague with whom you are likely to just vent. Then commit to a scheduled time that works for you and establish a routine for sharing and processing your dilemmas. It helps if you focus on only one dilemma each time you meet. Doing so keeps you from being overwhelmed and ensures that you devote enough time to the dilemma.

Establish Ground Rules for Discussing Dilemmas

Once you decide to examine your dilemmas with a trusted ally and schedule a regular meeting time, you need to establish some ground rules. Having ground rules will help you stay on task.

- *Suspend judgment.* We call it "Just the facts, ma'am." Tell the story, not how you felt or how this comes up all the time with this child or family. Stay with this event, even if it does happen all the time. Staying with one event, describing it deeply, and suspending judgment can increase clarity.
- *Honor confidentiality.* You may have access to information about a child or his or her family or a colleague that your partner does not. Honoring confidentiality can also help you to suspend judgment and avoid the pitfall of your partner's projecting his or her own frustrations onto what is puzzling you.
- *Avoid hasty conclusions.* You and your ally will need to work hard to avoid trying to solve the dilemma too quickly. Recognize that each child and each situation is unique. It will take time for you and your ally to determine all the factors that make this a dilemma.
- *Analyze the dilemma before brainstorming possible actions.* Remember that dilemmas involve difficult choices. Quickly jumping in to suggest actions may reduce the promise of creative decisions.
- *Honor the story.* A dilemma is your story of a challenging experience. When you tell it as a story, your ally will hear your truth about the experience. In telling the dilemma as a story, you place yourself in the story without editing or analysis.

Describing and Deconstructing Dilemmas

In working with dilemmas your first consideration in analyzing and examining them in detail—the deconstruction process—is to describe the dilemma using nonjudgmental language to tell the story. Use the examples in Figures 2.2 and 2.3 as guides for writing your story about the week's most perplexing situation.

You will need to reflect on all your dilemmas for the week and weed out those that may have lost their intensity. The weeding process is beneficial because it allows you to see a pattern of types of dilemmas that surface on a weekly basis. Once you select your dilemma, use the Cultural Dilemma Story form (Figure 2.1)

Figure 2.2. Cultural Dilemma Story

In a public elementary school, teachers became aware of a change in the behavior of their immigrant students as the media reported far-reaching changes in U.S. immigration policy. Some children were terrified of being separated from their parents because of their ethnicity and were missing school. Those who came to school became very quiet and withdrawn. The students seemed more cautious, more suspicious, more scared. This behavior was demonstrated in their reluctance to participate in class activities and to interact with their peers, and sometimes they even seemed shy around the teachers. Their classwork was suffering. The teachers began to better understand this behavior when a 5th-grader confided in his teacher that he and his sibling were fearful that their parents would be arrested and deported. Because of the recent executive actions targeting immigrants in the United States, all adults in his family and his friends' families were fearful, he said. The fear was widespread despite the fact that many people he knew were permanent residents or had siblings or relatives who were American citizens.

In an effort to help their students feel comfortable and safe again in their school environment, a group of teachers discussed this situation and explored various actions that the school might undertake. One suggestion was that the school become a sanctuary for immigrant children and their families. The teachers asked the principal for permission to raise the issue at a staff meeting. Because everyone who works in a school contributes to its environment, not only were teachers present at the meeting, but also present were school staff, such as custodians, cafeteria workers, and specialists who provided services to students on a regular basis.

Figure 2.3. A Cultural Dilemma Story

Setting (no names): Local public elementary school

People involved (descriptors or first name only): The immigrant children attending the public elementary school and their families, as well as the principal, all-grade-level teachers, school specialists, office staff, and other school services providers. Others playing a role are Immigration and Customs Enforcement (ICE) officials and other law enforcement officers.

The story—description of what happened: At a staff meeting a group of teachers discussed the idea of becoming a sanctuary school. They explained why they were trying to help the immigrant children and families in their school. The goal of sanctuary status is to afford undocumented immigrant children and their families a safe haven from community bias, but in particular to prevent ICE officials from entering the school's grounds to remove children or any family members who may be on the premises. The proposal for creating a sanctuary school also stated that those working in the school would not be able to ask the children about their immigration status or that of their families or their neighbors.

What perplexed me about this: At this point in any cultural dilemma story, we ask you to reflect on your feelings and ask why certain emotional reactions occur.

- What were your first thoughts? Why did these come up for you?
- Review your Cultural Lens (Figure 2.4).
    - » What links you to this dilemma?
    - » Are any of your beliefs and values being challenged? Why?
    - » What attitudes or assumptions are being questioned?

Figure 2.3. A Cultural Dilemma Story (continued)

- What are some hot-button issues for you?
  - » What experiences have contributed to these issues?
  - » How do they contribute to your reaction?
- Consider the perspective of others regarding this dilemma.
  - » How are they viewing the dilemma?
  - » What have you learned from their story?
  - » What experiences would help you further understand the situation?

Something I wonder: Remember that cultural dilemma work is a search for alternative views that are nonjudgmental and includes your understanding of your hot-button issues and the stories of others involved in the dilemma. Additionally, keep in mind that "it is in our discomfort that learning takes place" (Herr, as cited in Treinen, 2017, p. 13A).

- What is another way to view this dilemma?
- What additional information do I need to consider so that I can reframe my culturally influenced views?
- How can I adjust my cultural lens?

to describe your dilemma using descriptive and nonjudgmental language. Notice the difference between how you write the dilemma and how you describe it orally. Many teachers found that when a dilemma is shared orally, the description becomes more elaborate and complex, and judgmental, as the dilemma story appears to be overwhelming and in need of an immediate solution. It is important to be aware of this difference because dilemmas are opportunities for learning and not problems that need to be resolved immediately.

A second element to consider in deconstructing your dilemma is identifying the roles of all the people involved. Doing so will help you identify the focus of the dilemma, discussed below. It will also allow you to slow down the dilemma process and distance yourself from emotions that are typically associated with dilemmas.

In our experience as teacher educators, we rarely found any mention of interpreters in the written description of dilemmas presented by our student teachers. There are key factors to consider when an interpreter is involved in a dilemma. First, there is an underlying assumption that the interpreter provides a literal translation of the teacher's comments. However, even for professionally certified interpreters, a literal translation does not always capture jargon and the culturally and linguistically laden concepts used in the field of education. Additionally, interpreters are often immigrants themselves and bring their own cultural perspective, which may or may not be similar to that of the families or professionals involved in the dilemma. Even when people speak the same language, factors of class, race, education, gender, and immigration status can affect communication. While cross-cultural miscommunication can occur, remember that the cultural perspectives of everyone involved in a dilemma will affect the process.

A third element to consider is identifying the focus of the dilemma. Almost any dilemma can have several major issues. Recognizing this can help you understand that some elements of the dilemma are not as challenging as you at first perceived or that you have no role to play in some aspects of the dilemma. As you work to identify the focus of the dilemma, you also gain self-understanding about why you consider this situation a dilemma. It may remind you of a personal challenge you faced previously. For some people there is no dilemma where you believe one exists. The dilemma may solely be one that triggers a reaction or challenge for you. Thus, it's time to reflect on who you are in the dilemma (Why is this an issue for me?) and to work on your own self-awareness.

Dilemmas begin with you. When a dilemma occurs, you know it. There is that familiar feeling in the pit of your stomach, perhaps even a rush of anger or frustration or a sense of "Here we go again." This approach asks you to wonder why these feelings come up in your work with immigrant students and families. It is important to recognize that who you are as a cultural being influences how you experience a dilemma. The process of examining one's cultural perspective is not easy. As teacher educators, we consistently examined our own cultural lenses and openly shared with our graduate students what we learned about our own biases and misunderstandings. We state this here to let you know that being vulnerable is not comfortable; however, it is necessary. Learning takes place when we step out of our comfort zone and reflect on our work in diverse communities. We enhance our professional and personal growth by learning from our mistakes and from the views of others.

Explore your cultural lens. The elements that have made you a cultural being compose your cultural lens (Figure 2.4). Your cultural lens is the device through which you view all life experiences, especially those that feel the most challenging. It influences your opinions, your reactions, your assumptions, and your stereotypes. For example, your own immigration experience, as well as the immigration stories that have been passed down in your family, influence your view of immigrants, particularly those who may be undocumented. Do you see them as resourceful risk-takers or people who should not be here? Similarly, your own family history and cultural story form your view of families living in poverty, appropriate family size, child-rearing practices, language use, schooling, and school policies. These are just a few examples of what influences your cultural lens.

To explore your unique cultural lens, start by honestly voicing with your dilemma ally or in your journal why something is troublesome for you. This simple act honors you and acknowledges you as a cultural being. Your role is not to judge yourself but, rather, to become aware that you have a cultural view. Consider how each dilemma causes you to have a negative or guarded reaction and how it reminds you of earlier experiences and emotions with an issue. The memories and assumptions that surface in the present are informed by your inherent cultural nature. Your ally can support you in exploring earlier personal experiences that are similar to those in a current situation or dilemma.

Identify as many factors as possible that influence our daily beliefs, values, and practices. Figure 2.4 is one way to visualize our cultural lens. Some of the

Figure 2.4. Exploring Our Cultural Lens

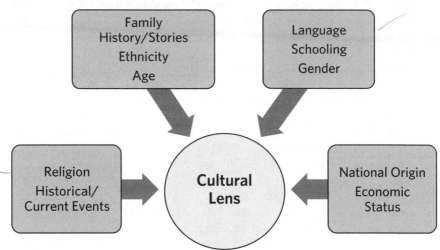

Culture is the accumulated and socially transmitted body of knowledge, behaviors, beliefs, values, and symbols that are learned through direct communication or imitation over generations, influenced by current experiences and social forces that impinge on ourselves and our community. Most of the dilemmas that challenge teachers contain a cultural dimension. Because we are all cultural beings, it is important to reflect on the characteristics that compose our cultural lens because they influence the way we interpret the world around us as well as how we relate to others.

factors that may make up your lens are race, ethnicity, language, family size, gender, economic status, education, generational history, major historical events, immigration, religion, country of origin, and level of educational attainment. Once you create your cultural lens, examine how each factor influences the assumptions and beliefs affecting your daily interactions with immigrant students, their families, and your colleagues. For each one, consider how it will positively influence your ability to manage the dilemmas you face as well as how each one might challenge your ability to do so. Over time your experience with dilemmas may cause your lens to change.

Explore stereotypes through your cultural lens. Your cultural lens also influences stereotypes you have about your own group and your view of other groups. Select one factor or element of your own cultural lens with which you really identify. Think about some of the negative or positive stereotypes you have of this trait and how it has shaped you. How might these views get in the way of or contribute to your work? For example, how might your family's immigration story, whether recent or in past generations, influence the stereotypes you have about today's immigrants?

In this brief overview, we are challenging you to explicitly commit to analyzing your cultural lens on an ongoing basis. When analyzing a dilemma, alone or with a dilemma ally, go back to that lens and wonder what role it might have in how you are experiencing the dilemma.

Explore your "hot buttons," or why this is a dilemma for you. Besides your cultural lens, another powerful factor that influences whether you experience a situation as a dilemma is what we call your "hot buttons." Our hot buttons cover a wide range of issues, including our views on immigration in general; on undocumented children and their families; on immigrant children in our schools; on culturally different parenting styles; on what is considered to be appropriate behavioral expectations; and on language use in the home, school, and community. Remember that a dilemma is triggered when there is a rush of feelings—anger, frustration, sadness, perplexity, and confusion about how to respond to a given situation. It's not that something is just perplexing but, rather, that you have some deep feelings about it. While not all dilemmas involve a hot button, the more emotionally charged an issue is for you, the more likely there is a hot button operating and it comes with a history of some pain you've experienced. Your emotional reaction to the dilemma may make it difficult for you to respond for a time. An emotional response usually surfaces when a situation or story is shared that embeds a message that conveys a judgment and assumes that you share that judgment with the person telling the story. Because you do not share the teller's perspective, you perceive a lack of understanding on the part of the teller about the injustice surrounding the event. For example, you hear a colleague speak with exasperation about the fact that a family has not shown any sign of participation in the school's at-home reading program. Your colleague says, "Well, what do you expect, the grandmother is the primary caregiver, and she can't even read or write in their home language, never mind in English." You are momentarily paralyzed, because you have a great deal of respect for this family, and you yourself had a wise grandmother who was not fluent in English but who worked hard and successfully raised children who were highly educated. You hear this comment as a judgment of the grandmother's general competence and are amazed by your colleague's unwillingness to explore other ways to interact with the grandmother. You are momentarily paralyzed because you also hear it as a judgment of your grandmother's competence. That's the hot button. At this moment, it's difficult to tap into your rational self and make a decision about the possible range of responses. When you feel this paralysis, look at the dilemma and ask, What is the hot button?

Seeing Dilemmas Through Another's Lens

Learn from others' stories. Gathering information is an important step in addressing a dilemma once the focus is identified. This is true for everyone involved. A teacher needs to learn about the relevant lives, hopes, and dreams directly from the family, the children, or other people involved. We can't know a family's story without being in an authentic relationship with the family. It is critical to do this through multiple relationship-building activities, which may include home visits and informal opportunities such as attending birthday parties, graduations, or sports events, and by including families in formal curriculum activities and making classrooms welcoming places for families.

Most dilemmas arise because the people involved do not know each other's stories. When relevant information is missing, misperceptions occur. In our experience, common dilemmas between educators and immigrant families are those that involve differing views of parent participation in school and homework, use of the home language, college planning, discipline, food preferences, and the role of students in caring for younger siblings, among others. To avoid making unnecessary judgments and to erase misconceptions, teachers must be willing to gather information about the parent's views of education. Thus when you experience a dilemma with a family, it is important to reflect on your relationship with them and to consider what else you may need to know, to be able to understand their expectations and experiences. This will help you to approach the dilemma in a less judgmental and more productive way.

Practice perspective taking. Perspective taking is another strategy that can enhance your self-awareness. It alerts you when others involved in the story do not react as you do.

A perspective-taking and reflective activity is charting (Figure 2.5). This activity can be done either as a journaling activity or with your dilemma ally. Two or more columns are drawn on a piece of paper, dry erase board, or journal page. You use the chart to reflect and write down the varying perspectives of all those involved in the dilemma. This is not a brainstorming activity; it is based on what is known from the perspective of those involved. Statements and questions about others' perspectives are listed on the chart. This part of the activity is especially eye opening since it is also an opportunity to identify what may be your assumptions, what are the actual facts, and what is known about others' perspectives. For example, in our work with student teachers we came across a dilemma in which the following assumption surfaced on the chart: an immigrant mother had no social network because her nuclear family lived in another country. Classmates informed the student teacher who had the dilemma that rarely do immigrant females leave their country for another without having a social network of family and friends, including community elders, waiting for them. The mother in the dilemma later explained to the cooperating teacher that she relied on a large social network that contributed to the overall well-being of the family. This network provided her with information on the educational system and how the U.S. legal system works. By getting to know some of the community elders and key members of the mother's social network, the teacher was able to work effectively and in a culturally responsive manner with the family. By developing an authentic relationship with some community elders, the teacher eventually was able to have a wider impact on the school's immigrant community. In this instance, charting the dilemma helped the teacher differentiate her assumptions from what was known, as well as from other possible interpretations.

Role playing also allows you to hear another's perspective by asking your dilemma ally to take on some of the various roles of the people in the dilemma. It is very helpful if you play the role of another person, especially the one who has been the most challenging to you, and the dilemma ally plays you. This activity can help challenge your assumptions and offer a window into how others perceive the dilemma. Before working with your dilemma ally, you should use your journal to list everyone involved in the dilemma and the various issues you feel are associated

Figure 2.5. Charting Activity

Write down what you know about the views of each participant in the dilemma. Your dilemma ally will take the position of the other participants. As you reflect on the views represented, is there something else you need to know? What questions arise about each view that can provide additional information? This activity allows you to identify your mindset versus the known facts of others' perspectives.

My Mindset	What I Need to Consider
My Dilemma: I have a mother who is not interested in her children's education. She isolates herself and has no one who can help her find out what's going on in school.	*Dilemma Ally:* Many immigrant families have a social network of extended family members and friends. Females, in particular, would not come here without some kind of assistance from a relative or friend.
Question(s): How can she expect to stay informed about school regulations, get meaningfully involved in school activities, or help her children with homework?	*Question(s):* Why do you think that the family has no way of staying informed? *Dilemma ally:* Some immigrants rely on community elders, religious leaders, for example, for assistance.
The mom doesn't seem to be aware of anything that's going on in school. She's hard to contact and won't come to meetings.	*Question(s):* Have you talked to the family, the mom, about this? Have you made a home visit?
No, I haven't. I'm concerned about visiting the home.	*Dilemma ally:* What are you worried about? Why is this a concern?
The process continues until the person with the dilemma feels that she has sufficient information to enable her to act in a manner that will help her and the parent work together.	*The dilemma ally proceeds in this fashion, providing known information and asking questions in a supportive manner.*

with the dilemma. Your dilemma ally can assist you in identifying the key people in the dilemma to ensure that the perspectives of those you did not even consider to be significant to the dilemma are heard. The use of nonjudgmental language is a key part of the role-playing exercise. Just as you described your dilemma using nonjudgmental language, you should practice asking questions in a nonjudgmental manner and also be an active listener. When you are listening to a particularly challenging perspective, it is important to slow down the role playing to give you time to wonder aloud and to practice gathering others' stories. Discussion and reflection with your dilemma ally after the role-playing exchanges allows more perspectives and clarifications to surface and will enhance your listening and perspective-taking skills.

Dilemma Challenges:
Dealing with Peers and Other Professionals

Not all dilemmas are directly related to a child or a family. We found that teachers often have dilemmas about how children and families are viewed by other faculty and staff. This occurs frequently with children who are immigrants, families who live in poverty, families who are not fluent in English, and families of color. Often you may witness a conversation that casts judgment on a child or family, making a negative assumption. Because you see yourself as an ally and advocate for undocumented children and mixed-status families, you feel uncomfortable witnessing these judgmental conversations. Without gathering a family story, there is no way to know what is really going on for the child and family who are the subject of these conversations. One strategy is to avoid them (flight); however, since they often occur in the copy room, the office, staff meetings, or the teachers' lounge, they cannot always be avoided. Further, avoidance creates a situation in which you continue to experience discomfort, and you have failed to explore the many options for different responses. Your discomfort could lead you to confront your colleagues in a nonproductive way that will not lead to a change in their behavior (fight). One dilemma strategy is to consider how to function as an ally and advocate on behalf of the children and families whose voices are not heard in these conversations.

A very useful resource for dealing with this type of dilemma comes from the National Coalition Building Institute (NCBI; Brown & Mazza, 2004; NCBI, 2015). NCBI offers training on prejudice reduction and coalition building. Several features of the training can assist you when you are wishing to provide an alternate view in these conversations. First, it is important to learn from the story of the person who is doing the judging. Remember, it is our assumption that our view of dilemmas is influenced by our own cultural lens and prior experiences. Thus, when someone speaks in judgment of a family and you want to understand, it is important to understand the meaning of the dilemma for that person by staying in a relationship with them. It can be helpful for you to suspend your own discomfort and judgment and ask them, "You hear people say that. I wonder why?"

It can be useful, then, to provide information to suggest an alternate view of what might be going on for the family. This is hard because it is important to avoid one's own lecturing or judgment and instead offer a differing perspective. Keep in mind that relationship building is the most important ingredient to changing minds and hearts.

Making Dilemmas a Habit of Mind

As you can see, the dilemma approach becomes a habit of mind, an almost automatic response to those perplexing situations that come up in your work with immigrant students and their families (Figure 2.6). The goal is to look for alternative views through your journaling and work with a dilemma ally and to consider alternative actions that are judgment free. You reach this goal by reflecting on

Figure 2.6. Cultural Dilemmas Framework

Principles of Cultural Dilemma Work

- Cultural dilemmas are everywhere
- It is process oriented, not product oriented
- Success requires a willingness to slow down the process

Strategies for Cultural Dilemma Work

1. Start a dilemma journal
2. Find a partner, a dilemma ally
3. Establish ground rules
    a. Suspend judgment
    b. Honor confidentiality
    c. Avoid hasty conclusions
    d. Analyze the dilemma before brainstorming possible actions
    e. Honor the story
4. Describe and deconstruct a cultural dilemma (Figures 2.1 to 2.3)
    a. Describe the cultural dilemma using nonjudgmental language
    b. Identify everyone involved
    c. Identify the focus of the dilemma
5. Explore your cultural lens (Figure 2.4)
6. Reflect on the dilemma using your cultural lens

Keep In Mind

- Cultural dilemma work is a search for alternative views that are nonjudgmental and includes your understanding of your hot-button issues and the stories of others involved in the dilemma.
- Reflection is a recursive and ongoing process.
- Cultural dilemma issues are interrelated and affected by the intersection of various factors, among them poverty, race, immigration status, education level, age, segregation, ethnic political power, class, and language.

your cultural lens, what you have come to understand about your hot buttons, and the stories of the others involved in the dilemma. To lead you in this direction, reframe how you initially stated the dilemma. How would you state it now? What might be possible courses of action? What have you learned by going through this process? Finally, it is important to recognize this as a recursive process and that you can always go back and work on other elements of the dilemma. As you work through the chapters of this book, we encourage you to begin to keep a journal of your dilemmas and to reflect on their meanings. We ask that you maintain a spirit of wondering: Why is this a dilemma for me? Where am I in the unfolding story of this child and family? What would it take for me to enter this dilemma as an ally or advocate?

Moving Forward as an Advocate and Ally

If the teacher is mindful of the community that his or her school serves, the opportunity to be an ally and advocate on behalf of immigrant children and families is always present. Sadly, we find ourselves in a politically charged atmosphere that has exposed undercurrents of prejudice and discrimination against immigrants. At the highest levels, injustices and legislation threaten DREAMers and their families, and these actions are reflected at the local and state levels as well. This growing insensitivity to the needs of the immigrant community makes it difficult for teachers to act on behalf of undocumented children and their families. The decision to become an ally and advocate is solely a personal one. While some will simply choose to turn their backs on the issue, others will not be able to turn away, because they believe that it is morally right to get involved.

It is important to know yourself and the level of commitment you are willing to make to address the issues facing the immigrant community. As educators, we are primarily aware of educational issues facing schools and classrooms. Unfortunately, in today's political, anti-immigrant climate the heated rhetoric has penetrated school walls in the form of bullying and attacks on immigrant children. Outside the school walls, we know that immigrant students and families face the actions of Immigration and Customs Enforcement (ICE) and state and local laws banning sanctuary policies.

Advocates and allies can work within the school community as well as at the local, state, and national levels. To make a decision about your level of involvement, first identify your interests and passions. Then research the many major institutions—educational, religious, economic, health, housing, and political—that have groups that advocate on behalf of immigrants. To develop your knowledge base about the various organizations, we encourage you to use the resources in Chapter 14 to find the groups and services that meet your needs.

The most important and critical aspect of working with marginalized communities is an awareness that your role is not to take ownership of the issues facing the immigrant community, but rather to be an ally and support the community's own self-advocacy and action. Ask yourself what the immigrant community wants and how you can support their hopes and dreams as they perceive them and what the implications for your work as a teacher of immigrant students are. Your teaching practice and every aspect of your professional role affords you a significant and powerful opportunity to be an advocate and an ally on behalf of your students and their families.

A Return to Our Vignette

You may wonder what happened to Tessa and Rafael. We used the dilemma process with Tessa, and she decided that the first step for her was to reach out to the family. However, she was only able to do that after engaging in self-exploration and a careful analysis of the stereotypes and the messages conveyed by the school. As she explored her own cultural lens, she was able to tap into her childhood experience living in a low-income family, with parents who worked multiple jobs and rarely had time for school involvement. She also wondered about the assumptions she was making about Rafael and his family. She recognized the role that stereotyping may have played when other staff informed her that the family would not be open to meeting with her. In order to reach out to the family, she also realized that she did not have the language skills to engage in a dialogue with the family necessary to establish a stronger relationship with them. She proceeded to invite a Spanish-speaking colleague to make a home visit with her. She was surprised by the fact that the family responded immediately and invited her to their home on a Sunday evening. She learned that Rafael's father had been a math teacher in his home country and that he was unaware of the challenges Rafael was experiencing. When he learned about the issues, he offered to gather texts that he had used back home and to become more active in helping Rafael. Rafael began to make dramatic progress but, more importantly, she developed a deeper understanding of how to engage with families as a teacher.

References

Brookfield, S. (1995). *Becoming a reflective teacher*. San Francisco, CA: Jossey-Bass.

Brown, C., & Mazza, G. (2004). *Leading in diverse communities: A how-to guide for moving from healing into action*. San Francisco, CA: Jossey-Bass.

Costa, A. L., & Kallick, B. (1993). New roles, new relationships: Through the lens of a critical friend. *Ed Leadership, 51*(2), 49–51.

Delpit, L. D. (2002). *Other people's children: Cultural conflicts in the classroom*. New York, NY: The New Press.

Kidd, J. K., Sánchez, S. Y., & Thorp, E. K. (2005). Cracking the challenge of changing dispositions: Changing hearts and minds through stories, narratives, and direct cultural interactions. *Journal of Early Childhood Teacher Education, 26*(4), 347–359.

Kidd, J. K., Sánchez, S. Y., & Thorp, E. K. (2008). Defining moments: Developing culturally responsive dispositions and teaching practices in early childhood preservice teachers. *Teaching and Teacher Education, 24*(2), 316–328.

National Coalition Building Institute. (2015). *The NCBI controversial issues process*. Retrieved from www.ncbi.org/wp-content/uploads/2017/05/controversial-issues-process-re-do.pdf

Sánchez, S. Y., & Thorp, E. K. (2008). Teaching to transform: Infusing cultural and linguistic diversity. In P. J. Winton, J. A. McCollum, & C. Catlett (Eds.), *Practical approaches to early childhood professional development: Evidence, strategies, and resources* (pp. 81–97). Washington, DC: Zero to Three Press.

Thorp, E. K., & Sánchez, S. Y. (1998). The use of discontinuity in preparing early educators of culturally, linguistically, and ability-diverse young children and their families. *Bulletin of Zero to Three, 18*(6), 27–32.

Thorp, E. K., & Sánchez, S. Y. (2008). Teaching to transform: Infusing cultural and linguistic diversity. In P. J. Winton, J. A. McCollum, & C. Catlett (Eds.), *Practical approaches to early childhood professional development: Evidence, strategies, and resources* (pp. 81–97). Washington, DC: Zero to Three Press.

Treinen, M. (2017, January 29). Seeking equality using dialogue. *The News Journal*, p. 13A.

CHAPTER 3

Teachers as Allies and Advocates for Students Living in Fear of Raids, Detention, and Deportation

Eva K. Thorp

The Fears That Touch Children's Lives: Three Dilemmas

I am a teacher educator. My work has focused on preparing teachers to work in diverse cultural communities. In turn, this work requires me to spend time in schools where there are large numbers of immigrant children and families, and I often observe the dilemmas that confront preservice teachers. I see my role as working with these teachers to help them better understand the challenges faced by immigrant children and families, especially those who are undocumented. My goal is to prepare the teachers to create culturally responsive curriculum that is informed by their understanding of children in immigrant families. Additionally, I encourage them to consider how to develop classroom and school climates that engage all the children in curriculum that recognizes the implications of current policies and embraces a climate of safety.

Immigration policies are increasingly a part of the American public discourse, and schools are becoming more affected by the ways in which current immigration policies touch the lives of the children enrolled in schools. As a result, the preservice teachers with whom I work are frequently confronted with the effects on their students of increased raids, detentions, and deportations of undocumented immigrants, both directly, as children become aware of peers in their midst who are at risk, and indirectly through what they see on television or hear discussed in their homes and communities.

Teachers report that some children are not coming to school because their parents are fearful of going out. Other children are food insecure because their parents are fearful of filling out any forms that would make them eligible for free and reduced-price lunch or other food support. Some families are missing critical health appointments for their children or are failing to attend a scheduled IEP (individualized education program) meeting out of fear of being picked up outside the meeting locale or fear that information they provide in a health department visit or a school

35

visit will be used against them. Some teachers report observing young children at play creating extended scenarios around the threat of ICE raids, acting out a sad variation on traditional hide-and-seek games. Many teachers report that immigrant parent participation in school-based or volunteer activities has decreased in part because of the broader climate of fear but also because of extra security measures, which may deter immigrant parents from feeling they can safely enter school buildings. Consider, for example, the message that is communicated to a family when any parent entering the school is required to leave a driver's license or other form of picture identification at the front desk prior to being able to go to his or her child's classroom. Such examples are common practice in schools where I work.

In this chapter, I discuss the implications for teachers when students in their elementary schools are faced with the reality of one or both parents having been detained or deported or who live in fear because of their family's mixed status. Detaining or deporting parents has a powerful impact on children whatever their age; however, for younger children, understanding the impacts and responding appropriately can be especially problematic. Younger elementary students are unlikely to even understand the notion of citizenship or immigration status. Even when older students have a rudimentary understanding of citizenship, they may be completely unaware of their own parents' undocumented status, a story that has been retold over and over by DREAMers.

It is critical that teachers understand how the threat of parental detention and deportation affects children's social-emotional development, their behavior, and their academic performance. These children have unique needs directly related to their family's mixed immigration status (Carnock, 2016). With this understanding, teachers can adopt strategies to support children who are living in fear. Social, emotional, and developmental challenges occur when students live in fear of separation from family members, particularly when students may have already been marginalized as immigrants living in poverty or linguistic isolation.

Children living in mixed-status families live in a climate of uncertainty, not knowing who in the larger community are their allies and who are their adversaries. They observe or are victims of hostile anti-immigrant messages. Teachers can communicate to these vulnerable children that their classrooms are safe spaces where they have allies and can safely voice their fears. Teachers can become skilled at addressing the behavioral and performance challenges that may arise when a child is experiencing separation or is living in an environment of heightened fear. Such skill will enable teachers to avoid problems associated with either over- or underreferral for special education services when a child's immigration status and parental separation are likely to become a part of the overall picture of his or her classroom academic performance and behavior. If teachers do not commit to integrating supportive strategies with children from families with vulnerable immigration status, such children's behavior may be completely misinterpreted, they may begin to underperform on academic tasks, and, sadly, they may just become silent.

Teachers can also commit to mindfully consider how any area of curriculum might be affected by the immigration dialogue. When teaching standard social studies units required for students to score at appropriate levels on high-stakes assessments, teachers can consider what these topics might mean for recent immigrants, students who have been historically marginalized, or students whose family's immigration status affects their ability to participate in the activities of citizenship covered by the assessment.

I have witnessed or been part of many dilemmas involving school-age children living with the fear of parental detention or deportation. For this chapter, I have chosen three stories that capture some of the challenges confronting teachers. These stories can help us explore how teachers can create safe, nurturing classroom communities for all children, including those living in fear; how they can refine their observation skills in order to be alert to behavioral and academic changes and to better interpret the possible meaning of these changes; how they can create curriculum that embeds issues of equity and addresses institutional forces that affect the current immigration climate; and how they can partner with families as allies and advocates for these children.

Does Afua Need a Special Education Referral?

Amanda was completing the final internship prior to graduation from her teacher education program. Amanda was a strong student, and as her supervisor, I had observed her leading several highly effective lessons in the 3rd-grade class where she had been placed to provide English as a second language (ESL) services. In preparation for her final observation, Amanda asked that I focus on her interactions with Afua and that I use this opportunity to notice Afua's behavior throughout the day. She noted that her cooperating professional was concerned about Afua's behavior. Afua had been acting differently in the classroom, sometimes lashing out aggressively, sometimes seemingly totally withdrawn. She refused to engage in conversation about what was going on. The teacher was wondering whether to make a special education referral, wondering whether Afua might have a behavior disorder. While observing this student teacher, I noted Afua's interactions with the teacher and others. On this day, she was quite withdrawn. While the lesson had been made accessible for children with varied levels of language proficiency and core knowledge, she did not seem willing to participate. Yet she seemed to be watching from afar and even seemed to be taking in what was happening. As part of debriefing, Amanda and I had a conversation about what she knew about Afua and about all the possible ways to interpret her behavior. As it turned out, Amanda's cooperative teacher had had a limited conversation with Afua's older sister and was told that Afua's father had recently been detained and was expecting to be deported to the African nation from which he had emigrated. Out of fear, Afua's mother had voluntarily returned to their home country. As a result, Afua now lived in the care of her older sister and her aunt. No one in the school knew where the father was being detained, or particularly what the family support needs might be for Afua. Looking into this story more deeply, Amanda was able to begin to identify many ways she could look at Afua differently and begin to explore ways to ensure that the classroom could be a safe haven for her. In the pages below, we will explore the opportunities for teachers that arise from this all too frequently occurring dilemma. It is important to consider why it is often suggested that a child's behaviors are related to a need for special education (Harry & Klingner, 2006).

What's Going On with Luna?

Another powerful dilemma that stays with me is that of Luna. Luna was a saucy 3rd-grader who participated in an after-school tutoring program staffed by graduate students in education. She was full of energy and enthusiasm for life. She loved to read, had a vocabulary well beyond her years, and displayed a dramatic flair that delighted all her teachers and tutors. She could retell anything she had read and do it with theatrical emphasis. She had a younger brother whom she treated with nurturing care, always making sure that he was where he needed to be before she settled into her school routine. She was highly conversational and appeared to enjoy talking about just about anything with teachers and tutors. When Luna entered 4th grade, things seemed to change. Her hair, which had always been impeccably cared for, was now less so. She freely said she hated school. She was not staying current on homework, and notes home from her teacher indicated the teacher's concern about Luna's lack of attention in school and her unwillingness to complete her work. One day, staff became concerned when Luna's mother was very late in picking up Luna and her brother. The graduate student waited and had a conversation with Luna's mother that led her to better understand what might be going on. Luna's mother's hours had changed at her job, and she was now working a later shift. The break her employer allowed her was barely long enough for Luna's mother to pick up her children, but even that was not consistent, so she could not be guaranteed to leave at a regular time, and sometimes she had to take the children to this night job, just to make it back in time. In the conversation, it became clear that Luna's mother's fear was that her undocumented status placed her in jeopardy if she were to request any accommodations from her boss. In the meantime, family stress and concern about her children in that context made it hard for her to find other solutions and caused her to rely on Luna to watch out for her brother.

Only Blue-Eyed People Get to Vote

Martin was a charming young 3rd-grader, quick to accomplish math and reading objectives. He loved to tell stories in one-on-one learning activities and enjoyed playing with his peers during recess. However, when it came to small-group social studies activites, it was nearly impossible to engage him. One day, during election season, he was placed in a small group composed of mostly children whose parents were immigrants. They were to work on an activity about voting that was intended to help prepare them for the upcoming grade-level, state-mandated assessment. The children read and discussed a short informative text, then offered their understanding of who can vote and what it means to vote in this country. Some of the children spoke with pride about the fact that their mothers or fathers had just been granted citizenship and obtained the right to vote; others seemed to know that their parents could not vote. Martin was noticeably silent and did not seem willing to respond. Shortly before the end of group time, he was encouraged to weigh in. He was reticent at first; then after a short time, he quietly whispered, "I heard that there is somebody who only wants people who are blue eyed and blonde to vote. I heard that those are the only people they want here." The teacher was taken aback. However, this statement was, in fact, a gift, presenting an opportunity to carefully consider the dilemmas associated with teaching the standard curriculum to students whose families are disenfranchised and who receive messages that they are not welcome.

In Chapter 2, we discussed the potential for using dilemmas to understand the many opportunities teachers have in a dilemma. Each of these stories describes a powerful dilemma, and each presents a teacher with many choices of whether and how to respond in a way that supports the needs of children who live in fear of the detention and deportation of their family members.

Who Are the Children?

There is no single profile of children affected by detention and deportation of their unauthorized parents. It is estimated that there are at least 5.1 million children under age 18 with at least one undocumented parent. In this group, more than 80% are U.S.-born citizens. Others are unauthorized themselves. Among the children who themselves are unauthorized, some accompanied their parents; others have come unaccompanied after lengthy separations from the parents who preceded them in their migration to the United States. These numbers represent nearly 30% of the children of immigrants and up to 7% of the total United States child population. Further, up to 40% of these children are age 5–11 and part of the fabric of elementary schools. While it is still the case that the largest numbers of families living under the shadow of threat of deportation are concentrated in a few states—California, Florida, Illinois, New York, and Texas—the elevated emphasis on immigration enforcement has meant large increases in detention in other states. These changes in enforcement have also meant that detentions and deportations are being carried out where immigrants targeted for deportation may have been long-term residents, firmly established in their local communities and not known to have been involved in any criminal activities. Capps, Fix, and Zong (2016) report that of those deported in the 2010–2012 period, 205,000 had one or more U.S.-citizen children. This has led to a climate of fear among communities, even among those who themselves are not at risk for deportation; Rosenblum and Meissner (2014) report, for example, that 24% of all Latinos say they know someone who was deported or detained in the past year; and nearly half worry about themselves, a family member, or a friend being deported. This climate of worry can have lasting effects on children, on their school performance, and on their sense of security and emotional well-being.

Many tangible factors affect immigrant children living under the shadow of detention and deportation. Immigrant families in which one or more family member is undocumented are more likely to be living in poverty. When there is a threat of deportation or a family member has actually been deported, income is further reduced. Families are less likely to avail themselves of the services that are available for their U.S.-born children, fearful of discovery of the status of one or more members of the family. Employed unauthorized parents often do not have access to benefits such as insurance. Families are faced with disruptions that temporarily, or in some cases permanently, affect the family structure. Sadly, there were estimates that at least 5,100 children in the United States were currently in foster care because a parent had been detained or deported. Children living under the threat of deportation have been reported to finish fewer years of school (Anderson, 2016).

While these tangible factors have long-term impacts, perhaps even more significant are the less tangible emotional and mental health consequences of the threats to family stability and child well-being that accompany detentions and deportations. The threat of deportation creates a circumstance of chronic stress that affects all family members. This may add to the chronic depression or anxiety experienced by parents whose motivation for immigrating was to escape violence and terror in their home countries. The detention and deportation of one or both parents contributes to trauma with results not unlike those associated with post-traumatic stress for U.S.-born children. Some children have witnessed the frightening arrest of a parent; others have experienced the equally frightening disappearance of a parent. Some children, themselves undocumented, may have already experienced the fear of their initial migration, or they may relive the trauma of an earlier separation from their parent or parents who preceded them in migrating to the United States. Visitation programs at some detention facilities offer only partial relief. In school, children may lose all motivation, as a result of the loss of a parent but also following the shattering of their beliefs about their life in the United States.

What's a Teacher to Do?

Because schools cannot inquire about, or deny services based on, immigration status, teachers have an opportunity to create a safe haven for children who are threatened by immigration enforcement and who live under the cloud of family separation. Doing this work takes a willingness to be a leader for social justice (Long, Souto-Manning, & Vasquez, 2016). Unfortunately, many teachers are unaware of the climate of fear that surrounds children they teach. They may be woefully uninformed that certain dramatic behavior changes they observe may be attributable to this climate of fear. To create a safe haven for students, teachers can take many steps.

Know yourself. In Chapter 2, we stressed the importance of knowing yourself. As a teacher affected by the climate that increased enforcement creates, you must consider how committed you are to better understanding the challenges confronting students and their families. You must know who you are as an advocate and ally. Having committed to making your classroom a safe haven, you will have many things to do. A Baltimore teacher, Tom Smith, provides a good model for us when he says, "When I hear where they're from, I can imagine their stories and I don't want to do anything that will add to their pain" (Bowie, 2015).

Become informed. Often schools operate as their own microcultures; teachers benefit when they learn about and from the community around them. Who are the families? What are the immigration pressures in the community? How is immigration enforcement affecting the life of the community? Learn about the community groups that provide information and resources to families experiencing the crisis of deportation. Gather your own information about the legal rights of immigrant children and families. Share this information with other staff in your schools.

Use your child development knowledge. Teachers must be alert to the signs of distress and emotional trauma in the children they teach and be aware of the ways that these signs may be exhibited across students of different ages. Younger children may have very little understanding of what is happening, though they have an awareness of changes in the life of their family. They may be feeling a sense of loss but not be able to express it. They may show signs of withdrawal. Consider how to engage children in developmentally appropriate conversation that enables them to express their emotions. By contrast, older students may show overt signs of stress through anger or by acting out. Older students may also have been placed in positions of taking on additional responsibility. They can benefit from someone who can hear their concerns.

Find ways to engage with families, learning from families while honoring privacy and confidentiality. In the current climate of fear, families may be avoiding schools. They may not be responding to teachers' requests for information. They may be uncertain about whether it is safe to come to school. Find ways to connect with them. Do not assume that a family member's nonresponsiveness means disinterest. All too often that is exactly what school staff assume. Explore with them ways to be in contact. A teacher's presence in the community, at community events, signals his or her interest in the children and families and may create opportunities for further collaboration. Invite families into the classroom and find meaningful ways for them to share their stories.

Embrace a strengths-based approach. Consider what you know about the children and their families and what that suggests about their strength and resilience. The act of immigration itself requires phenomenal strength on the part of individuals and families. In the current climate, a deficit approach is far more common.

Critically analyze your curriculum from an equity perspective. Consider the messages conveyed by the curriculum. Recall the story of Martin. He did not see himself in the lesson about voting and democracy. Not only that; he did not see himself as being welcome in this country. He was not belligerent; he just did not see himself. Teachers must wonder how to ensure the required content is taught in a way that is relevant to the students. Relevant content—exploration of the immigrant experience—will increase student's motivation.

Advocate for appropriate supports and services. As noted above, families living under the threat of deportation are less likely to seek the services to which they are entitled. Find ways to inform them about available services.

Engage all children in equity curriculum in a supportive classroom. Immigrant children experience hate messages in their communities, from the media, and from their peers. Teachers have an opportunity to create classroom space where all students become aware of these messages and explore how to be allies.

It is easy to make suggestions, but the hard work starts with teachers and families. There is so much that can be done to help one become an ally and an advocate for these children and their families. Their contributions to our communities warrant our dedication. There are those who would ask us to look at the driving forces of immigration and understand the heartache involved (Nazario, 2013), but the reality is that teachers are in the best position to make a difference in the immediate challenges that undocumented students and students from mixed-status families encounter every day.

References

Anderson, M. (2016, January 26). How fears of deportation harm kids' education. *The Atlantic.* Retrieved from www.theatlantic.com/education/archive/2016/01/the-educational-and-emotioal-toll-of-deportation/426987/

Bowie, L. (2015, October 30). Unsettled journeys: Torn between two worlds. *Baltimore Sun.* Retrieved from data.baltimoresun.com/news/unsettled-journeys/part-1

Capps, R., Fix, M., & Zong, J. (2016). *A profile of U.S. children with unauthorized immigrant parents.* Migration Policy Institute. Retrieved from mpi.org

Carnock, J. T. (2016). *Growing up with undocumented parents: The challenges children face.* Retrieved from www.newamerica.org/education-policy/edcentral/undoc-parents/

Harry, B., & Klingner, J. (2006). *Why are so many minority students in special education?* New York, NY: Teachers College Press.

Long, S., Souto-Manning, M., & Vasquez, V. M. (Eds.). (2016). *Courageous leadership.* New York, NY: Teachers College Press.

Nazario, S. (2013, October 14). The heartache of an immigrant family. *The New York Times,* p. A27.

Rosenblum, M. R., & Meissner, D. (2014). *The deportation dilemma: Reconciling tough and humane enforcement.* Washington, DC: Migration Policy Institute.

The Urban Institute. (2006). *Children of immigrants: Facts and figures* (Issue brief No. 51111/900955).

Part II

REACHING STUDENTS FROM IMMIGRANT FAMILIES THROUGH TRANSFORMATIVE CULTURALLY RESPONSIVE EDUCATION

Carollyn James

CHAPTER 4

Antiracist Practices

Strengthening Students' Sense of Self to Promote Hope and Confidence for Student Success

Sandra Duval

Out of my desire to hear the echo of my voice in America
and see my footprints in its landscape,
my songs extol the cherished memories of there
While my feet respond to the fluid rhythms of here.
And in between a new configuration emerges
Which is neither Here nor There.
This novel form was born of my struggle
to unearth who I was there and to assert who I am here.
The delicate co-mingling of these two worlds,
each richer because of the other
has produced a new place for me.
This world that is in-between that I inhabit
has transformed me.

—Sandra Duval

Since the passage of the 1965 Immigration and Naturalization Act and the shift in immigration patterns, the education of children of immigrants of color has been a debate filled with contention. Zéphir states, "Haitian educators believe that many of these problems stem from racial and ethnic discrimination and Haitians are perceived to be nothing but a source of problems for American society and American education, in particular" (Zéphir, 1996, p. 151). The debate continues today and is directed by the public's strong opinions on many issues, including how to educate immigrant populations and the process of their assimilation into U.S. culture. The awareness of and array of sentiments about immigrants with undocumented status augment and add a new dimension to the debate. As Chomsky explains, "Today's immigration debate is rife with myths, stereotypes, and unquestioned assumptions. . . . It's clear to me that many of the arguments currently being cir-culated are based on serious misconceptions not only about how society and economy function, but also about the history of immigration, the law, and the reasons for immigration" (Chomsky, 2007, p. xi). The controversies are heightened as schools struggle with not only how to educate children of immigrants but also how to decipher the roles and responsibilities of teachers in working with students who may be undocumented.

Educational agencies at all levels—federal, state, and local—may, like the general public, have the very best intentions, but they are suffering from having an incomplete understanding of students whose future we are charged to chart. This incomplete understanding, also fueled by our narrow understandings of each other's stories, propels policymakers and educators to design educational strate-gic plans and use practices that were created with the objective of educating all students but that unintentionally, because of their lack of relevance, often fail the children of immigrants when implemented. This is because the plans frequently begin with the erroneous concept of a homogeneous immigrant population, thus the plans are not successful at taking into account the complexities of the stressors that can affect the educational experiences of different immigrant student popula-tions. As Brookfield explains, "One of the hardest things teachers have to learn is that the sincerity of their intentions does not guarantee the purity of their practice" (Brookfield, 1995, p. 1).

These failed educational plans perpetuate stereotypes and create a lens through which immigrant students are viewed as "the other." This sense of "otherness" fur-ther negatively influences our beliefs and in turn our educational decisions and policies where immigrant children are concerned. In the dichotomy that exists in education, the "othering" of immigrant children stunts our capacity to tackle the challenges of all students through critical voices and diverse perspectives. This lens also prevents us from recognizing the knowledge, skills, and multitude of experi-ences that the students and their families bring to U.S. schools.

Today, there are over 13 million children of foreign-born parents in U.S. schools (U.S. Census Bureau, 2011), including those with undocumented sta-tus. For many of these students, school is their only hope of a promising future. Culturally competent educators hold the key to that promise. This chapter presents a model that can support transcultural practices for transformative educational experiences in our schools for immigrant students, especially those who are Black and have an undocumented status. Using a self-study approach, the *Roots and Wings Transformative Model* was designed. My goal is to identify the mindset and practices that can contribute to successful outcomes for our students.

The model stems from the value of personal narratives. It identifies edu-cational strategies to affirm the culture and lives of our immigrant students in order to ensure their success. Schools and other educational agencies can sup-port building educators' cultural competency by providing a platform for pro-fessional development that is rooted in knowledge construction from diverse perspectives.

Urgency

Since teaching is not neutral, teachers need to understand students' lives beyond the schoolhouse in order to avoid hegemonic practices. This way they can address complex challenges with the necessary urgency. Educators should create an environment that takes into consideration that one or more of their students may be undocumented, may become undocumented during the course of their academic life, or may live in a multi-immigration-status home. Educators who are aware that students can feel the impact of immigration policies, especially those aimed at the undocumented, understand that students may be traumatized because of one or more of seven possible scenarios:

1. They are undocumented or may become undocumented when their visa expires.
2. A family member is affected by his or her status or fear of being deported.
3. They feel an eerie familiarity or connection to groups of immigrants who are being persecuted.
4. They experience other's beliefs, micro-aggressions, or actions as a result of the hurtful language used to describe them or communities they love—words such as *alien, illegal,* and *criminal.*
5. Their educators are silent on issues that cause them stress.
6. Their parents' mistrust of institutions discourages them from participating in programs that can support their academic and social development.
7. They do not see their place in their world and rapidly move from being hyper-visible to invisible.

The detrimental impact takes root when schools and teachers do not have the cultural competency to build a positive social relationship that promotes a supportive climate and culturally responsive instruction. As Hammond (2015) puts it, "It becomes imperative to understand how to build positive social relationships that signal to the brain a sense of physical and psychological and social safety so that learning is possible" (p. 45). As a result we understand that there is no way around using instruction that is culturally responsive because it serves as a catalyst for student learning.

As I was, many school-age children were brought by their parents to, or reunited with them in, the United States. For example, today, approximately 20% of the Haitian immigrant population is of school age (5–17 years; U.S. Census Bureau, 2015). Eighty-five percent of children immigrating to the United States experience a separation during the migratory process, often for several years, from one or both parents (Suárez-Orozco, Suárez-Orozco, & Todorova, 2008). Such situations activate children's stress response, which can be lessened through the presence of supportive relationships with caring adults. Children from Central America, the Dominican Republic, and Haiti are most adversely affected, as they might have to wait 5 or more years before reuniting with their father, mother, or both (Suárez-Orozco et al., 2008). No matter how and why they come, the children are often affected by the trauma of immigration and current immigration policies, as they often reside in multi-immigrant-status homes or communities. It is that population—vulnerable, precious, and with a lot of potential—this chapter focuses on. I want to tell their story by reflecting on my own, using a self-study approach, knowing that the lessons learned will leave us better equipped to know them and help them achieve their full potential.

Rationale for the Model

Flor Ada and Campoy (2004) advise that "to increase our ability to think clearly about these issues, we need to be willing to reconnect with our own early experiences. Although we may encounter some painful feelings in the process, we are also regaining our capacity to feel a deeper sense of joy and connection with ourselves and others" (p. 15). This time, I dig for artifacts so as not to rely on memories to study what were the components of my transformative and transcultural education.

As Brookfield (1995) explains, one form of critically reflective process happens when teachers are able to have autobiographical reflections. The author contends that although disparaged, "our autobiographical experiences as learners and teachers provide a rich source of materials for us to probe." So I probed. The more I probed the more I realized that this type of self-study could provide invaluable insight. So I asked many questions, including, What practices affected my educational experiences as an immigrant student in New York City public schools in a positive way? In which ways do caring adults diminish the impact of toxic stress from immigration trauma on the developing brain? How might insights gained from self-study and counter-storytelling support my growth as a teacher educator to serve as an ally for immigrant students, including undocumented students? How can I apply my self-study insights in professional development to build teachers' cultural competence? In the end, I want to open a different type of dialogue by sharing bits and pieces of my story. "Consulting our autobiographies as learners puts us in the role of the 'other.' We see our practice from the other side of the mirror, and we become viscerally connected to what our own students are experiencing" (Brookfield, 1995, p. 29). There are three reasons why I selected the process:

1. My public elementary school, which provided an education overwhelmingly to children of immigrants, was considered one of the best in the nation when I attended it. An article, "U.S. Honors Brooklyn School," in the *New York Times* noted that "a public elementary school in Brooklyn is among 270 public and private elementary schools nation-wide being honored by the federal government for excellence. . . . [It] is the only public school in the New York City metropolitan area to receive the honor." The then U.S. secretary of education, William J. Bennett, congratulated the schools that were recognized:

"They're good schools. They provide the young with a solid foundation for later life" (Rangel, 1986). In addition to government accolades, data collected about alumni and staff strongly presented the same sentiments.

Testimonies:

- "Amazing—dedicated teachers."
- "Thank you for caring and never giving up."
- "Principal always made it her duty to tell me how smart and special all of us are."
- "Amazing—we had no idea at the time the caliber of excellence they instilled in us."
- "Amazing educators."
- "Creative, involved, energetic."
- "Brilliant educator."
- "Thank you for teaching me to 'think outside of the box.'"
- "The Best thing that ever happened to education."
- "Outstanding educators."
- "They have changed my life."

2. Teachers and staff knew how to support parents with negotiating for their children a racialized United States. Coming from a country where race classification did not exist, they needed to adapt.
3. Since teachers valued my sharing of narratives as an immigrant student during professional development opportunities, I wanted to reflect on my experiences and provide a broader and more accurate picture of my elementary school experiences.
4. Educators can perpetuate racist ideas about other people's children no matter what color they are, and none of us are immune.

As a way to support teachers in building their capacity to meet the needs of culturally and linguistically diverse immigrant students, the "power of a single story," a phrase coined by researcher Margaret Mitchell Armand (2015), has personal meaning for me because it supports the idea of bringing many single voices together to build multiple perspectives about the education of immigrant students.

I began evaluating my bilingual multicultural education from Grade 5, the year I arrived in the United States to reunite with my family. The experience of having great teachers prompted me to become a general education teacher as well as a teacher who taught English learners (ELs). Early in my career, during my doctoral work at George Washington University, I started working as a teacher trainer. Over the years, as I reviewed the feedback from teachers after the delivery of different professional development modules, such as "Educating Caribbean Students in U.S. Schools," it became evident that sharing my educational experiences as an immigrant student in U.S. schools and as an ESOL/ESL teacher supported their ability to grasp the information and navigate and negotiate the meaning of cultural dynamics as they learned how to best meet the needs of their students. The conversations were deepened by the sharing of personal narratives. We often reflected on what had made my own teachers and school culturally competent. This openness invited many teachers to also share their own stories.

During the early 2000s, I worked for an educational association, where I was exposed to the plight of DREAMers. During visits on Capitol Hill, my colleagues and I would listen to the stories of the students as they pleaded their cases, looking for allies and policy changes. During those years the power of a "single story" became even more obvious to me. Today, during professional development I continue to remember the power of a single story as well as policy.

A staff member at my elementary school reminded me that "having immigrant teachers was a big plus" for me as a student. The self-study allowed me to also analyze the narratives of many of my elementary school educators who were themselves immigrants. My goal was to reconceptualize the intersection of immigrant teachers' and students' identities as pedagogy for elevating teacher practice and professional development, thus promoting cultural competence that combats implicit biases. These strides serve as a catalyst for teacher agency and student advocacy. In the end, teachers can develop the mindset and use the practices presented in the model below to promote their capacity to provide a transcultural and transformative education. Finally, our collaborative effort is to equip immigrant students of color with *roots and wings* for success by implementing culturally responsive practices.

Design of a Self-Study Approach

The self-study approach pushed me to collect data from multiple sources that could provide invaluable insight on how to affirm the lives of our immigrant students though the practices used in our schools. Educators can replicate the approach to gather additional knowledge.

Step 1: I brainstormed many questions and selected a few, including, What practices influenced my educational experiences as an immigrant student in New York City public schools in a positive way? In which ways did caring adults diminish the impact of toxic stress from immigration trauma on my developing brain? How can I use my reflections on the analysis of the data gathered to refine my practice? How can I share the findings to build the cultural competence of other educators?

Step 2: I systematically reviewed and analyzed data from diverse and multiple sources: my diaries, yearbooks, essays, student artifacts, letters, student academic records, and school records. To add objectivity to the analysis, I analyzed data from other sources: interview scripts, online posts from alumni of various classes who were answering questions about the impact of staff on their lives, posts from teachers sharing information on educational models, old pictures posted by alumni sharing celebrations of culture, and newspaper articles (e.g., Rangel, 1986). I also did an extensive literature review about the education of Haitian immigrants.

Step 3: Four readers were selected to review my analysis of the data and the findings to be sure that the analysis was objective.

Step 4: I used a focus group to address these questions: (1) How might insights gained from the self-study approach support my growth as a teacher educator to serve as an ally for immigrant students, including undocumented students? (2) How can I apply my self-study insights in professional development to build teachers' cultural competence?

Findings from the Data Analysis

In the end, the decision to build a model to gather the information derived from the analysis was made. Providing students with a strong sense of identity and affirming their worth and intelligence were salient themes when analyzing the data. Matthew Lieberman affirms that our brain is wired to feel connected and respected because our survival depends on it. He adds, "Our basic urges include the need to belong, right along with the need for food and water. . . . Someday we will look back and wonder how we ever had lives, work, and schools that were not guided by the principles of the social brain" (Lieberman, 2013, p. 299, 303). For students who may experience anti-immigrant sentiments, school can act as a buffer. This is even more imperative for students who may have undocumented status and feel a deep sense of rejection or isolation from their countries.

Ultimately, I want to open a different type of dialogue by sharing bits and pieces of my educational experiences in an organized way. This would allow dialogues containing perspectives that are so wide that divergent thoughts are not silenced or delegitimized. As Reagan (2000) stresses, "Discourse itself—the way that one talks, thinks about, and conceptualizes educational thought and practice—that is the issue" (p. 3). In my opinion, the goal is for educators to ask different kinds of questions that augment our ways of making meaning of complex educational challenges from multiple perspectives. These strides serve as a catalyst for teacher agency and student advocacy. In the end, teachers develop the mindset and use tools that promote their capacity to provide a transcultural education that equips immigrant students of color with roots and wings for success.

The Roots and Wings Transformative Model

There are many ways to incorporate counternarratives in a framework for transformative education for immigrant students. The most basic way to look at this model (Figure 4.1) is to see it as a way to give students roots and wings. The roots are mindsets, knowledge, and skills that build a strong sense of identity. The wings are mindsets, knowledge, and skills that promote academic growth and success as well as life skills. Figure 4.1 is a quick reference chart to identify and organize the educational practices.

Figure 4.1. The Roots and Wings Transformative Model

Transcultural Educational Practices for Immigrant Students

Build an understanding of deep culture and of sociopolitical context as they apply to both teachers and students; thereby building relationships that make it possible to bring to the classroom relevance and rigor that leads to excellence.

Individual-Student-Level Practices	Educator-Level Practices	Environmental-Level Practices
• Make each student feel visible. • Develop a mindset that promotes a strong and positive self-identity for each student. • Encourage each student to discover and nurture his or her gifts. • Promote hope and confidence about the future for each student.	• Teach with rigor and discuss the complexities of concepts in different content areas. • Encourage students to read a diversity of texts and to write their own history. • Communicate high expectations. • Teach academic work habits that explicitly foster student ownership of learning. • Be an inspiration.	• Create a nurturing school climate that provides access and success to all. • Align the school with community values. • Prepare students to be contributing and collaborative global citizens. • Provide an array of opportunities for transcultural and transformative experiences in and outside of school.

Build an Understanding of Deep Culture

Where do we start? The Roots and Wings Transformative Model demands that teachers build an understanding of deep culture—theirs and their students'. Discourse about deep culture moves us beyond heroes and holidays and invites us to talk about expectations, childrearing practices, concepts of beauty, family, and community. The diversity of our students challenges us to be honest about this "othering"; understand the impact of our own cultural understandings on our teaching; and explore the complexities of the cultures, histories, and experiences of our students. "As we begin the process of trying to broaden our perspectives on the history of educational thought and practice, it is important for us to understand that the activity in which we are engaged will inevitably involve challenging both our own ethnocentrism and the ethnocentrism of others" (Reagan, 2000, p. 3). What we know well about our immigrant students is country of origin and level of English proficiency, but, often, knowledge of their families and communities is limited. There is a strong urgency to understand more about the true stories of our students and families and the dynamic of our interactions in order to address the educational and socioemotional needs of our immigrant students.

Counter-Storytelling In Context

The insights suggest two strides to bring a paradigm shift in educating the children of immigrants. First, educational models must be constructed in ways that are inclusive of the cultural lenses of the marginalized in order to address the persistent disconnect sensed by immigrant students and their families. As an example, many teachers understood that nearly three-quarters of Haitian students were reuniting with their parents. Being raised by grandparents and then reuniting creates a sense of isolation and longing no matter where you are. Adjusting to different norms and expectations can lead to conflict. The impact of immigration policy that separates parents from children is strongly felt through the reunification process. The self-study approach allows such groups to share their stories.

Storytelling can be used to provide an additional lens because as a methodology it deliberately considers cultural values and behaviors. Historically, Haitians have been portrayed as a problem to be solved, as the focus is typically on disaster relief and poverty. However, we did not see ourselves this way because our teachers helped us explore our history and contributions to freedom in the Americas, including the United States, as Haiti was the only country to end slavery and gain their freedom from colonial powers through revolution. In my hometown, examples of how inspirational the Third World liberation movement that began in Haiti can be found in historical landmarks. One such place tells the history of Mother Mary Elizabeth Lange, a Haitian immigrant who founded the first African American Catholic community that included a school to educate black girls with music, the classics, and fine art as part of the curriculum.

Educators can conduct an analysis of personal narratives related to the contributions of their ancestors to create a transcultural and transformative educational model that equips immigrant students, especially DREAMers, with the academic and socioemotional skills needed to negotiate and navigate their worlds successfully. Integral to the model is the development of a strong sense of dignity and cultural identity where cultural and linguistic diversity is recognized as a gift, not a deficit. One alumna remembers being inspired by a principal who believed that we should all strive for perfection so we can settle for excellence.

Educators can invite students to discover with them which knowledge is silenced and how new narratives can be created about their world while addressing the curriculum standards. For example, the concept of Christopher Columbus discovering America carries different meanings for different groups. For people from the Caribbean, it brought the disappearance of the natives and brought enslaved Africans to replace them. My teachers did not allow the world to define us. They lifted the weight of a definition of blackness rooted solely in U.S. history and replaced it with a comprehensive, diasporic meaning of blackness.

The practices are by no means inclusive of all possibilities and can be divided into three distinct categories: individual student level, educator level, and environmental level. At the *individual student level*, educators and the school must always seek to know their students by honoring who they are and supporting the development of students' positive self-identity. At the *educator level*, teachers must build their cultural competence and identify equitable strategies that engage students and give them access to rigorous, culturally relevant educational experiences so they gain ownership of their own learning and become lifelong learners. At the *environmental level*, the school and stakeholders must create a culturally responsive environment that reflects both students and their community so that students become responsible and contributing citizens at local, national, and global levels.

For each of these categories, we must keep relationship building, rigorous and relevant education, and high expectation for excellence at the core. I must emphasize that transcultural mindset and education happens when educators have an understanding of deep culture—their own and their students. This includes an understanding of the sociopolitical context of the communities they serve. Knowing and building relationships with our students and their families is the only way to start if we are willing to give transcultural education a try. It is the primary way to reach and affirm the lives of our students and their families.

Below is an example of how educators might use the first component of the Roots and Wings Transformative Model, individual-student-level practices, to elicit counterstories, personal narratives, and guiding questions to facilitate discourse and gain an authentic understanding of their students.

Make Students Feel Visible—Know Their Names

One of the simplest ways to acknowledge students is to make them feel visible. In school, almost everyone knew my name and where I came from. My friends remembered the same thing. Eve remembers the way the teachers took time to teach her to say her name with Haitian phonetics. As stated in *The Language of Names*, "It seems obvious that name and self-identity are permanently wed. No one is more aware of this than a child. Names weren't just names. . . . Names penetrate the core of our being, and are a form of poetry, storytelling, magic and compressed history" (Kaplan & Bernays, 1999, p. 13). As one classmate recalled, "One of my fondest memories is of how Mrs. Bruno, the principal, pronounced each person's name correctly. In doing so, she showed us that she valued who we were and how important our parents' culture should be to us."

My Testimony and Analysis: Over the years, I remember many instances of being invisible or, worse, being reconstructed into someone I barely recognized by ideologically dominant discourses in the media. It started with the distortion of my name and then, later on, my memories of the first place that I called home. Fortunately, the teachers at my elementary school honored my name, my history, and my parents' spirit. This set a strong example for my peers of the importance of demonstrating respect for us as individuals with unique qualities and histories. This kind of respect quickly builds a positive classroom climate. As an educator, I value showing respect and honoring students by being able to greet them by their name each day.

Guiding questions: Are we taking the time to pronounce our students' names correctly, or do we create abbreviated versions for our convenience? Do we know what our students' names mean to them and their families? How do we support students whose names can be used for racial profiling or make them a target for bullying?

Implications:
Creating Policies with a Future Workforce in Mind

I believe that only by sharing and learning from students' stories, from Congress to the classroom, can we prevent education that dehumanizes or extinguishes others instead of affirming them. Education that dehumanizes students of color leads to disengagement, academic failure, and dropout, and sometimes facilitates the school-to-prison pipeline.

Listening to youths' testimonies of anti-immigrant sentiments and reflecting on my own experiences, I wondered about those who did not view policies that make it possible for immigrant children, especially undocumented children, to go to college as a moral obligation. Could they at least see them as obvious social and economic imperatives? One cannot ignore the fact that the foreign-born population grew from approximately 5% in 1970 to approximately 13% in 2010 (U.S. Census Bureau, 2013). Of that population, the Latin American population exhibited the largest growth—from 9% of the foreign-born population in 1960 to 53% in 2010 (U.S. Census Bureau, 2013). This suggests that "among immigrant families, communities, and workers, languages other than English offer a potential resource to individuals and employers" (Moore, Fee, Ee, Wiley, & Arias, 2014, p. 45).

I thought of my students who were undocumented or living in multistatus homes and are now college age. For my students and me, there is a part of our stories that is the same—we are children displaced in a land, never feeling a natural part of the mainstream, living where our community is often viewed as a "problem to be solved." Today, there are 1,662,550 individuals who identify themselves as Haitian, making them 25% of the Caribbean population (4,165,453) in the nation (U.S. Census Bureau, 2015). For them there can be an alternative narrative, where we understand the connectedness of our history with the United States and are able to celebrate our contributions. Do Americans know that Haitians fought in the Revolutionary War during the Battle of Savannah to support America in securing her freedom? Do they know that a monument is erected in Savannah to commemorate the event? American secretary of state Cordell Hull dedicated a commemorative plaque at a cathedral in the Haitain city of Saint Marc, my grandmother's hometown, on April 25, 1944. The plaque reads, "Today we pay tribute to the courage and spirit of those Haitian volunteers who in 1779 risked their lives for the cause of American Liberty." I share with teachers about the connectivity of our histories and that it is a way to engage students meaningfully—that is what my teachers did. My teachers shared that Alexander Hamilton, one of the Founding Fathers of the United States, was born in the Caribbean. But unfortunately many of the histories are not told. As stated by Baptist, "Even today, most U.S. history textbooks tell the story of the Louisiana Purchase without admitting that slave revolution in Saint/Domingue (Haiti) made it possible" (Baptist, 2014, p. 49). Teachers must seek that knowledge.

For the Caribbean parents who guided the model above, they started the tie between ethnicity and educational institutions early. For them, "whether the motive is the wish for better educational quality or for stronger ethnic identity, the result is that school becomes an institution in which the ethnic culture is maintained rather than a vehicle for assimilation" (Kasinitz, 1992, p. 74). Teachers who are culturally competent and culturally relevant can achieve that by being authentic in using the connections all around us. In trainings, I share these connections with my peers. I often ask, Do they know that the founder of Chicago was from Haiti? Do they know that a Haitian philanthropist contributed enormous sums to the building of St. Patrick's Cathedral in New York City? Immigrants contribute to the social richness and the vibrancy of the economic fiber of the nation in many ways—then and now. Haitians are achieving the American dream with each passing generation. As noted by the Migration Policy Institute (2014),

> The Haitian diaspora is not as well educated as the general U.S. population, but children of Haitian immigrants (the second generation) have made significant educational advances, graduating from college and earning advanced degrees at rates above the general U.S. population.

My elementary school opened its doors specifically to educate the children of immigrants. Their narratives and mine created the model. I look at our elementary school class picture—and the majority of us went on to college. I count among us physician, engineer, entrepreneur, architect, educator, and military officer, to name a few. We too are America. We benefited from *Lau vs. Nichols*, as we have been educated in a bilingual multicultural school. We love this country because the school taught us that we are a part of its fabric and our histories are interconnected.

This chapter does not provide the answer, but it offers a model that can be adapted to support a school's needs in moving closer to creating a transcultural and transformative program for students. There are many like me who came to the United States with the potential to change not only our lives but also our community. For example, Dr. Rose-Marie Toussaint, who immigrated to the United States from Haiti with her parents, became a liver and kidney surgeon in the United States (Toussaint & Santaniello, 1998).

The hope is that the model creates opportunities for us to ask more and deeper questions in order to come to more balanced perspectives, a common lens, about educating immigrant students to be contributing, successful world citizens. My goal is to teach toward freedom by dispelling negative myths about the educability of immigrant children, their ways of knowing, and their communities' contributions. This challenge is enormous with colleagues who refuse to enter conversation or who address the impact of race from a deficit perspective. Ayers suggests, "Teaching towards freedom goes beyond presenting what already is, it is teaching toward what could be, what ought to be and what is not yet" (Ayers, 2004, p. 156). For example, when I was in school my 5th-grade teacher was forced to teach me English with texts that were not always relevant, so she infused relevance herself when she taught me. When I was at the beginning of my teaching career she sent me a Haitian folktale book that she had published. The front page reads, "Dear Sandra, it is because of students like you that I thought of writing this story. Please read it to your class and enjoy it. Love, Adrienne Jeudy" (Jeudy, 2000). She inspires me to contribute and be an ally. We all need to contribute, in our own way, to be culturally responsive educators to all our students for as long as we can so they can become the people we've been waiting for.

References

Armand, M. M. (2015). *Healing in the homeland: Haitian vodou tradition*. Lanham, MD: Lexington.

Ayers, W. (2004). *Teaching toward freedom: Moral commitment and ethical action in the classroom*. Boston, MA: Beacon Press.

Baptist, E. E. (2014). *The half has never been told: Slavery and the making of American capitalism*. New York, NY: Basic Books.

Brookfield, S. (1995). *Becoming a critically reflective teacher*. San Francisco, CA: Jossey-Bass.

Chomsky, A. (2007). *"They take our jobs!": And 20 other myths about immigration*. Boston, MA: Beacon Press.

Flor Ada, A., & Campoy, F. I. (2004). *Authors in the classroom: A transformative education process*. Boston, MA: Pearson.

Hammond, Z. (2015). *Culturally responsive teaching and the brain: Promoting authentic engagement and rigor among culturally and linguistically diverse students*. Thousand Oaks, CA: Corwin.

Jeudy, A. (2000). *Miyon and the mountain spirit*. n.p.: Vantage Press.

Kaplan, J., & Bernays, A. (1999). *The language of names*. New York, NY: Simon & Schuster.

Kasinitz, P. (1992). *Caribbean New York: Black immigrants and the politics of race*. Ithaca, NY: Cornell University Press.

Lieberman, M. D. (2013). *Social: Why our brains are wired to connect*. New York, NY: Crown.

Migration Policy Institute. (2014). *RAD Report 2014. Haitian diaspora in the United States*. Washington DC: Migration Policy Institute.

Moore, S. C., Fee, M., Ee, J., Wiley, T, & Arias, M. B. (2014). Exploring bilingualism, literacy, employability, and income levels among Latinos in the United States. In R. M. Callahan & P. C. Gandara (Eds.), *The bilingual advantage: Language, literacy, and the U.S. labor market* (pp. 45–76). Bristol, United Kingdom: Multilingual Matters.

Rangel, J. (1986, June 30). U.S. honors Brooklyn school. *New York Times*. Retrieved from www.nytimes.com/1986/07/01/nyregion/us-honors-brooklyn-school.html

Reagan, T. G. (2000). *Non-Western educational traditions: Alternative approaches to educational thought and practice*. Mahwah, NJ: L. Erlbaum Associates.

Suárez-Orozco, C., Suárez-Orozco, M. M., & Todorova, I. (2008). *Learning a new land: Immigrant students in American society*. Cambridge, MA: Belknap Press of Harvard University Press.

Toussaint, R., & Santaniello, A. E. (1998). *Never question the miracle: A surgeon's story*. New York, NY: One World, Ballantine.

U.S. Census Bureau. (2011). *Foreign-born population in the United States*. Retrieved from census.gov/newsroom/pdf/cspan_fb_slides.pdf

U.S. Census Bureau. (2013). *How do we know? America's foreign born in the last 50 years*. Retrieved from www.census.gov/library/visualizations/2013/comm/foreign_born.html

U.S. Census Bureau. (2015). *American Community Survey (ACS)*. Retrieved August 2017 from factfinder.census.gov/faces/nav/jsf/pages/searchresults.xhtml

Zéphir, F. (1996). *Haitian immigrants in Black America: A sociological and sociolinguistic portrait*. Westport, CT: Bergin & Garvey.

CHAPTER 5

An Examination of the DREAM Act from the Classroom to Capitol Hill

Analyzing the Arguments

Tiffany Mitchell and Brett Burnham with Gaby Pacheco

During the spring of 2013, eighty 7th-grade students at Cesar Chavez Preparatory Public Charter School for Public Policy (Chavez Prep PCS) in Washington, DC, embarked on an incredible journey to analyze the arguments for and against the DREAM Act. This journey took students from the classroom to the offices of the United States Senate. Of these students, 28 were English learners and immigrants or children of immigrants. Chavez Prep PCS is a school for public policy where each year students address different social issues, ranging from health care, to immigration, to gun control. Each year students are offered an array of issues from which to choose; a classwide democratic voting process occurs to allow students to choose the public policy topic that they wish to address. The students with whom we worked chose to learn about and advocate for the DREAM Act. With student buy-in around the topic of immigration reform, teachers planned a 3-week unit that involved using a complex text, videos, and a student workbook for critical thinking and academic vocabulary. Additionally, community activists were invited into the classroom to teach students about the history and traction of the federal DREAM Act. These activists also shared their experiences, many of which included the speakers' personal stories of educational struggles and triumphs in a country that considers them, or their immediate family members, as "illegals." The unit culminated with students writing an argumentative essay–style paragraph that would be presented and delivered to some Senate offices.

The unit began with lessons on social justice, a brief history of immigration in the United States, and reading of the DREAM Act bill. Additionally the text *Right to DREAM: Immigration Reform and America's Future*, by Dr. William Schwab (2013), was introduced. This book was chosen to serve as the anchor text for the unit primarily because it contains highly relevant information, which we believed our students could use to frame their arguments. *Right to DREAM* was published just a few months before the unit began, and its content contained recent critical immigration issues and legislation. Also, although the book is noticeably biased in favor of the DREAM Act, it does present both the pro and con sides of the U.S. immigration debate, and we felt that it would provide opportunities for our team to present information to our students in a way that would allow them to reach their own conclusions concerning the DREAM Act. Further, the book covers a wide range of salient immigration topics such as the history of immigration in the United States, the economic impacts of immigration, legal issues associated with immigration, xenophobia, and the notion of America as a cultural melting pot. Furthermore, using *Right to DREAM* met one of the project's important aims: to have our students read a comprehensible yet upper-level (high school) text that challenged them to learn new and difficult vocabulary, grammar, and syntax through context clues and graphic text annotation and dissection.

Last, our decision to use *Right to DREAM* to teach about immigration and the DREAM Act was finalized when its author agreed to hold a Skype conversation with our entire 7th-grade class about his book. We believe that having access to the author was enticing to our students and transformed somewhat abstract information into a very personal learning experience for them.

Advocacy Unit and Standards

One of the core values of Chavez Prep PCS is that all teachers will incorporate civic lessons into curricular content and, more specifically, will teach students the academic and advocacy skills necessary to influence public policies and make a difference for others. The school has a public policy team that supports teachers in this work. However, even without this support teachers will find that it is very easy and natural to incorporate an advocacy project as a unit. Each year, at Chavez Prep PCS, usually after the completion of standardized testing, between mid-May and June, students conduct an interdisciplinary advocacy project. This is an opportune time to combat the lethargy that many teachers and students face at the end of the school year. For teachers, participating in an advocacy project is an engaging and meaningful way to assess what students have learned throughout the year by involving them in a social action project based on an issue that is important to them. For students, it is a meaningful way to learn the importance of advocacy and how they can make a difference on issues they care about.

The advocacy unit was conducted primarily in our history class; however, it was a collaborative effort supported by other content teachers on the team. For example, in math and science classes students analyzed and interpreted data on the DREAM Act. In English, students were able to refine their writing for the argumentative paragraph. At the time, Chavez Prep PCS incorporated learning-goal scales (similar to a rubric) to assist teachers in assessing learning and to help students track their own learning through the course of the unit. We crafted a learning goal scale (see Table 5.1) for our advocacy unit on the DREAM Act. This goal stipulated that at the end of the unit students would understand the pros and cons of the DREAM Act bill and would write an argumentative paragraph on whether the DREAM Act should or should not pass as a bill and become law.

Table 5.1. Learning Goal Scale

Score	Criteria
	Learning Goal: I can understand the pros and cons of the DREAM Act bill and write an argumentative paragraph on whether the DREAM Act should pass as a bill and become a law.
4.0	In addition to a 3.0, I am able to go beyond what I was taught. For example, I can do the following: • Use the strategies for making political change and adjust them creatively to fit new situations.
3.0	In addition to a 2.0, I can do the following: • Evaluate whether suggested solutions are reasonable for Congress to achieve. • Evaluate pros and cons of the DREAM Act bill. • Write a clear argumentative paragraph targeted to a specific audience using evidence to support a claim.
2.0	I can define terms in my own words, such as the following: • Immigration • DREAM Act • Economics • Culture • Assimilation • Legal • Common good I can perform basic processes, such as the following: • List pros and cons of the DREAM Act • Identify key components of the DREAM Act
1.0	With help, I can achieve some of a 2.0 and some of a 3.0.

The first half of the book *Right to DREAM* was used in this unit and is divided into chapters on culture, economics, legal matters, immigration, and assimilation of both documented and undocumented immigrants. After receiving a brief overview of all the chapters in the first half of the book, students selected a chapter that they were interested in learning more about. Strategies on how to read a complex text and tools to interpret and understand academic vocabulary were taught and modeled. Karine Welsh, our English for Speakers of Other Languages (ESOL) teacher, was essential in developing strategies to teach academic vocabulary and make the content accessible for all students. With these strategies mastered, students had time to read their selected chapters in groups and to answer questions in order to ensure comprehension. This worked extremely well and our teaching team was impressed with how students were able to grasp the big ideas from a text that was well above their grade level.

One of the culminating activities for 7th-grade students at Chavez Prep PCS involves a trip to Capitol Hill. At the start of this unit, students were made aware that our DREAM Act advocacy unit would come to a close by presenting their edited work orally and in writing to members of Congress as well as various political pundits during their Capitol Hill field trip. Thus, as the final component of the unit, students wrote an argumentative essay–style paragraph in which they were tasked with articulating and supporting, using compelling evidence, their own stance on the issue of immigration reform as well as that of the opposing viewpoint. For students, the opportunity to have their voices heard by powerful decisionmakers motivated them to authentically engage in the learning and preparation processes.

With argumentative paragraphs as the culminating product, we decided to use Literacy Design Collaborative (LDC; www.ldc.org/) curricula development tools to build our unit. LDC provides methodologically rigorous teaching and learning frameworks with built-in Common Core standards for curriculum design. Our team selected Template Task 2, which incorporates multiple Common Core Reading (Table 5.2) and Writing State Standards (Table 5.3), listed below:

> Template Task 2: [Insert question] After reading _____ (literature or informational texts), write _____ (essay or substitute) that addresses the question, and support your position with evidence from the text(s). L2: Be sure to acknowledge competing views.

Table 5.2. Common Core Reading Standards for Argumentation

"Built-in" Reading Standards	"When Appropriate" Reading Standards
Standard 1. Read closely to determine what the text says explicitly and to make logical inferences from it; cite specific textual evidence when writing or speaking to support conclusions drawn from the text.	**Standard 3.** Analyze how and why individuals, events, and ideas develop and interact over the course of a text.
Standard 2. Determine central ideas or themes of a text and analyze their development; summarize the key supporting details and ideas.	**Standard 5.** Analyze the structure of texts, including how specific sentences, paragraphs, and larger portions of the text (e.g., section, chapter, scene, or stanza) relate to each other and the whole.
Standard 4. Interpret words and phrases as they are used in a text, including determining technical, connotative, and figurative meanings, and analyze how specific word choices shape meaning or tone.	**Standard 6.** Assess how point of view or purpose shapes the content and style of a text.

Table 5.2. Common Core Reading Standards for Argumentation (continued)

"Built-in" Reading Standards	"When Appropriate" Reading Standards
Standard 10. Read and comprehend complex literary and informational texts independently and proficiently.	*Standard 7.* Integrate and evaluate content presented in diverse formats and media, including visually and quantitatively, as well as in words.
	Standard 8. Delineate and evaluate the argument and specific claims in a text, including the validity of the reasoning as well as the relevance and sufficiency of the evidence.
	Standard 9. Analyze how two or more texts address similar themes or topics in order to build knowledge or to compare the approaches the authors take.

Table 5.3. Common Core Writing Standards for Argumentation

"Built-in" Writing Standards	"When Appropriate" Writing Standards
Standard 1. Write arguments to support claims in an analysis of substantive topics or texts, using valid reasoning and relevant and sufficient evidence.	*Standard 2.* Write informative/explanatory texts to examine and convey complex ideas and information clearly and accurately through the effective selection, organization, and analysis of content.
Standard 4. Produce clear and coherent writing in which the development, organization, and style are appropriate to task, purpose, and audience.	*Standard 3.* Write narratives to develop real or imagined experiences or events using effective technique, well-chosen details, and well-structured event sequences.
Standard 5. Develop and strengthen writing as needed by planning, revising, editing, rewriting, or trying a new approach.	*Standard 6.* Use technology, including the Internet, to produce and publish writing and to interact and collaborate with others.
Standard 9. Draw evidence from literary or informational texts to support analysis, reflection, and research.	*Standard 7.* Conduct short as well as more sustained research projects based on focused questions, demonstrating understanding of the subject under investigation.
Standard 10. Write routinely over extended time frames (time for research, reflection, and revision) and shorter time frames (a single sitting or a day or two) for a range of tasks, purposes, and audience.	*Standard 8.* Gather relevant information from multiple print and digital sources, assess the credibility and accuracy of each source, and integrate the information while avoiding plagiarism.

Source: National Governors Association Center for Best Practices & Council of Chief State School Officers (2010)

To organize all the information students used throughout the unit, the team created a student workbook. The workbook contained a gallery walk, pros and cons of the DREAM Act, graphic organizers for chapter readings and writing, vocabulary resources, and reference materials that we used. Figure 5.1 shows the table of contents from the student workbook.

The Power of Discussions

It was important that as educators we remained objective throughout the unit. Our goal was not to invoke our own opinions, but to have students develop their own based on the variety of evidence we reviewed. As students began to read and digest information on the DREAM Act, a critical component of this unit was to allow a safe space for students to process their ideas and thoughts about their reading and learning. We knew that not all students agreed that the DREAM Act should be passed. Therefore, we wanted to make sure that all opinions were valued and discussed in a constructive way. During discussions, students were required to state evidence-based opinions. This technique drew upon what had been taught throughout the year: Don't argue with the person, but do debate the ideas/evidence. Having structured, evidence-based discussions, similar to a Socratic seminar, helped to create a safe environment for students to practice advocacy skills. Discussions in both small and whole groups were a regular part of this unit as a means for students to process the complex text, presentations, and legislation. Often it would happen organically, as students wanted to share their ideas, revelations, or personal experiences.

Figure 5.1. Student Workbook Table of Contents

Part 1—VIDEO: U.S. Immigration in 10 minutes

Part 2—DREAM Act gallery walk

Part 3—Pros and Cons of the DREAM Act

Part 4—The Complete Guide to Service Learning, Ch. 12

Part 5—Where Are We From? Activity

Part 6—Introduction to *Right to DREAM*

Part 7—Reading Outline for Your Chapter

Part 8—Vocabulary List for Your Chapter

Part 9—Detailed Chapter Summaries

Part 10—What Questions Would You Ask?

Part 11—SPEAKER(S): What Have You Learned? What Questions Do You Still Have?

Part 12—SPEAKER(S): Appendixes

Part 13—Template: Writing an Argumentative Essay

Part 14—Exemplar: Writing an Argumentative Essay

Finding Resources

Although schools are a part of the community, as educators we do not always perceive the many resources available to us as part of that community. It is in fact amazing how many resources are available right under our proverbial noses. Indeed, as the team began to look for supporting resources for this project, the work took on a life of its own. We were surprised to find that community organizations are very open to coming to schools and speaking to students. By emailing organizations and tapping our personal networks, we were able to secure presentations from several DREAMer activists, a program assistant for the Immigrant Children's Legal Program at the U.S. Committee of Refugees and Immigrants, a number of U.S. Senate staffers, and a representative from the Heritage Foundation. Our journey through this unit was a truly organic process.

Our team, composed of two content teachers, Brett Burnham and Tiffany Mitchell, as well as an ESOL teacher, Karine Welsh, met and discussed how to transform this unit into a dynamic experiential learning opportunity through the use of guest speakers. This work became a collaborative process across our team, across the grade-level team, and across the entire school. Certainly, securing Dr. Schwab as a digital media guest speaker prior to designing the unit was critical to this effort. However, the process of garnering other key volunteers to assist in teaching our students about the DREAM Act was truly a serendipitous process. For instance, Mr. Burnham, using his social network, was also able to gain collaboration from a highly acclaimed DREAMer activist named Gaby Pacheco (who organized the Trail of DREAMS civil rights immigration reform march from Miami to Washington, DC). The path to Ms. Pacheco was not direct, however. One of Mr. Burnham's graduate colleagues is a close friend of the famous DREAMer activist Jose Magana. Mr. Magana is a lawyer who graduated from Baylor Law School and has fought for immigration rights in various capacities, including as past president of the DREAM Bar Association. Mr. Magana listened to our plan and we won his support, but he was unable to participate directly. Therefore, he reached out on our behalf to several other DREAMer activists in his network, including his friend Ms. Pacheco, who enthusiastically welcomed our invitation to work with our students. The project grew organically as Ms. Pacheco, several other DREAMers, and a few immigration reform organizations heard through their social networks what we were learning and doing. They were inspired by our project and their support proved crucial to this teaching and learning process.

Each team member worked to set other networks in motion. For instance, Ms. Mitchell contacted Teaching for Change and the Zinn Education Project, which provides a wealth of resources for teacher advocates. In addition, a math teacher on our team suggested that we contact her friend Lisa Swanson, who works at the U.S. Committee for Refugees and Immigrants. Ms. Mitchell made arrangements for Ms. Swanson to speak to the students. At a WATESOL (Washington, DC, Area Teachers of English to Speakers of Other Languages) conference, Ms. Welsh, the ESOL teacher on the team, contacted additional DREAMers from Northern Virginia who were enrolled in a local community college. They agreed to speak to our students about their personal experiences as immigrants in mixed-citizen-status families, as well as their activism around the issue of immigration reform.

We had a phenomenal response to our call for presentations on this project all within the DC metro area and at no cost to the school. Resources are available—it just takes persistence and sending out emails to your personal networks and to various organizations that align with your project. We felt it was imperative that we meet with all presenters before their presentations to discuss their ideas and ensure their presentation would be interactive. We wanted the presentations to be an enriching experience and accessible for all students. Having the opportunity to meet and hear from presenters with different perspectives helped to strengthen student understanding of the issue and their own position.

Ultimately, our community partners and activists transformed this experience. Our efforts were made possible with the help of Gaby Pacheco, First Focus Campaign, the Bridge Project, and the National Immigration Law Center—which volunteered to compile and print the student paragraphs; arrange opportunities for students to meet and share their ideas with key Senate staff; and organize a discussion panel composed of congressional staffers, immigration reform pundits, and a representative from the Heritage Foundation. Students went in small groups of 4 or 5 to visit Senate offices to share their thoughts on whether the DREAM Act should pass. The unit was powerful and authentic and met many Common Core standards in reading, writing, and critical thinking.

The Final Product: Student Voices on the DREAM Act

The culminating product that students prepared for this unit were persuasive paragraphs shared orally and in writing with members of Congress, congressional staffers, and immigrant reform pundits. Students drew upon all that they had learned through unit texts, their student workbook, videos, and guest speakers in order to answer the following prompt: Should the bill for the DREAM Act pass and become law? This is how some of the students answered that question:

> I think the Dream Act should pass and become a law because this will help many students that are immigrants get a college education. The book *Right to Dream: Immigration Reform and America's Future* by Dr. William A. Schwab said "Education contributes to the common good and democracy." Every person should be able go to college. Some people think the Dream Act shouldn't pass because immigrants will take away citizens' jobs. Another thing some people think is that immigrants are criminals. Children of immigrants didn't decide to come here. They didn't make the decision, their parents decided to come here. One of the reasons they came here was to look for a better job or have better housing. Many immigrants come so their children can have a better future. Immigrants are regular people who want

the same things as everyone else, so they deserve to have the same rights as citizens. Many immigrants are very smart and they don't break the laws. Just because one immigrant does something bad does not mean it's okay to stereotype every immigrant. I think it isn't fair for some people to say bad things about immigrants as a whole group. Everyone who lives in America has ancestors that immigrated here too. By talking bad about immigrants, they are also talking bad about their own ancestors, too. These are some of my reasons the Dream Act should be passed. —Valery

Commentary: This student's voice was selected, as she produced a compelling argument about how and why passage of the DREAM Act holds the potential to promote the greater good and democracy within the United States vis-à-vis equitable education, housing, jobs, and other opportunities for DREAMers. Moreover, this student argued that many immigrants are unfairly stereotyped as criminals, while she also points out that America is a nation of immigrants.

I believe that the DREAM Act should be passed because kids need a chance to succeed in life and in their education even if they're undocumented. However, critics say that we (immigrants) are changing the culture and nation of the U.S.A. in a negative way and that we are destroying their nation. In addition, critics say that immigrants are criminals and that we're breaking the law because we can't come to this country without papers. Yes, that can be true, but it is not our fault because we came here as children and our parents want a better life for us. Immigrants come here for a reason and that reason is because they need a future by going to college and jobs. Right now, we need to focus on immigrant's future because there are 11 million people that are undocumented. This will help the country in many ways because there would be more professionals that can pay higher taxes. They can also improve our economy by working in high quality jobs. Lastly, because immigrants want a good future, they will work hard and be productive in life, this is why I support the DREAM Act. —Obdulio

Commentary: This student's voice was selected as he highlighted that if the DREAM Act were to be passed, the United States as a whole would benefit via a more educated workforce that will in turn increase the national tax base and economy. Additionally, he suggested that children who immigrate to the United States are deemed criminals, but came with their families and are not at fault for this.

I think the Dream Act should be passed because families won't be separated and kids of all ages will get the education they dreamed of. Though, critics argue about passing the Dream Act because "they could take our jobs, and not pay the necessary taxes." Based on that, I think that the critics view is stereotypical. I say this because not every immigrant will take your job and pay the taxes needed. If we pass the Dream Act, immigrants will be able to have a great life for them, their families, and generations to come. In chapter one of *Right to Dream* by William A. Schwab, it talked about children's right to education. This chapter interested me because I never knew how hard it was to get an education if I were an immigrant. I never thought about the many people suffering out there, willing to take dangerous risks to just be a welcomed citizen in a country you all call "liberty and justice for all." In conclusion, I believe the Dream Act should be passed, so that the United States could be one step closer to promoting the common good for everyone, and everyone could have a shot at having successful careers. Just think about it. Think about the millions of people fighting and taking risks for something you already have. —Jayla

Commentary: This student's voice was selected, as she emphasized that critics of the DREAM Act often stereotype undocumented workers as job thieves and tax evaders. She provides a rebuttal to this worldview by claiming that providing DREAMers with a good education will afford them opportunities for successful careers, which in turn will bolster the common good.

The United States congress should pass the dream act because there are 11.1 millions of undocumented immigrants in the whole U.S.A. The critics say it is a crime and amnesty and the bill faces long odds in the Senate. On the other hand, half of the immigrants are children that have been brought here from their country to have a better education, and some of them have been brought when they were only babies. They start their lives here and begin school in US elementary, middle and high school. My name is Jazmin and I was born in Mexico, and I was brought to the US when I was 3 years old, and never knew that I was undocumented. Sometimes my dreams disappear knowing that if the DREAM Act doesn't pass then my dreams won't come true. My dream is to become a doctor or join the Marines to help the country where I grow up or to save lives. I would like to be the first person from my family to graduate college; I want to make my parents happy I want to hear them say "that's my daughter." I want to be up there getting my diploma saying thank you to everyone that believed in me. In conclusion, this is why I feel they should pass the DREAM Act to help young students accomplish their dreams. —Jazmin

Commentary: This student's voice was selected, as she provided a very eloquent and compelling argument about why she believes the DREAM Act should be passed— so that students' dreams can become a reality. In her argument, Jazmin retorted that if the DREAM Act is not passed, the dreams, including her own, of many un-documented immigrant students of a successful future attained through education could be shattered. Furthermore, this argument highlights that DREAMers are often unaware that they are not citizens of the United States, and that they consider this country to be their home—a place where they aspire to a quality education, career opportunities, and fulfilled lives.

Moving Forward in Anti-Immigrant Times

The complexity of our students' lives is more apparent now due to current events, such as the Charlottesville Unite the Right rally, professional athletes kneeling for social justice, Twitter storms that are insensitive to the human toll of tropical storms and hurricanes, the Muslim travel ban, ICE raids that feed the for-profit prison system, and numerous local legislative efforts aimed at spreading fear in immigrant communities. Now more than ever, we must seize opportunities to use the model provided in this chapter to critically engage students in working at local, state, and federal levels on the most important legislative issues of the day.

References

Education World. (2012). How laws are made. Retrieved from www.educationworld.com/a_lesson/02/lp284-02.shtml

Immigration Law Resource Center. (2012). Comparison chart: DACA, California Dream Act, AB 540, and DREAM Act. Retrieved from www.sjsu.edu/people/julia.curry/AB540/s2/ilrc-daca_comparison_chart-2012-10_10.pdf

Kaye, C. B. (2004). *The complete guide to service learning: Proven, practical ways to engage students in civic responsibility, academic curriculum, and social action.* Minneapolis, MN: Free Spirit.

National Governors Association Center for Best Practices & Council of Chief State School Officers. (2010). *Common Core State Standards for English language arts and literacy in history/social studies, science, and technical subjects.* Washington, DC: Author.

National Immigration Law Center. (2011). DREAM Act: Summary. Retrieved from www.nilc.org/issues/immigration-reform-and-executive-actions/dreamact/dreamsummary

Schwab, W. A. (2013). *Right to DREAM: Immigration reform and America's future.* Fayetteville, AR: University of Arkansas Press.

U.S. Immigration. (2011). Pros and cons of the DREAM Act. Retrieved from www.usimmigration.com/prosconsdreamact.html

CHAPTER 6

First-Person Narratives

Recognizing the Hidden Challenges Faced by STEM DREAMers of Color

Anita Bright and G. Sue Kasun
with Dario Lopez

> I came with the plan of working 1 or 2 years to save money to then go back to México to finish university. But destiny or life had other plans for me.
>
> —Dario

There is often a great desire among educators to maintain a focus on lighthearted, joyful, and fun aspects of our professional practice as teachers. As K–12 professionals and teacher educators who work with standards-based curriculum, we may have a genuine appetite for pleasant and entertaining "do tomorrow" activities that can capture the attention of our students and for pragmatic and efficient uses of time to scaffold literacy and content-based instruction (Au, 2011). As such, it can, at times, be a challenge to find ways to address and authentically engage students with more serious, emotionally charged, and politically fraught concerns that may be layered into our daily classroom routines. These are often issues that are of deeply urgent importance to our students. In each of our classes there may be undocumented students who face hidden challenges, including emotional and physical abuse and trauma that interfere with their learning and academic achievement (Houser, 1996).

While some students may unwittingly reveal their undocumented status, others may be extremely skillful in avoiding certain topics that would bring unwarranted attention to themselves or their families (Patel, 2013). Pre-K–12 teachers may not hear about these challenges because their students are unaware of or too young to understand immigration status. If teachers are asked to maintain fidelity to the curriculum, they might not think to ask their students to share their stories, especially if the textbook or mandated curriculum is uninformed about the realities that undocumented students and U.S. citizen students with an undocumented family member experience.

Another reason why teachers may not hear about the hidden challenges their students face is that the students themselves may be reluctant to discuss their vulnerabilities (Pandya, Pagdilao, & Kim, 2015). Many immigrant students work to help their families (Valenzuela, 2003). Immigrant students without documentation may be unwilling to reveal domestic or work-related abuse, such as being cheated by an unscrupulous employer or being injured on the job without compensation, out of fear that they will be reported to the authorities (Milkman, 2006).

In addition, given the current polarized rhetorical political climate, teachers themselves may consciously avoid "trigger topics" such as immigration, race, and religion. Some educators have been told that it is not permissible to ask about a student's status, as explained in the Dear Colleague Letter distributed to principals (U.S. Department of Education & U.S. Department of Justice, 2014). Others may not want to ask about a student's personal life because that might make him or her feel uncomfortable. Instead we may focus on "safe" topics, not realizing that by not facing the concerns experienced by students directly, we may inadvertently contribute to the problem.

Pre-K–12 teachers may also not hear about the problems our students may be experiencing, not because they are not concerned but because under the context of needing to prepare students for high-stakes exams, they may feel the pressure of directing every minute of class time to the mandated curriculum. Some teachers might even fear censure or sanction from a supervisor concerned about aligned curricula, test scores, and closing the achievement gap. When teachers are asked to maintain fidelity to a curriculum that is uninformed about the realities their students are living, they might think they don't have time to ask their students to share their stories. But in times of increasing economic and political inequality between haves and have-nots, and increasing deportations and indefinite detention without right to counsel, listening to the stories of immigrant youth is made all the more urgent (Vitali, Glattfelder, & Battiston, 2011).

While there are various ways of listening to our students to better ascertain their needs and support their learning, in this chapter we propose the use of *testimonio*, a Spanish term for a first-person narrative that originates from a member of a marginalized group or community. We offer the personal narrative of Dario Lopez, a first-generation college student in science, technology, engineering, and mathematics (STEM) education as an example of how *testimonio* can be used by educators of all subjects and content areas (1) to increase awareness of the challenges and realities lived by undocumented students in our schools; (2) to contrast the racialized and dehumanizing portrayal of immigrants in the media and public discourse and reflect on the effect of these stereotypes and bias on ourselves as teachers and on our students' academic lives; and (3) to identify concrete antiracist and antioppressive steps and strategies that teachers can use to create more inclusive classrooms, schools and communities, and pedagogical practices for the academic achievement of all students—refugee, immigrant, and U.S. born alike (Bright, 2014).

Testimonio: Definitions

Testimonio is intentionally a first-person "narration of urgency" (Jara, 1986), with a purposeful use of "I" to speak directly to the audience, to claim the attention of the listener or reader of a written text. Just as actors may choose to break the metaphorical fourth wall of the stage and step outside the scene to directly address the viewing audience, the use of testimonio is similarly intended to both engage and provoke the audience to lament, to action, to change.

Testimonios are the stories told by the holder of the story, who has first-person experience of marginalization (Menchú, 1984); these are always stories that the dominant society cannot hear or resists hearing (Cervantes-Soon, 2012; Yúdice, 1991). With roots in Latin American studies of literature, the testimonial narrative invokes the spirit of historical figures to speak publicly of their oppression (Beverley, 2008), individuals such as Rigoberta Menchú (1984), the indigenous Guatemalan Nobel Peace Prize winner who wrote about the horrors inflicted upon her family and community during the Guatemalan Civil War.

Our Process for Using Testimonios in Teacher Education

We invited Dario as a guest speaker to a quarterly university workshop of preservice teachers. Dario shared his testimonio, live, with three dozen bilingual teacher candidates in the same city in Oregon where he studied. Dario was invited because he and many of the preservice teachers in the audience were contemporaries and would have many of the same frames of reference. As bilingual teachers they had shared with Dario many of the same experiences of culture shock and the challenges of learning a second or foreign language. What made his testimonio most valuable was that most of the audience—teachers and university supervisors, graduate students and professors alike—had operated with the many privileges of being documented.

His presentation produced an immediate reaction: quiet, perhaps stunned, reverence, interrupted by occasional sniffles, before the future teachers burst into applause at the end of his talk. While the group was surely not applauding Dario's graphically tenuous life situation, it was clear that those assembled were moved by the candor he expressed despite the risk he bore in revealing his undocumented status and that they were affected by his creative tenacity in the face of desperately obstructive circumstances. Their response may also have been a way to mitigate their sorrow, pain, and awkwardness from knowing there was no ready answer to his pleas and requests.

Weeks later, we went through Dario's notes, which he had provided, and developed a set of follow-up questions. We interviewed Dario some months later and transcribed his remarks. We co-created a master narrative, incorporating the original remarks as well as the follow-up interview, weaving his words together into a coherent story that Dario felt represented his thinking.

Dario's Testimonio, Part 1: Challenges in the United States

My name is Dario Lopez. . . . Let me repeat it again: Dario Lopez. I am from Tapachula, Chiapas, México. It is a beautiful agricultural area where we grow coffee, and, relative to life in the U.S., it is a poor place where about one-fourth of the people live in houses with dirt floors.

I came here, to the United States of America, in December 2001, after finishing high school in México when I was 18. I came with the plan of working 1 or 2 years to save money to then go back to México to finish university.

It's hard. Leaving your family for many years. People come here like me, for 2 or 3 years, and then they end up staying longer, longer, and longer. They get hooked into the system in that they'll never be able to escape if they don't go to school.

I have experienced a cultural shock. I missed my family and friends and still miss them because I have not been back to México since 2001. I cannot go back because I have no papers.

Coming here is like, I don't know, it's like . . . another world. People are different, there is a different culture, different . . . We don't have culture in México like the United States.

I have the obstacle of money. Money has always been an issue. Ever since I was 7 years old I started working to pay for school and help my mother and my brothers. It was hard to find a job in the U.S. In fact, it took me about 5 months to find my first job.

I was misled by an adviser at PCC into taking a technician's program instead of the electrical engineering degree program. I did not know the difference. At that time, I trusted the adviser since I did not know anything else. I was very naive.

No work, no money, no honey. No financial aid. Not enough scholarships to pay for school.

On top of that, on December 19, 2010, I was almost taken by the ICE. They came; it was about 8 in the morning. I wasn't scared at the time. They asked me, "Do you know this guy?" They had a big picture of my brother's face, my oldest brother, and I said, "Yeah, that's my brother." They said, "We are looking for him"—I don't think he did anything too bad, didn't pay child support; he was paying the wife, but according to them he wasn't, but he was paying rent too. They asked if they could look [in the house for him] and I said, yeah. At that point I didn't know what to say or what to do, but I knew he wasn't there so I said they could look.

I didn't know my legal rights—that I could say no. I said yes. And they went in there. They were three people, a team. My brother didn't live with us, he just used the address; that's why they came there. They asked my sister about him, and we said we didn't know, we hadn't seen him. Then they asked for his phone number and I gave them the number.

They said, "What do you do?" and I said, "I'm a student, studying electrical engineering." And they said, "Oh, cool." And then one of the guys says, "So you have a green card?" And I couldn't say no, so I said "Yes, I do." And they asked to see it, and I said, "Yeah, you can see it." So then I'm just making time, just slowing down. So I walk into my room and I'm just looking for it in my drawers, anything, just making time. At that point I wasn't nervous, not really nervous.

It's funny to me now, but it wasn't really funny then.

It was my sister that saved me, my sister, because she said, "Just show them your [driver's] license; give them your license, and they should be able to look it up in the computer." And I did, and then they said, "OK," and he gave me back my license. And then the main guy just said, "Let's go." And they left. They were probably just too lazy to go into the computer. If they would have taken their time, they probably would have found out my status and taken me.

This uncertainty sometimes creates some stress on me so I tried not to think about it and think positively.

Discussing the Realities and Perils of Being Undocumented: Implications for Educators

From learning a completely new language after childhood, to the stresses of missing home, to feeling forced to stay in the United States, to fearing immigration raids, to experiencing an encounter with law enforcement investigators, the list of challenges as exemplified in Dario's narrative grew over time. These are the realities for many undocumented students and their families, and we as educators are often unaware of these challenges if we have not faced them in our own lives.

An implication of Dario's narrative is for us as educators to become more informed about immigrant rights. Would you advise a beloved friend to tell Immigration and Customs Enforcement (ICE, the new name for Immigration and Naturalization Service, INS) the truth about not having a green card? Green card holders have the right to live and work in the United States with the protection of local, state, and federal law. Would you support someone who doesn't have a green card who is, nonetheless, trying to pursue his or her dream of becoming a doctor, engineer, or artist while contributing to the society in which he or she lives?

Would you do your best to teach undocumented students that without a search warrant, officials do not have the right to search someone's property? Could you imagine how your entire life could hang in the balance regarding the possession—or lack thereof—of one single document to prove citizenship or the right to residency? As teachers listening to Dario's testimonio we can gain a greater understanding of the realities of our students' lives and this will enable us to build bridges between the experiences of our students' lives and the resources presented in the school curricula.

A challenge to educators is to design more relevant curricular connections between students' lives and content subject matter in math, science, and social studies and to provide safe environments designed to support student success. Dario, and students like him, need to be made aware that K–12 students have a protected right to an education; however, the right to a higher education is less well defined. Some colleges and universities are identifying themselves as "sanctuary" institutions that will not support immigration raids on campus while immigration policy questions are being debated at the federal, state, and local levels of government.

In what might be perceived as an expression of a culture of low expectations or a tendency to track students by subtle or subconscious reflex, the college counselor provided Dario with incorrect program information. Teachers and other educational professionals can actively work against this subconscious tendency by learning the true stories of students like Dario. The classroom teacher can incorporate topics of law, policy, and self-advocacy into curriculum research projects, writing assignments, debate challenges, and more. All students, especially those with similar challenges expressed in Dario's testimonio, can then apply this knowledge and skill as they navigate higher education.

Countering Stereotypes and Bias

We are bringing in people from backward, primitive cultures expecting them to turn into middle-class Americans.

—Ann Coulter (Media Matters, 2017)

Testimonios provide a counternarrative to myths in the media and public discourse about "illegals." Labeling undocumented people as "illegal" and portraying them as "rapists" and "gang members" serve to criminalize and dehumanize immigrants discursively. When immigrants are labeled as "cockroaches" the unconscious message is that they should be "exterminated." If immigrants are seen as animals, the subliminal message is that they are not deserving of human rights. If they are viewed as lazy, they are not deserving of a teacher's efforts to differentiate instruction.

Dario's Testimonio, Part 2: The Story of My Mom and Papa

My mother lives in México. Even though she did not go to school, when it comes to making money calculations she is very good. She is so good that when I was young I tried to sneak 5 or 10 pesos for me here and there, but she always caught me, so I gave up. My dad grew up in a farm. Went to school 3 years, and he was a hardworking and clever man. He told me he took apart and fixed a huge corn mill and put it back together. I share this story because I love my parents and because it has to do with math. Math is very important in their life, my life, and the life of everybody to survive; we can't function without math.

Discussion of Dario's Narrative, Part 2: Funds of Knowledge. Dario demonstrates the rich tradition of educational research called *funds of knowledge*, or the accumulated cultural knowledge shared by people, passed on through generations (González, Moll, & Amanti, 2005; Moll, Amanti, Neff, & González, 1992). By weaving students' funds of knowledge into the curriculum, educators may further engage the students' interests by valuing their experiences, voices, and contributions. In this case, Dario's shared funds of knowledge includes an agricultural background, an ability to read socioeconomic conditions, and his family's skills in using mathematics. Specifically, Dario illustrated how despite his mother's lack of a formal education, she could calculate financial transactions and could catch him when he tried to keep extra change as a child. His father showed great skill in three-dimensional mathematics and engineering in his work with agricultural equipment. Also, it is clear that his family is supportive and loving, another source of his funds of knowledge.

Dario's story offers examples of topics his teachers could use to make connections to his learning environments, which is the primary purpose for identifying and drawing upon funds of knowledge. For instance, if Dario were a high school student today, his teachers could develop project-based learning experiences related to the design of agricultural equipment. They could relate science education to agriculture, including through topics such as climate, irrigation, and the nitrogen cycle, as well as connections to native science, or the indigenous-knowledge orientation of understanding the interconnectedness of all things (Kasun & López, 2017; Medin & Bang, 2014). In pre-K–12 contexts, students' families can be invited to share, demonstrate, or teach about something they value in their knowledge of the world (Aguilar-Váldez et al., 2015). And at all levels, the students themselves can be positioned as experts. This positions the students' knowledge and being as valuable, rather than deficient (Valencia, 1997); it is in the latter way that undocumented youth are so often discussed and framed in the school context.

The teacher made a big difference. It was in my first class, we were about 25 students, everyone was from a different country; there were a whole bunch of Americans, couple of Vietnamese, one Latina girl, and me. And so the teacher, in this first class, said, "Does anyone know about what we're talking about here, this 'gate' in electronics?" And only one person raises the hand, and everyone else, we didn't know nothing about what he was talking about. So I think, "Ok, I'm not the only one who doesn't know nothing about these things." And the second thing, the teacher says to us, "Don't worry, it will make sense. After the first week, it will all make sense, to the point that you will love this stuff." And later he would say to us, "Don't you love this stuff?" And he meant it when he said that. He would make it funny, and fun, and wouldn't make it hard or difficult for me to learn.

My family supported me and inspired me. My engineering teacher, Gary Hecht, who is very inspiring and made digital electronics lectures and lab fun and easy. My math teacher, Emiliano Vega, who has lent me math books and answered math questions any time. My best friend who is also my wife who has believed in me and I am very blessed for having her in my life.

Teachers hearing or reading Dario's testimonio can tap into that student passion and create curricular connections to foster learning that is relevant to his stated understanding of the world and his expressed needs. He tells us that his curiosity was nurtured by his family, his experiences, and his teachers. He was compelled to pursue his educational dreams in spite of the obstacles before him. A single, committed teacher has the potential to have life-changing effects on students (Ladson-Billings, 2009; Michie, 2005; Valenzuela, 1999).

His testimonio could inspire secondary students to likewise find the tenacity to persist in the face of challenges that may initially seem insurmountable. K–12 teachers could engage their own students' backgrounds by asking them to make personal connections to Dario's strengths and challenges as he follows his dream to become a professional in STEM and, by implication, can see that the path is possible for them, too. Dario, at an early age, showed a love for math that evolved into the pursuit of a degree in engineering. K–12 educators can ask themselves how they can engender such passion. Immigrant students who manage to succeed in U.S. schools often attempt to encourage other immigrant youth to experience the same success (Kasun, 2015).

In addition, teachers can use testimonios like Dario's to have all students explore and better understand the functions of government, issues of rights and responsibilities and policy and law, and self-advocacy and community services, among other subjects, to appreciate the concept of "the greater good" for a humane and conscientious society. Perhaps most vividly exemplifying his cultural wealth and deep understanding of the intense delicacy of his status and situation, Dario acted with an exceptional nimbleness, coolly maintaining his composure when, almost in passing, he was questioned by government officials about his nonexistent green card. His story can be used to make connections to other students' lives with or without the situation of immigration.

In education, *grit* has been defined as persistence, determination, and resilience. While research extols the value of grit in education (e.g., Duckworth, Peterson, & Matthews, 2007), we worry about how this is actually just grittiness at times (Kasun, 2015). Actually, Dario demonstrated what Yosso (2005) refers to as "cultural wealth" in her reframing of the kinds of capital that circulate among immigrants in the United States. Dario's grittiness forces a perhaps uncomfortable question: What is each educator doing to support students like Dario while working to upend constructs that limit people's life potentials when they are perceived by some as mere "aliens" (Ngai, 2004)?

The teacher candidates reflected on Dario's testimonio at the end of the workshop, providing brief written reactions. One response was quite clear:

Testimony was very inspiring and motivated. I was thinking about dropping out of the teacher education program. However, now I am ready to take on

this journey with everything that is going on in my life :) Thank you :)
—Reflection by Luis (a pseudonym), bilingual teacher candidate

We wanted our teacher candidates to gain a sense of urgency with regard to the barriers that legal status may erect in education. Also, we wanted our preservice teachers to see their own students as more than just working toward bilingualism and biliteracy. By inviting Dario, we wanted the teacher candidates to see what happens when a child's curiosity in STEM has been nurtured and cultivated, and to see how this youthful passion can translate into a mature desire for deeper and more intensive learning. In short, we saw Dario as an exemplar of what can happen when young folks have their curiosity supported by their teachers, and we wanted his story to serve as a call to action for our teacher candidates.

Further, we wanted our teacher candidates to pause and consider, for all their students, the students' history, journey, and family, and the successes and defeats each has encountered. With a focus on funds of knowledge and contextualizing the lived experiences of each student, we wanted our preservice teachers to think deeply about their own roles in fostering and nurturing each student, including students with academic curiosity and hunger in areas different from their own.

Finally, we chose to invite Dario to share his narrative as a way to provide witness to his journey, his frustration, his sorrow, and his optimism. We wanted our teacher candidates to engage in this work of thinking holistically about our students, and to consider the long-lasting impacts teachers may have on the lives of students. We wanted our future teachers to engage in authentic listening, recognizing that the lives of our students are at times wrought with pain. This humanization of their future students can inspire preservice teachers to become curricular change agents and allies in K–12 education. They are better positioned to critically analyze the curriculum and find ways to incorporate testimonios and other forms of student voice in the objectives outlined in a traditional curriculum. A deeper understanding of their students can lead to better-informed materials selection. Assignments and assessments can become more student focused and celebratory of strengths in the face of challenges. Curriculum can expect deeper critical analysis and application to the lives of the students in each classroom as they prepare to contribute their ways of knowing to our broader communities.

Becoming an Ally

Certainly, the challenge of becoming an ally is not easy. We may not know the realities of our students' lives without specifically designing ways to create safe spaces within the curriculum and the classroom for students to share their stories. DREAMers often comment on how a teacher was the first person who knew they were undocumented or that someone in their family was facing deportation (DreamTeam LA, 2014). What makes these students share? Is it a disposition fostered in the teacher education process? The dispositions we look for in teacher candidates are an orientation toward respect, fairness, flexibility, collaboration, and a belief that everyone can learn. As authors, we can write about how difficult this situation would be in *academic terms*, but reading it from the embodied experience of Dario helps provoke the empathy we desperately need to do our best work with immigrant youth. At this time of increasing violence against immigrants and people of color that reveals a paucity of insight on the dynamics of our diverse society, we are called, now more than ever, to find ways to foreground true stories of true grit. We offer this work as an appeal to our broader humanity, one in which the inspired ideal of *making a difference* becomes reality by being an ally. Dario's testimonio is a rich account of an individual typically silenced in the college setting, providing a narrative that can be used in a variety of educational environments. Similar to Luis, quoted above, how might hearing this testimonio inspire some of your students to persist through their own *sobrevivencia*, (struggle for survival; Kasun, 2015; Trinidad Galván, 2006)? This is a process and outcome that can be replicated by teachers in all settings.

Future Implications

As we wrote this chapter, we were unable to reach Dario, to contact him to check this manuscript. We appreciate Dario's contribution to this chapter through his careful reading and feedback to previous versions of his testimonio. As university professors and teachers with U.S. citizenship and other racial and class positions of privilege, we acknowledge that this chapter would be stronger had we had Dario's feedback before the book went to press and we take full responsibility for the shortcomings in this text.

References

Aguilar-Valdez, J. R., López Leiva, A., Roberts-Harris, D., Torres-Velásquez, G. Lobo, & Westby, C. (2013). Ciencia en Nepantla: The journey of Nepantler@s in science learning and teaching. *Cultural Studies of Science Education, 8*(4), 821–858.

Au, W. (2011). Teaching under the new Taylorism: High-stakes testing and the standardization of the 21st century curriculum. *Journal of Curriculum Studies, 43*(1), 25–45.

Beverley, J. (2008). Testimonio, subalternity, and narrative authority. In S. Castro-Klaren (Ed.), *A companion to Latin American Literature and Culture*, 571–583. Chichester, West Sussex, England: Blackwell Publishing Ltd.

Bright, A. (2014). Trust me on this. *Journal of Middle Level Education in Texas, 1*(1), 25–36.

Cervantes-Soon, C. G. (2012). Testimonios of life and learning in the Borderlands: Subaltern Juárez girls speak. *Equity and Excellence in Education, 45*(3), 373–391.

DreamTeam LA. (2014). *Underground undergrads: The journey*. Retrieved from www .undergroundundergrads.com/

Duckworth, A. L., Peterson, C., & Matthews, M. D. (2007). Grit: Perseverance and passion for long-term goals. *Journal of Personality and Social Psychology, 92*(6), 1087–1101.

González, N., Moll, L. C., & Amanti, C. (2005). *Funds of knowledge: Theorizing practices in households, communities, and classrooms*. Mahwah, NJ: Lawrence Erlbaum Associates.

Houser, N. O. (1996). Negotiating dissonance and safety for the common good: Social education in the elementary classroom. *Theory and Research in Social Education, 24*(3), 294–312.

Jara, R. (1986). Prologo. In R. Jara & H. Vidal (Eds.), *Testimonio y literatura* (pp. 1–3). Minneapolis, MN: Institute for the Study of Ideologies and Literature.

Kasun, G. S. (2015). "The only Mexican in the room": Sobrevivencia as a way of knowing for Mexican transnational students and families. *Anthropology and Education Quarterly, 46*(3), 277–294.

Kasun, G. S., & López, D. (2017). Native science in practice: Cases for broadening understanding and engagement of science in education as a plea for future generations. *The Journal of Multicultural Affairs, 2*(1), 1–19.

Ladson-Billings, G. (2009). *The dreamkeepers: Successful teaching of African American children* (2nd ed.). San Francisco: Jossey-Bass.

Media Matters. (2015, May 27). Ann Coulter on immigration: "We're bringing in people from backward, primitive cultures" expecting them to turn into middle-class Americans. Retrieved from mediamatters.org/video/2015/05/27/ann-coulter-on-immigration -were-bringing-in-peo/203791

Medin, D. L., & Bang, M. (2014). *Who's asking: Native science, Western science, and science education.* Cambridge, MA: MIT Press.

Menchú, R. (1984). *I, Rigoberta Menchú, an Indian woman in Guatemala* (Ann Wright, Trans.). London: Verso.

Michie, G. (2005). *See you when we get there: Teaching for change in urban schools.* New York, NY: Teachers College Press.

Milkman, R. (2006). *L.A. story: Immigrant workers and the future of the U.S. labor movement.* New York, NY: Russell Sage Foundation.

Moll, L. C., Amanti, C., Neff, D., & González, N. (1992). Funds of knowledge: Using a qualitative approach to connect homes and classrooms. *Theory into Practice, XXXI*(2), 132–141.

Ngai, M. M. (2004). *Impossible subjects: Illegal aliens and the making of modern America.* Princeton, NJ: Princeton University Press.

Pandya, J. Z., Pagdilao, K. C., & Kim, E. A. (2015). Transnational children orchestrating competing voices in multimodal, digital autobiographies. *Teachers College Record, 117*(7), n7.

Patel, L. (2013). *Youth held at the border: Immigration, education, and the politics of inclusion.* New York, NY: Teachers College Press.

Trinidad Galván, R. (2006). *Campesina* epistemologies and pedagogies of the spirit: Examining women's *sobrevivencia.* In D. Delgado Bernal, C. A. Elenes, F. E. Godinez, & S. A. Villenas (Eds.), *Chicana/Latina education in everyday life: Feminista perspectives on pedagogy and epistemology* (pp. 161–180). Albany, NY: State University of New York Press.

U.S. Department of Education & U.S. Department of Justice. (2014). *Dear colleague letter: School enrollment procedures.* Retrieved from www2.ed.gov/about/offices/list/ocr/ letters/colleague-201405.pdf

Valencia, R. R. (1997). *The evolution of deficit thinking: Educational thought and practice.* London, England: Routledge.

Valenzuela, A. [Abel]. (2003). Day-labor work. *Annual Review of Sociology, 29*(10), 307–333.

Valenzuela, A. [Angela]. (1999). *Subtractive schooling: U.S. Mexican youth and the politics of caring.* Albany, NY: State University of New York Press.

Vitali, S., Glattfelder, J. B., & Battiston, S. (2011). The network of global corporate control. *PLOS ONE, 6*(10), 1–6.

Yosso, T. J. (2005). Whose culture has capital? A critical race theory discussion of community cultural wealth. *Race Ethnicity and Education, 8*(1), 69–91.

Yúdice, G. (1991). Testimonio and postmodernism. *Latin American Perspectives, 18*(3), 15–31.

Part III

ACCESSING, SURVIVING, AND THRIVING
DREAMERs GO TO COLLEGE

Carollyn James

CHAPTER 7

Getting Ready for College

Navigating Undocumented Status,
College Applications, and Financial Aid

Samantha Spinney with Danna Chávez Calvi

From 2007 to 2011, I worked in two large public high schools with many documented and undocumented immigrant students in the Virginia suburbs of Washington, DC. For three of those years, I taught English to high school seniors and required my students to learn about the college application process and write college essays. Many times throughout the school year, my students would have emotional breakdowns because of the stress of college applications and financial aid. Indeed, transitioning to college is a struggle for all students, especially for students who are the first in their families to go to college or who are completely dependent on scholarships and loans. At that time, however, I knew only a couple of openly undocumented students and so did not fully understand that their struggles were infinitely more complicated and challenging than those of their documented peers.

As a teacher, I was not equipped with knowledge about the difficult circumstances faced by undocumented students. My educational training never provided me with insights into the actual lived struggles faced by DREAMers or with knowledge of the ways that educators can support undocumented students in their struggles. I did not learn more about this until 2012, when my doctoral research led me to talk to numerous undocumented college students about their high school experiences and their transition to college (Spinney, 2015). Through this process, I formed many acquaintances—and friends—among undocumented students and activist allies; furthermore, I became involved in advocating for legislation to grant residency to young undocumented immigrants, known as the Development, Relief, and Education for Alien Minors (DREAM) Act (DREAM Act, 2001). I participated in actions to lobby members of Congress and local representatives, attended marches, and strategized with other immigration activists on how to raise awareness about this topic at the school level.

Barriers to Higher Education Access

Through my experiences working with undocumented students, I came to learn about the numerous hurdles undocumented students face in gaining access to higher education. Specifically, undocumented students face a variety of legal, financial, academic, and social-emotional barriers that inhibit and complicate this access—each of which is discussed in further detail below.

Legal Barriers. Prior to 2012, all undocumented youth were eligible for deportation upon turning 18 years of age—even though many of them did not know or remember their countries of origin and may not have had familial connections there (Gonzales, 2009). On June 15, 2012, President Barack Obama signed an executive order for a new program, Deferred Action for Childhood Arrivals (DACA), which deferred the deportation of young undocumented immigrants in good standing and allowed them to apply for temporary work permits renewable at 2-year intervals (U.S. Department of Homeland Security, 2012). More than 750,000 DREAMers applied for and received DACA status (Krogstad, 2017). With the inauguration of President Trump, who ran a campaign rife with anti-immigrant policies and rhetoric, the hard-earned future of DACA recipients is again in limbo (Alvarez, 2017). On September 5, 2017, the U.S. Attorney General announced that Congress had 6 months to address the status of DACA recipients. No new applications would be accepted and renewals would only be available until October 5 for those whose status would expire by March 5, 2018. In fact, prior to this announcement, some DACA recipients had been detained and deported without due process under the current administration (United We Dream, 2017).

Financial Barriers. Most undocumented students come from families living in poverty, as a result of unjust economic and social policies. Undocumented immigrants are paid well below average wages in the United States, with a median annual household income of $36,000, compared with the median household income of $50,000 for U.S.-born residents (Passel & Cohn, 2009). Despite contributing billions of federal, state, and local tax dollars annually, undocumented immigrants are locked out of poverty alleviation and social welfare programs, such as the Earned Income Tax Credit (EITC), the Social Security retirement benefit, Medicare, nonemergency Medicaid, the Children's Health Insurance Program, the Supplemental Nutrition Assistance Program, and the Housing and Urban Development Public Housing and Section 8 programs (Lipman, 2007; National Immigration Law Center, 2011). In fact, by not receiving the EITC, undocumented immigrant families bear a higher marginal tax rate than high-income households (Lipman, 2007).

Considering these conditions, the cost of college tuition is too high for many undocumented families (Abrego, 2006; Diaz-Strong Gomez, Luna-Duarte, &

Meiners, 2011). Although most students in the United States finance their higher education through federal student aid, undocumented students are banned from this essential education financing program (Morse & Birnbach, 2012). In addition, in most states, undocumented students are required to pay out-of-state tuition rates at public universities and community colleges (Diaz-Strong et al., 2011). Although Flores and Horn (2009) and Flores (2010) suggest that in-state tuition rates in Texas may have led to increased enrollment and retention rates in that state, students interviewed in Diaz-Strong et al. (2011) who received in-state tuition in Illinois explained that even in-state tuition rates often could not be borne by undocumented students and their families. As a result of these factors, of the students who do start college, many drop out or take classes sporadically, whenever they can afford to do so (Diaz-Strong et al., 2011).

Academic Barriers. Undocumented students pursuing higher education are faced with systemic academic barriers that have the potential to hinder their academic success and college access. As with other low-income student groups, undocumented students often attend low-performing K-12 schools, which may not adequately prepare them for higher education (Conway, 2009; Garcia & Tierney, 2011; Gonzales, 2009). Additionally, some undocumented students, like other immigrant students, are English language learners (ELLs) and have not been adequately prepared in the academic literacy that is required in higher education (Curry, 2004), which may ultimately place them at a disadvantage (Garcia & Tierney, 2011). Furthermore, many undocumented students are first-generation college-goers (Garcia & Tierney, 2011; Gonzales, 2009; Pérez, Espinoza, Ramos, Coronado, & Cortés, 2009) and, thus, may not receive adequate or timely college preparation information and resources (Garcia & Tierney, 2011). Moreover, the college information and resources they do receive may not be customized to their unique needs as undocumented students (Garcia & Tierney, 2011).

Social-Emotional Barriers. Undocumented young adults also experience social-emotional barriers to higher education attainment related to their undocumented status and the systemic barriers that society confers on individuals with such status. Migration is a radical life change (Pérez et al., 2009) that may be fraught with trauma for many immigrants to the United States—related to the migration process itself, acculturation, learning the English language, loss of family and community, a downturn in socioeconomic status, and several other stressors (Perez Foster, 2001). After arriving in the United States, immigrants face anti-immigrant xenophobia, not only from extremists, such as racist nativist hate groups (Southern Poverty Law Center, 2014) and anti-immigrant grassroots mobilizations (Fox, 2014), but also from mainstream U.S. society— from racist and xenophobic discourse about immigration issues and immigrants (Allexsaht-Snider, Buxton, & Harman, 2012; Catalano, 2013; Lawton, 2013; Santa Ana, 1999) to racist and xenophobic policies and practices at a variety of institutions (Lipman, 2007; Pérez Huber, 2011; Seif, 2011; Ybarra, Sánchez, & Sánchez, 2015). Such conditions have negative mental health consequences for immigrant students. Exposure to racism not only causes poor mental health, anxiety, and stress (Priest, et al., 2013) but also leads racism to become internalized (Hipolito-Delgado, 2010; Padilla, 2001; Taylor & Grundy, 1996). Internalized racism, that is, the acceptance of inferior stereotypes about one's racial group, may reinforce self-fulfilling negative stereotypes and lead to self-destructive behavior (Padilla, 2001).

Undocumented young adults may also experience depression, anxiety, stress, and feelings of hopelessness related to a fear of deportation, financial struggles, and other issues connected to their undocumented immigration status (Abrego, 2006; Contreras, 2009; Diaz-Strong et al., 2011; Garcia & Tierney, 2011; Pérez, Cortés, Ramos, & Coronado, 2010). Many undocumented students learn about their legal status only when they are in high school—when they attempt to reach milestones such as acquiring a driver's license or applying to college—which is a trauma in and of itself (Lawrence, 2011). Further, many undocumented students do not let teachers, counselors, and their friends know of their status, so they do not get the adequate educational and emotional support needed to navigate this trying process (Pérez et al., 2010).

Strategies for Educators

To help undocumented students navigate barriers to attaining a college education, many education and immigrant rights organizations have developed resources and initiated services promoting college access. Such resources and services are widely available in the public domain and include, for example, lists of scholarships for DREAMers; mentorship, internship, and tutoring programs available to DREAMers; information on state-level tuition policies; and legal organizations that assist DREAMers. Such resources and services are critically important for undocumented students because they provide them with information, direction, and advice that caters to their unique circumstances (Enriquez, 2011).

Despite the prevalence of resources and services to support DREAMers, however, many educators are unaware of this information. I know about this anecdotally, primarily from speaking with educators. For example, after coming across a list of scholarships available to DREAMers a few years ago, I forwarded it to a high school counselor with whom I used to work. She thanked me profusely and let me know that she had been unaware that such a list of scholarships existed. She passed this list along to all the other counselors in her department, who also had not previously seen a list of scholarships catering specifically to DREAMers. In the past few years, I have continued to share lists of scholarships for DREAMers with other college access professionals from different schools who work with undocumented students. Each time, the educators have mentioned that they had never seen or heard of such a list of scholarships—despite such lists being widely available through the websites of organizations that support DREAMers. This suggests that a gap exists between educators and DREAMer advocacy organizations that needs to be bridged.

There is an urgent need for educators to learn how to better support their undocumented students in accessing higher education. Informed and compassionate high school educators can take small steps to enormously benefit DREAMers pursuing their higher education goals. Three simple strategies that high school educators can use to support their undocumented students are as follows:

1. *Be knowledgeable.* Educators should be knowledgeable about the plight of undocumented students in the United States and be aware of the tools available to help DREAMers. Educators should learn about national, state, and local policies related to the education of undocumented immigrant students, and they should familiarize themselves with scholarships and university transition programs available to undocumented students. An easy way for educators to become knowledgeable about critical information supporting their undocumented student population is to identify local community-based organizations that assist DREAMers and their families, or even larger organizations that post key information online. An additional benefit of identifying these organizations is that educators can point DREAMers to these organizations for additional help and support.

2. *Be compassionate, build rapport, and stay positive.* It is important for educators to build rapport and trust with all their students and create a safe, nonjudgmental space so that students feel comfortable opening up to them when they need help. This is true when working with all students, but especially so when working with students who may be DREAMers. Educators who learn they have DREAMers in their classrooms should demonstrate compassion and understanding, without singling out these students who may already feel stigmatized. Further, educators should always be positive and encouraging with DREAMer students regarding the college application process, in the awareness that many DREAMers have great difficulty with stress, anxiety, and depression related to the pursuit of higher education. Educators should help DREAMers problem solve when navigating the college application process. If an educator is unsure about how to solve a college access problem, he or she should reach out to an organization that mentors undocumented students for additional guidance.

3. *Advocate for your students, and promote a culture of advocacy in your school.* If an educator learns of his or her student's undocumented status, and believes that the student is facing an unjust situation, that educator should advocate. Advocating can take many forms, including holding meetings within the school on how to better support undocumented students and families; raising awareness within the school and broader community; raising funds for local scholarships that support DREAMer students or creating a scholarship in the

name of a local DREAMer; lobbying local, state, and national elected leaders through phone calls, letters, and meetings; participating in marches and other demonstrations; and volunteering at a variety of organizations that support DREAMers. Advocating will both help to change policy—to bring justice for DREAMers and their families—and demonstrate to undocumented students that educators are willing to not just help them but also stand with them in their struggle. A demonstration of solidarity is an important symbolic message that will help to counter some of the xenophobic and racist nativist messages that are inundating undocumented students.

In addition to being advocates themselves, educators should encourage students (documented and undocumented alike) to create school-based student-led organizations in support of DREAMers, and then educators should consider sponsoring those organizations. Members and sponsors of such student organizations should connect to local and national organizations that provide information and support to DREAMers—which may help to fill any resource and information gaps left by educational institutions. Student organizations will also help to promote networking among undocumented students. Several studies have demonstrated the critical importance of networking for DREAMers (Enriquez, 2011; Garcia & Tierney, 2011; Gonzales, 2010; Silver, 2012). Networking among DREAMers can help promote the exchange of information that is unique to DREAMers' needs and can function as a way for DREAMers to support one another emotionally (Enriquez, 2011).

It does not necessarily take an excessive amount of time or effort for educators to support their undocumented students. Using the simple strategies described above, educators can support DREAMers in profound ways to ease the transition from high school to college.

When a DREAMer Becomes an Educator, Advocate, and Advisor

by Danna Chávez Calvi

It has been 17 years since I last set foot in "the city of eternal spring," Cochabamba, Bolivia—my native homeland. I was 8 years old when I boarded a plane and arrived in the United States under a visa—one that soon after expired. Unable to rectify or change my status at the time, at 8 years of age, I first became acquainted with the term *undocumented*.

Much like many others in my same predicament, though I knew the term pertained to me in some way, I had little idea what it truly meant. It was only later, when I reached my teen years and high school, that I quickly learned to what degree an immigrant status had affected and would continue affecting my future. A cumulative GPA above 4.0, an advanced diploma, and early admission to a variety of universities within the state of Virginia appeared to have little weight against an immigrant status that seemed to define me. My character, academic record, and volunteer involvement were outweighed by who I was not—or really, in this case, *what* I was not.

It was for this reason that I originally planned to take what some might consider a practical route: pursue a major that could secure a stable living for myself and my family, regardless of an immigrant status. I started out as a business administration student. After high school, I made my way through the local community college and later transferred to a 4-year institution, all of which would not have been possible without considerable help from my family and scholarships. I lived through the pre-DACA days—the ones where individuals like me were subjected to out-of-state tuition rates, despite having paid local and state taxes (for purchases and property) from the moment my family and I had set foot in the state over 10 years before.

Then came June 12, 2012. In my 24 years of living, it stands among the three dates I remember most (the other two being December 11, 2000, and September 11, 2001). I think I recall each of these dates because each had a significant impact in shaping me and my future. The first signifies the beginning of the end of my childhood; the second was the first time I had conflicting thoughts of what I "should" feel or where I belonged; and the last: a long overdue permit to dream. On June 12, I received that. It is for this reason that upon graduating from community college, I took a year and a half off to immerse myself in field experience in my chosen branch of work and to also accumulate money for my remaining 2 years of undergraduate. It was during this period that I realized I could not deal with the corporate world, or rather, I did not *want* to deal with the corporate world all my life—at least, not solely. I needed, wanted, and missed meaningful engagement with my community. I needed, wanted, and missed being with students.

This is why, despite all the challenges and mishaps that have occurred over the years, I would still consider my experience as an undocumented individual among the biggest blessings *in disguise* I have ever received. It has allowed me to learn how to look at the world differently, taught me the value of an education, helped me recognize and understand privilege, and fortified me to handle the unconventional. And, most important, it has led me to find a purpose and passion in working with students.

It is for all of these reasons and more that I have sought to become so involved in education and advocacy. Through my experience and the experiences of all whom I have had the pleasure to meet along the way, I find it unfortunate and shameful that in a country that often refers to itself as the most powerful in the world, access to a quality education is still more of a privilege than a right. Nevertheless, I recognize that we get little from complaining and much more from taking action. This is why I joined Mason DREAMers, a student organization at George Mason University that aims to create a more inclusive environment for undocumented students through education and advocacy, first as a student leader and now as an advisory board member. I am also working for Manassas City Public Schools within the AVID program, a college prep program where I advise and support students in Grades 7–12. Interestingly enough, in both of these organizations and programs I first started out as a student, and now I have taken on the role of the educator and advisor. I give each of these opportunities much credit for helping me become the individual I am today. Had it not been for them, I would have felt even more lost and less supported navigating my way through college as a first-generation immigrant student.

Guidelines

This section is meant to help educators understand and support their undocumented students, so that they, too, have a chance at earning a college degree. It is important for every educator to recognize and remember that no two immigrant stories are the same, and as a result, there exists no "single way" to provide support to all. Every student will always have varying needs and varying obligations to fulfill—and most important, you do not need to be a psychologist, an academic adviser, a financial aid counselor, a lawyer, a minority, or formerly undocumented to find ways to support your students. Oftentimes what these students seek is not an adult who has all the answers but rather an adult who cares enough to work alongside them. This is why the first and most crucial step in helping an undocumented student is learning their full story.

In order to gain an understanding of your student's immigrant story, which often involves the sharing of sensitive information, it is important to emphasize the following as you begin the conversation:

1. **Student Voluntary Choice.** From the very start, the student should be made aware that he/she has the option to skip or not answer any particular question you as an educator may ask.
2. **Absolute Confidentiality.** The student should be made aware that nothing discussed during the session will be shared with others unless he or she authorizes it. However, emphasize that certain questions will be asked in an effort to better grasp his or her particular situation and how the faculty member will be able to best assist.
3. **No legal advice will be provided.** The student should understand that whatever the staff/faculty member will be saying should be interpreted not as legal advice or the definitive answer to most questions the student may have but rather as input based on the current knowledge of the faculty member.
4. **Your current knowledge and understanding.** If you have had experience working with undocumented students before, be sure to mention it to the student. If you have not had that experience, be honest and let him or her know. Nine times out of ten, the student will take careful note of that and

appreciate it. Why? Because, in spite of any lack of experience, the student will recognize that you are opting to invest your time and effort in working with him or her in particular.

5. **Explain that your aim and role is to serve as a support and connector.** As a faculty member, you are more likely to serve as the best version of such if you are able to learn as much as you can about the student. Explain that to him or her. In an ideal situation, after talking with the student you should be able to draw and explain connections between the student's interests/aspirations and his or her past/present choices. You should also be able to provide some insight on organizations, particular contact names and emails, and/or available financial resources.

6. **Don't make assumptions; make introductions.** As an educator it is your duty to introduce students to ideas they may not have considered pursuing before (i.e., an alternative major/career path based on demonstrated work you have seen from the student, a government program like DACA, double majoring, minoring, an accelerated master's program, honors college, particular clubs, etc.). Know that the student and his or her family will always be seeking to make each dollar spent on education worth it. Never assume that they are fully aware that certain programs or options exist.

7. **The order and manner** in which the following questions are asked is subject to change based on a case-by-case scenario.

To best assist a particular undocumented or DACAmented student, a staff member should seek to focus and ask questions in the areas outlined in Table 7.1. Acquiring answers to these questions will help build a more personal connection with the student and enable a trusting relationship to develop. It may also help educators most easily fulfill their role as "connectors" to resources the student may not be aware exist. For example, in the last few years Latin American organizations like some in Mexico have established unique study-abroad programs and funds for exemplary students. In addition, becoming acquainted with community organizations will allow educators to more easily make connections between financial opportunities a student may be eligible for and also to provide career/professional guidance.

As an undocumented and later as a DACAmented student, I believe I would have had no problem answering these questions. If anything, it would have made sense to me that the faculty member wanted to first know where I am, where I have been, and where I seek to go—and, perhaps more important, the many reasons why. Along with their reiteration of the above guidelines (student choice, absolute confidentiality, etc.), their vested interest in learning my "whys" would have helped me to grow more comfortable in sharing my story with them.

Table 7.1. Questions for Advisors

Area	Related Questions
If the Student Is a Transfer Student....	• What exactly has made this student transfer? • At the student's former institution, was he/she considered an in-state or out-of-state student? • At the student's institution/college will he/she be considered an in-state or out-of-state student? • How was the student able to afford his or her tuition at the former institution and how does he or she plan to do so at the new institution? • How many credits is the student planning to take this semester? Do these plans coincide with the number of credits the student would take in his or her ideal world? • Is the student a current DACA recipient or not?
Scholarships and Financial Aid	• What scholarships has the student received? • What scholarships (if any) has the student applied for but is waiting to hear back about? • What financial resources for DACA or undocumented students does he or she know about?
Student Background* **The answers to these questions may reveal themselves as the relationship develops between the advisor and the student*	• Where was the student born? * • What year did the student arrive? * • At what age did he or she arrive? * • Under what circumstances did the student leave his or her native homeland? (i.e., war, famine, political turmoil, economic depression, etc.)* • How did the student arrive in the United States? (i.e., the border or visa)* • What was his or her student involvement like back in K–12 afterschool/club activities? • What was his or her student involvement like back in the old institution? • What personal or family obligations does he/she have? (i.e., paying rent/car/utilities, taking care of children, working X number of hours, etc.) • Does he/she have any siblings or close family members who have previously attended college under similar circumstances? If so, how was their experience? Did they also transfer? Did they finish school? • Has the student ever attended a lawyer consultation about his or her case?*
Professional Background and Aspirations	• What major is he/she pursuing? • What career does he/she intend on pursuing? • What has led to his or her career choice? • How familiar is he/she with research opportunities, internships, and fellowships in that field? • Has he/she considered honors college, a minor, double majoring, an accelerated master's program, etc.? • Are there any particular goals the student has for the remainder of his or her undergraduate career? (i.e. take part in research, study abroad, attain a particular internship/fellowship, join a particular honor society, etc.)
Personal Interests/ Aspirations	• What does he/she enjoy doing during leisure time? (i.e., sports, singing/dancing, reading/writing, photography, video games, volunteering, etc.) • What academic areas does the student consider to be his or her strongest? (i.e., math, English, science, etc.) • How does the student's personal interests align with his or her choice in major? With his or her choice in career? • In an ideal world, would the student be interested in joining a club, sports, or Greek life?

References

Abrego, L. J. (2006). "I can't go to college because I don't have papers": Incorporation patterns of Latino undocumented youth. *Latino Studies, 4,* 212–231.

Allexsaht-Snider, M., Buxton, C. A., & Harman, R. (2012). Challenging anti-immigration discourses in school and community contexts. *International Journal of Multicultural Education, 14,* 191–217. doi:dx.doi.org/10.18251/ijme.v14i2.649

Alvarez, P. (2017, April). Trump's quiet reversal on deporting young undocumented immigrants. *The Atlantic.* Retrieved from www.theatlantic.com/politics/archive/2017/04/trumps-quiet-reversal-on-deporting-young-undocumented-immigrants/524367/

Catalano, T. (2013). Anti-immigrant ideology in U.S. crime reports: Effects on the education of Latino children. *Journal of Latinos and Education, 12,* 254–270. doi:10.1080/15348431.2013.785408

Chomsky, A. (2007). *They take our jobs!: And 20 other myths about immigration.* Boston, MA: Beacon Press.

Chomsky, A. (2014). *Undocumented: How immigration became illegal.* Boston, MA: Beacon Press.

Contreras, F. (2009). Sin papeles y rompiendo barreras: Latino students and the challenges of persisting in college. *Harvard Educational Review, 79,* 610–639. doi:dx.doi.org/10.17763/haer.79.4.02671846902gl33w

Conway, K. M. (2009). Exploring persistence of immigrant and native students in an urban community college. *Review of Higher Education, 32,* 321–352. doi:10.1353/rhe.0.0059

Curry, M. J. (2004). UCLA community college review: Academic literacy for English language learners. *Community College Review, 32,* 51–68. doi:10.1177/009155210403200204

Diaz-Strong, D., Gomez, C., Luna-Duarte, M. E., & Meiners, E. R. (2011). Purged: Undocumented students, financial aid policies, and access to higher education. *Journal of Hispanic Higher Education, 10*(2), 107–119. doi:10.1177/1538192711401917

DREAM Act. (2001). S. 1291, 107th Cong. (21).

Enriquez, L. E. (2011). "Because we feel the pressure and we also feel the support": Examining the educational success of undocumented immigrant Latina/o students. *Harvard Educational Review, 81*(3), 476–499.

Flores, S. M. (2010). State "Dream Acts": The effect of in-state resident tuition policies on the college enrollment of undocumented Latino students in the United States. *The Review of Higher Education, 33,* 239–283. doi:10.1353/rhe.0.0134

Flores, S. M., & Horn, C. L. (2009). College persistence and undocumented students at a selective public university: A quantitative case study analysis. *Journal of College Student Retention, 11,* 57–76. doi:10.2190/CS.11.1.d

Fox, L. (2014, July). Anti-immigrant hate coming from everyday Americans. *US News and World Report.* Retrieved from www.usnews.com/news/articles/2014/07/24/anti-immigrant-hate-coming-from-everyday-americans

Freire, P. (1970). *Pedagogy of the oppressed.* New York, NY: Herder and Herder.

Garcia, L. D., & Tierney, W. G. (2011). Undocumented immigrants in higher education: A preliminary analysis. *Teachers College Record, 113*(12), 2739–2776.

Gonzales, R. G. (2009). *Young lives on hold: The college dreams of undocumented students.* The College Board. Retrieved from professionals.collegeboard.com/profdownload/young-lives-on-hold-college-board.pdf

Gonzales, R. G. (2010). On the wrong side of the tracks: Understanding the effects of school structure and social capital in the educational pursuits of undocumented immigrant students. *Peabody Journal of Education, 85*(4), 469–485. dx.doi.org/10.1080/0161956X.2010.518039

Hipolito-Delgado, C. P. (2010). Exploring the etiology of ethnic self-hatred: Internalized racism in Chicana/o and Latina/o college students. *Journal of College Student Development, 51,* 319–331. doi:10.1353/csd.0.0133

Krogstad, J. M. (2017). Unauthorized immigrants covered by DACA face uncertain future. Pew Research Center. Retrieved from www.pewresearch.org/fact-tank/2017/01/05 /unauthorized-immigrants-covered-by-daca-face-uncertain-future/

Lawrence, C. (2011). *Advising undocumented students: FAQs for college counselors.* Retrieved from www.nacacnet.org/globalassets/documents/knowledge-center/undocumented -students/counselor_faqs_advising_undocumented_students_2014.pdf

Lawton, L. (2013). Speak English or go home: The anti-immigrant discourse of the American "English only" movement. *Critical Approaches to Discourse Analysis across Disciplines, 7,* 100–122. Retrieved from www.lancaster.ac.uk/fass/journals/cadaad /wp-content/uploads/2015/04/Volume-7_Lawton.pdf

Lipman, F. J. (2007). Bearing witness to economic injustices of undocumented immigrant families: A new class of "undeserving" poor. *Nevada Law Journal, 7,* 736–758. Retrieved from scholars.law.unlv.edu/cgi/viewcontent.cgi?article=1449&context=nlj

Morse, A., & Birnbach, K. (2012). *In-state tuition and unauthorized immigrant students.* National Conference of State Legislatures, Immigrant Policy Project. Retrieved from www.ncsl.org/issues-research/immig/in-state-tuition-and-unauthorized-immigrants. aspx

National Education Association. (2015, March). *ALL IN! How educators can advocate for English language learners.* Retrieved from colorincolorado.org/sites/default/files/ELL _AdvocacyGuide2015.pdf

National Immigration Law Center. (2011). *Overview of immigrant eligibility for federal programs.* Retrieved from www.nilc.org/issues/economic-support/table_ovrw_fedprogs/

Padilla, L. M. (2001). "But you're not a dirty Mexican": Internalized oppression, Latinos, and law. *Texas Hispanic Journal of Law and Policy, 7,* 59–113. Retrieved from connection.ebscohost.com/c/articles/6236245/but-youre-not-dirty-mexican -internalized-oppression-latinos-law

Passel, J. S., & Cohn, D. (2009). *A portrait of unauthorized immigrants in the United States.* Pew Research Center. Retrieved from www.pewhispanic.org/2009/04/14/a-portrait -of-unauthorized-immigrants-in-the-united-states/

Pérez, W., Espinoza, R., Ramos, K., Coronado, H. M., & Cortés, R. (2009). Academic resilience among undocumented Latino students. *Hispanic Journal of Behavioral Sciences, 31,* 149–181. doi:10.1177/0739986309333020

Pérez, W., Cortés, R. D., Ramos, K., & Coronado, H. (2010). "Cursed and blessed": Examining the socioemotional and academic experiences of undocumented Latina and Latino college students. *New Directions for Student Services, 131,* 35–51. doi:10.1002 /ss.366

Perez Foster, R. (2001). When immigration is trauma: Guidelines for the individual and family clinician. *American Journal of Orthopsychiatry, 71,* 153–170. doi:10.1037/0002-9432.71.2.153

Pérez Huber, L. (2011). Discourses of racist nativism in California public education: English dominance as racist nativist microaggressions. *Educational Studies: A Journal of the American Educational Studies Association, 47,* 379–401. doi:10.1080/00131946.2011. 589301

Priest, N., Paradies, Y., Trenerry, B., Truong, M., Karlsen, S., & Kelly, Y. (2013). A systematic review of studies examining the relationship between reported racism and health and wellbeing for children and young people. *Social Science and Medicine, 95,* 115–127. doi:10.1016/j.socscimed.2012.11.031

Santa Ana, O. (1999). "Like an animal I was treated": Anti-immigrant metaphor in US public discourse. *Discourse and Society, 10,* 191–224. doi:10.1177/0957926599010002004

Seif, H. (2011). "Unapologetic and unafraid": Immigrant youth come out from the shadows. *New Directions for Child and Adolescent Development, 2011*(134), 59–75. doi:10.1002/cd.311

Silver, A. (2012). Aging into exclusion and social transparency: Undocumented immigrant youth and the transition to adulthood. *Latino Studies, 10,* 499–522. doi:10.1057/lst.2012.41

Southern Poverty Law Center. (2014, February 25). *"Nativist extremist" groups decline again.* Retrieved from www.splcenter.org/fighting-hate/intelligence-report/2014/%E2%80%98nativist-extremist%E2%80%99-groups-decline-again-0

Spinney, S. (2015). *Effects of participation in immigration activism on undocumented students in higher education* (Unpublished doctoral dissertation). George Mason University, Fairfax, Virginia.

Taylor, J., & Grundy, C. (1996). Measuring Black internalization of White stereotypes about African Americans: The Nadanolization Scale. In R. L. Jones (Ed.), *Handbook of tests and measures of Black populations* (Vol. 2, pp. 217–226). Hampton, VA: Cobb & Henry.

United We Dream. (2017, August 28). Trump announces an end to DACA. Here are 5 things you should know. Retrieved from weareheretostay.org/resources/daca-update-five-things-you-should-know

U.S. Department of Homeland Security. (2012). Secretary Napolitano announces deferred action process for young people who are low enforcement priorities [Press release]. Retrieved from www.dhs.gov/news/2012/06/15/secretary-napolitano-announces-deferred-action-process-young-people-who-are-low

Vargas, J. A. (2011, June 22). My life as an undocumented immigrant. *New York Times Magazine.* Retrieved from www.nytimes.com/2011/06/26/magazine/my-life-as-an-undocumented-immigrant.html

Vargas, J. A. (2012, December 10). Actions are illegal, never people. *TEDxMidAtlantic.* Retreived from www.youtube.com/watch?v=tmz9cCF0KNE

Wong, S. (2011). *Dialogic approaches to TESOL: Where the ginkgo tree grows.* New York, NY: Routledge.

Wong, S. & Grant, R. (2009). Nurturing cultures of peace with dialogic approaches to language and literacy. *TESOL in Context, 19,* 4–17.

Ybarra, V. D., Sánchez, L. M., & Sánchez, G. R. (2015). Anti-immigrant anxieties in state policy: The great recession and punitive immigration policy in the American states, 2005–2012. *State Politics and Policy Quarterly.* Advance online publication. doi:10.1177/1532440015605815

CHAPTER 8

Mentoring and Retaining College-Bound DREAMers

Establishing the Dream Project, a Nonprofit Organization in Virginia

Emma Violand-Sánchez and Marie Price

DREAMers, undocumented youth with or without Deferred Action for Childhood Arrivals (DACA) relief, face unique challenges navigating their way through the higher education labyrinth. The majority are often the first in their families to consider college, and so there are few precedents on which they can rely, including social networks, alumni networks, parental counseling and understanding, and access to information. Many must balance jobs with schoolwork. Many others have entered the high schools from which they will graduate midstream, and so must struggle with cultural and social nuances, while others have had the continuity of their educations disrupted. Given the precarious legal status of many DREAMers and their families, undocumented undergraduates report elevated levels of anxiety and high levels of being treated negatively, because of their status, by faculty, counselors, other students, or university administration (Suárez-Orozco, Teranishi, & Suárez-Orozco, 2015).

In June 2012, President Obama and his administration presented an executive order to the Department of Homeland Security (DHS) regarding young people who came to the United States as children—often called the "1.5 generation"—and who are now considered unauthorized immigrants. DACA has provided them with temporary relief from immigration enforcement and deportation proceedings, as well as the authorization to work, obtain a driver's license, and, in some states, eligibility for in-state tuition. To obtain DACA relief an applicant must have arrived in the United States before his or her 16th birthday and before June 15, 2007. Successful applicants also must be in school or have a high school degree or its equivalent. DACA recipients must reapply every 2 years, have no criminal record, and pay an application fee. As of June 2016, approximately 750,000 young people had received DACA protections (United States Citizenship and Immigration Services, 2016). Moreover, it is estimated that 250,000 undocumented students are currently in or trying to gain access to higher education (Suárez-Orozco et al,

2015), with California having the largest number of undocumented students in higher education.

DREAMers have been politically organized for nearly 2 decades (Rincón, 2008), but their political activities in U.S. southern states such as Virginia are more recent. The Dream Project, a nonprofit organization that is the focus of this chapter, began with parents who could not bear to see their children's academic achievements and futures undermined by the barriers of being undocumented. Leaving the relative safety of public schools, these students had begun what Roberto Gonzales terms the "transition to illegality" (2011, p. 607).

Afraid and powerless, about a dozen parents and students in Arlington, Virginia, came together in 2010 to become a force for change. The intent of this chapter is to share the Dream Project story as it may be instructive for others, especially in those states and localities where DREAMers struggle to find support and recognition (Pérez, 2014). After discussing the context for the formation of the Dream Project, the chapter will turn to three fundamental activities that allow the students in the Dream Project to beat the odds: (1) mentoring of students in high school and in college, (2) sustaining a scholarship program that is renewable for up to 6 years, and (3) community building through partnerships with parents, institutions, and volunteers. We will conclude with a discussion of student results based upon annual surveys of mentees and college students and focus groups.

The Virginia and Arlington Contexts

Virginia is an example of a new destination state with regard to immigration, and it is especially representative of a "new geography of Latino migration and settlement that now stretches into many southern cities and towns" and that, at times, has led to repressive reactions by state governments unaccustomed to racially diverse immigrant streams (Winders & Smith, 2012, p. 221). In the early 2000s Virginia state legislators passed or attempted to impose measures to limit access to state universities for DREAMers or to treat them as international students who pay higher fees. Even with the creation of DACA in 2012, DREAMers who graduated from Virginia high schools were still considered out-of-state students.

On April 29, 2014, Attorney General Mark Herring transformed this political landscape for DREAMers by announcing that the Commonwealth of Virginia would become the 19th state to offer DACA students in-state tuition. The rationale for doing this was linked to the overall well-being of the state economy and the recognition that making education accessible to eligible DREAMers would increase Virginia's competitiveness. As stated by Attorney General Herring at the time of his executive order,

> If the Commonwealth is to remain competitive in a global economy, we must embrace a strategy that maximizes our talent pool and helps all Virginians reach their full potential. . . . These "DREAMers" are already Virginians in some very important ways. In most cases they were raised here, they graduated from Virginia schools, and they have

known no home but Virginia. They might be the valedictorian or salutatorian of their high school, but because they were brought here as children many years ago, an affordable education remains out of their reach. Instead of punishing and placing limits on these smart, talented, hard working young people, Virginia should extend them an opportunity for an affordable education. It's what the law requires, it makes economic sense for Virginia, and it's the right thing to do. (Cohen, 2014)

This was a monumental change for Virginia; since this decision the number of undocumented youth in Virginia community colleges and universities has steadily increased to several hundred.

Unlike many parts of Virginia, counties such as Arlington that form part of the Washington, DC, metropolitan area have been receiving large numbers of immigrants and refugees since the 1970s (Price, Cheung, Friedman, & Singer, 2005). Arlington Public Schools is a highly diverse school system that enrolls 26,241 pre-K–12 grade students from 96 countries who speak 81 languages. Civil rights statistics indicate that 46.9% of students are White, 28% are Hispanic, 10% are African American, 9.5% are Asian, and 5.7% have other ethnic origins (Arlington Public Schools, 2017). The *Washington Post*'s Challenge Index is one measure of how effectively a school prepares its students for college. In 2017, the index listed all of Arlington's public high schools in the top 3%. However, even though Arlington schools are high performing, there are substantial gaps in achievement between students who are English proficient and classified as English language learners (ELL).

In this diverse and high-performing school district, the expectation to go to college is the norm and one that undocumented youth also embrace. Unfortunately, ethnic and racial gaps still exist in enrollments for rigorous college preparatory programs such as Advanced Placement and International Baccalaureate. Arlington has many initiatives designed to support students in their preparation for college. The Dream Project, as a 501(c)3 nonprofit, came out of a context of undocumented students' aspiring to attend college but facing serious barriers posed by their legal status, lack of financial resources, and unfamiliarity with the college admissions process. Recognizing these barriers, Arlington Public Schools was supportive of the Dream Project from the beginning to find ways to overcome these barriers. It is this partnership that has been fundamental in the Dream Project's success.

Creating the Dream Project

The Dream Project empowers students whose immigration status creates barriers to education by working with them to gain access to and succeed in college through scholarships, mentoring, family engagement, and advocacy. The organization was founded in 2010 around the kitchen table of Emma Violand-Sánchez along with immigrant parents and concerned community members. By 2011 the Dream Project was a registered legal entity with 501(c)3 status and it began accepting donations. That same year it gave four scholarships to undocumented high school seniors to assist them in attending college.

The grassroots ethos of the Dream Project is still evident in its reliance on community support and volunteers. The mission of the Dream Project has been formalized to accomplish the following:

1. Guide, support, and empower high school students from low-income, immigrant families to identify and achieve their postsecondary education dreams.
2. Engage and empower parents and families to take an active role in the college admission process and successful transition to higher education programs.
3. Increase community awareness and support for immigrant students and their families before and after college admission.
4. Assist in the retention and ultimate graduation of program participants.

More than 100 Dream Project scholars have enrolled in university since 2011 and 24 students have graduated from college as of 2017. Dream Scholars (individuals who receive a scholarship from the Dream Project) hail from 20 different Virginia high schools and have attended 20 colleges in six states. In 2017 the Dream Project awarded 77 scholarships, 47 of which were renewals. NOVA (Northern Virginia Community College) and George Mason University are the top institutions where Dream Scholars study, but students are enrolled in Virginia Tech, Virginia Commonwealth University, Marymount, Radford, James Madison, William and Mary, and Georgetown. More than half the Dream Scholars are pursuing college careers in engineering, science, and business.

Although 90% of Dream Scholars are from Latin America, DREAMers from South Korea, Mongolia, Ethiopia, Sudan, and the Philippines are also among the scholars and mentees. Based on our 2016 fall survey, 71% of our Dream Scholars have DACA. And, most important, 85% of our Dream Scholars have stayed in college or graduated.

A key to the program's success is partnerships with individuals, faith-based communities, community organizations, and private foundations. Also, the Dream Project has a "working" board of directors. These board members write grants, fundraise, manage the scholarship selection, and staff the mentoring program. The board includes community members, educators, lawyers, former Dream Scholars, and a parental advisory group. With this volunteer base, most funds raised go directly to initiatives and not to staff costs. Partnerships with public schools, particularly Arlington Public Schools, and colleges and universities is a multiplier of the Dream Project's resources. Arlington Public Schools provides a place for the Dream Project to operate, meet with students, and host events. Colleges and universities know that Dream Project students are prepared for the rigors of college education and these institutions are willing to take a chance on them in terms of admission and additional financial support. What follows is a brief discussion of the mentoring, scholarship, and community-building programs sustained by the Dream Project.

The Necessity of Mentoring

The Dream Project Mentoring Program was established in 2011 with four students and one mentor in a Georgetown University dorm room and has grown into the formal mentoring program that today serves more than 35 students and 12 volunteer mentors. The demand for the Dream Project's mentoring services has grown—this year the program received 60 applications.

Reaching High School Students. The current mentoring program consists of 2-hour weekly sessions in the evening from September until April, held in APS facilities. The mentees are current high school seniors from Northern Virginia. The volunteer mentors are current college students or professionals who have experience navigating the college application process, transitioning to higher education, and excelling in college. We also have current Dream Scholars who work with high school students.

Before each program year begins, students and parents are required to attend an orientation meeting. For many family members, this meeting is a crucial first step in taking an active role in the students' academic futures. Also, prior to the start of each year, a training session is held for all mentors. The program coordinator and members of her team provide volunteer management, training, and support to the mentors throughout the length of the program.

Each session of the mentoring program begins with all students working together on a curriculum topic, such as Understanding the College Application Process, Exploring Financial Assistance Open to DACA and Undocumented Students, Essay Writing, Confidence Building, and Transitioning into College. After the group work, each mentee in the program works with an assigned volunteer mentor. During these mentor-mentee sessions, mentees receive personal attention to complete college and scholarship applications, essays, and résumés. They form a relationship and often communicate with each other outside the mentoring sessions. Over the year, mentees and mentors develop a lasting relationship that positively enhances the college experience for both.

As part of the family engagement program, parents and family members participate in informational sessions to discuss the transition to college and take leadership roles in planning and executing community and fundraising activities. Special funds are raised to rent a bus and conduct college tours in the fall. For many of our mentees and their parents, this is their first experience on a college campus. What makes these college tours especially impactful is that current Dream Scholars meet the mentees and show them around the campuses.

Finally, the Dream Project has a partnership with Northern Virginia Community College (NVCC) to provide mentees with a Dual Enrollment Student

Development Orientation class, or SDV 100, during the last 6 weeks of mentoring. This course provides students with skills in time management, academic planning, note taking, study skills, financial literacy, and other necessary skills for college students. This one-credit course is required for incoming freshman at NVCC and is provided free of charge to all mentees, saving them between $161.75 (in state) and $359 (out of state), depending on their immigration status.

Summer Summit for College Students. Survey results revealed that Dream Scholars sought continued guidance while in college from the Dream Project. This led to the creation of a day-long summer summit open to all Dream Scholars. For the past 3 years, the event has taken place at George Washington University, where Marie Price, a board member, organizes the event with help of other board members, interns, and current and former Dream Scholars.

This specialized workshop is free of charge and consists of several distinct panels. Students have access to computers, meeting rooms, and lunch. Some 25 to 30 students participate in the panels that focus on résumé and portfolio development, legal issues, mindfulness, building community and creating change, financing education, and finding mentors in college. Student satisfaction with this event is very high (4.8 on a scale of 5.0). The summer summit is one of the ways the Dream Project continues to mentor its scholars while they are still in college.

Renewable Scholarships

Scholarship support, even at modest levels, can be essential in enabling DREAMers to attend college. Aside from constituting a critical financial resource, scholarships are a confirmation that the student can indeed succeed in higher education, and that someone genuinely believes in his or her potential (Enriquez, 2011).

In order to receive a scholarship from the Dream Project, applicants must have graduated from or be a senior at a Virginia high school, have been born outside the United States, and will attend a 2- or 4-year college or university. Students participate in a rigorous application and interview process during which their academic record, service to community, and proven ability to overcome obstacles are assessed. Students may submit renewal applications for up to 5 consecutive years, provided that they meet the academic requirements set by the scholarship committee and participate in Dream Project activities throughout the year.

In 2016–2017, the Dream Project received 112 applications and awarded 77 scholarships, of which 47 were renewals. Scholarships of $1,200 are paid directly to the student's institution. If for some reason the student does not enroll, the funds are returned to the Dream Project. All scholarships are renewable for up to 5 times, as noted above, as long as the recipient remains a student in good standing at an accredited college or university. Six years of support is crucial, because many of our students often take reduced course loads because of the need to work to pay for college.

Named Scholarships. The greatest challenge for a small, mostly volunteer organization such as the Dream Project is fundraising. Throughout the year various fundraising events are held, among them a holiday party, a spring concert, small gatherings at homes, and food sales. The creation of named scholarships that allow donors recognize a loved one or target a particular student group (based on area of study or country of origin) has been a significant fundraising tool.

Twenty-two individuals or organizations have established named scholarships that supported 39 students in 2017. In order to establish a named scholarship, the Dream Project asks for $1,000 per supported student and that the donor agree to continue this level of support until the student graduates from college. Through the named scholarship program, donors get to meet individual students and learn of their accomplishments. It is often a way for donors to remember a loved one with a living tribute. Establishing this funding mechanism sustains the Dream Project's fundraising goals and creates networks of donors and scholars that are mutually beneficial.

Emergency Loan Fund. In addition to scholarships, the Dream Project maintains an emergency no-interest loan fund to respond to critical short-term needs that may threaten a student's ability to remain in school, such as a parent's losing a job or a computer that needs replacement. It is modeled as a pay-it-forward program, with the intent that a student repay the loan within 2 years of graduation, although several students have repaid loans before graduating. The Dream Project has a Loan Committee to oversee the program and review applications. The maximum loan amount is $2,000. With support from two local area foundations, $12,000 is available each year. The goal is that as loans are repaid, the loan fund will be self-sustaining by 2020.

Community Building and Forging Partnerships

A small nonprofit that supports DREAMers could not operate without strategic partnerships. Partnering with Arlington Public Schools was instrumental in getting the organization running and having a place to meet with students. Support from faith-based groups and collaborations with local public and private universities in Virginia added resources and improved student access to college. In particular, the Dream Project has strong relationships with Marymount University, George Mason University, and William and Mary. We recommend that nonprofits supporting undocumented youth form partnerships with school districts to establish mentoring programs and work with local community colleges and universities to establish pathways that undocumented students might follow. In addition, reaching out to public officials and having Dream Scholars share their stories of exclusion and hope, in the end, is crucial for advocacy and change (Andrade-Ayala, Torres, Violand-Sánchez, Price, & Sojo, 2016).

In annual surveys, the students consistently express the value of meeting other undocumented youth like them. In addition to the financial help from the Dream

Project, students highly value being part of a supportive network. Many express relief after years of hiding their immigration status from even their closest friends. As one Dream Scholar said in a 2015 focus group: "The network is definitely good and it also gives you hope, knowing that there are people in the same situation as you and getting to know more people who can help you with recommendations."

Board members, Dream Scholars, and mentees all play a critical role in creating partnerships. The board acts to formalize these relationships with memoranda of understanding. The board engages dozens of volunteers in the application review and interview process as well as in the mentoring program. Volunteers receive an intimate look at compelling stories of undocumented students and often become advocates and fundraisers by reaching out to their community of friends and associates.

Some of the most important outreach work is done by the Dream Scholars themselves in sharing their stories at Dream Project events. One student recalls sharing her story for the first time:

> The first time I shared mine publicly was at the scholarship acceptance ceremony in 2012. I had just graduated from high school and at that point basically none of my friends had known about my circumstances. And then from there I realized that one way to take what the Dream Project was doing a step further was to actually advocate and write Congress, so I started to get involved with other groups.

This engagement has spread to campuses across Virginia as Dream Scholars learn the value of advocacy. In the fall 2016 survey, 46% of respondents stated that they were involved in DREAMer organizations at their universities.

Survey Results

Each fall an extensive online survey of all current and former Dream Scholars is conducted to assess how the students are doing and find ways to better support them. Eighty-six percent of respondents credit the Dream Project with helping them get into and succeed in college. In addition to the financial help, 77% of students valued being part of a supportive network and 41% valued the advocacy work. Two-thirds of Dream Scholars had paid employment while in college. To date 85% of the Dream Scholars have stayed in college or graduated, which far exceeds national percentages for first-generation, minority and undocumented students.

Mentoring high school students is critical to the success of undocumented students who aspire to attend college. The aspects of the program that are most beneficial are revealed in the mentee survey, which showed that

- 95% of mentees ranked learning about college scholarships as one of the most beneficial aspects of the mentoring program;

- 84% found meeting other students in a similar situation to be valuable;
- 79% of mentees stated that learning about the college application process was important;
- 79% thought that visiting college campuses was beneficial;
- 74% of mentees said that attending Dream Project events was important to them;
- 74% found that working closely with their mentor was the most beneficial part of the program; and
- 69% of mentees stated that specific help with writing their college applications was useful for them.

Interestingly, mentees ranked advocacy work for DREAMers and public speaking ("Telling Your Story") the lowest, at 31% and 26%, respectively. Yet once in college, Dream Scholars tend to value advocacy work and public speaking more highly.

The Dream Project acknowledges areas for improvement. Three-quarters of those surveyed would like the Dream Project to provide more guidance while they are in college, so programs like the summer summit should be expanded. Sixty percent of students would like explicit career guidance, and 58% of students would like to see the amount of the scholarships increased.

Financial challenges are very real for all students, but especially undocumented undergraduates. For those two-dozen students able to graduate, in-state tuition (available since 2014 in Virginia), financial support from other scholarships or institutions, and financial support from family and friends were the most-cited reasons for successful college completion. Similarly, two-thirds of students unable to remain in college cited the lack of financial resources as the main barrier.

Making a Difference

Our experience has shown that participants in the Dream Project benefit from mentoring, scholarships, expectations of college attendance and graduation, community building, parent engagement, and networking. Mentees as well as Dream Scholars left the program stronger, more connected, and more committed to making a positive change, both in their own communities and far beyond.

We believe that the success of these students hinges on the maintenance of programs such as DACA. Under the current DACA program, Dream Scholars receive in-state tuition, and they are able to work and obtain a driver's license. As many as 12,100 young DACAmented Virginians (Interfaith Worker Justice, 2017) would be left in legal limbo unless the DACA program is redesigned or comprehensive immigration reform is legislated through Congress.

As we encourage our Dream Scholars to do, we are sharing the story of the Dream Project in this chapter. Our hope is that it can be helpful for other educators of undocumented students, especially in areas where DREAMers struggle to find support and recognition. Educators have an important role in understanding the barriers undocumented youth face and supporting them in their pursuit of higher education. The Dream Project is one example of a community-led and school-supported effort that has made a difference in the lives of scores of Virginians.

References

Andrade-Ayala, H., Torres, D., Violand-Sánchez, E., Price, M, & Sojo, G. (2016, February). Living the Dream? Virginia's undocumented youth and the Dream Project. *Virginia Journal of Education*, pp. 18–19.

Arlington Public Schools. (2017). APS quick facts. Retrieved from www.apsva.us/wp -content/uploads/2015/03/QuickFacts-1.pdf

Cohen, M. (2014). Virginia attorney general says "DREAMers" can qualify for in-state tuition. Retrieved from dcist.com/2014/04/virginia_attorney_general_says_drea.php

Enriquez, L. E. (2011). "Because we feel pressure and we also feel support": Examining the educational success of undocumented immigrant Latina/o students. *Harvard Educational Review, 81*(3): 476–499.

Gonzales, R. G. (2011). Learning to be illegal. *American Sociological Review, 76*(4), 602–619.

Interfaith Worker Justice. (2017). *Virginia and DACA: The facts.* Retrieved from iwj.org /resources/state-by-state-daca-fact-sheets/DACA_Fact_Sheets/Virginia_DACA.pdf

Pérez, Z. J. (2014). *Removing barriers to higher education for undocumented students.* Washington, DC: Center for American Progress.

Price, M., Cheung, I., Friedman, S., & Singer, A. (2005). The world settles in: Washington, DC, as an immigrant gateway. *Urban Geography, 26*(1): 61–83.

Rincón, A. (2008). *Undocumented immigrants and higher education: Sí se puede.* New York, NY: LFB Scholarly.

Suárez-Orozco, M. M., Teranishi, R., & Suárez-Orozco, C. E. (2015). *In the shadows of the ivory tower: Undocumented undergraduates and the liminal state of immigration reform.* The UndocuScholar Project, Institute for Immigration, Globalization, and Education, University of California, Los Angeles.

United States Citizenship and Immigration Services. (2016). Number of I-821D, consideration of Deferred Action for Childhood Arrivals by fiscal year, quarter, intake, biometrics and case status: 2012–2016. Retrieved from www.uscis.gov/sites/default/ files/USCIS/Resources/Reports%20and%20Studies/Immigration%20Forms%20Data/ All%20Form%20Types/DACA/daca_performancedata_fy2016_qtr4.pdf

Winders, J., & Smith, B. E. (2012). Expecting/accepting the South: New geographies of Latino migration, new directions in Latino studies. *Latino Studies, 10*(1–2): 220–245.

CHAPTER 9

DREAMers in Double Exile
Teachers Can Be Allies of LGBTQ Students

Juan A. Ríos Vega and Sonja Franeta

Being an adolescent is a very difficult time in life with many rites of passage for most teenagers, since they are constantly looking for acceptance and love. While being an English as a Second Language (ESL) high school teacher for over 15 years, working primarily with undocumented students from Mexico and Central America, I, together with my students, learned to fight invisibility, racism, and intolerance; however, there were undocumented students who struggled with another challenge as a result of their sexual orientation. Although I realized some of my former students were gays and lesbians or heard rumors about their sexuality, my classroom became the nurturing place where every student felt included and loved.

I never talked to former high school students about my sexual orientation; moreover, some of them questioned my being single at my age, which in most Latin American countries is an indication of being gay or lesbian. It was not until my doctoral studies, when I could talk to my peers about my sexuality, when I finally accepted my sexual orientation in public without feeling targeted or oppressed. I always felt that being marginalized for being a Latino immigrant with brown skin was enough and that being openly gay represented another layer of oppression from mainstream society, my students, and their parents.

My personal experiences as a self-identified queer of color in this country and my undocumented LGBTQ former ESL students have compelled me to discuss how different intersectionalities of race, gender, language, immigration status, and sexual orientation shape the educational experiences and well-being of undocumented students. There are few studies that address how undocumented LGBTQ students live in double exile from mainstream society and their families. It is important to document how this group learns to resist and to navigate double oppression and marginalization, but it is more important to provide teachers and school administrations with culturally relevant tools and resources to support undocumented LGBTQ students. Undocumented LGBTQ students need to know that the classroom and school culture represent nurturing environments where their diverse cultural backgrounds, as well as their sexual orientation, do not represent obstacles for them to experience academic achievement and social upper mobility.

—*Juan A. Ríos Vega*

Since DREAMers do not always identify themselves, the strategies we recommend in this chapter can be used by teachers of both K–12 and postsecondary students. We encourage educators to learn about LGBTQ DREAMers and their struggles, become their allies, and give them a safe place to tell their stories. The complications arising from a student being LGBTQ and also hiding or going public about just one of their dual identities make life very difficult for them. We hope teachers will be more aware of these specific problems.

The rationale for these strategies is the hidden nature of both the DREAMer identity and the LGBTQ identity. Some students feel they have to hide their undocumented status and if they are LGBTQ they may repress or hide their sexuality as well. During puberty and late adolescence this may be very a difficult and complex situation for the student. I have given students the opportunity to talk with me privately and have referred them to get help. I have also been public about my sexuality and my political alliance with minorities. I have introduced them to my own writings about being a lesbian, and found support for them for both undocumented and LGBTQ issues. This can help bolster their confidence.

Finally I have gained insights from fellow teachers and my own political activism. I have been an activist for LGBTQs in Russia and recently published a book about my own and their struggles around sexuality. I have also learned strategies from my interviews with LGBTQs over a long period of time and from my own advocacy for minority issues.

—*Sonja Franeta*

In July 2014, Pulitzer Prize–winning journalist Jose Antonio Vargas was detained at an airport for being undocumented. He was born in the Philippines but came to the United States in 1993, when he was 12. He was in high school when he learned he was undocumented (a DREAMer) and came out as gay soon after. Many people have suffered humiliating treatment at the U.S. borders, especially since Immigration and Customs Enforcement (ICE) activity has intensified under President Donald Trump's administration. Countless people are being deported or detained. Not only the undocumented but also those who thought their papers were in order are also being barraged with harassment and threats of deportation. We are living through terrible reactionary times and immigrants and refugees seem to be the biggest targets. A gay or transgender person in prison suffers untold harsh conditions, abuse, and even solitary confinement, because of his or her sexuality and gender. In the United States, being undocumented generally means hiding, keeping out of trouble, avoiding racial profiling, and much more, in other words, an extremely stressful life. This is increased when one is LGBTQ.

As teachers, it is important to become more acquainted with LGBTQ immigrant struggles and learn as much as possible about policy and the law to help these students when they need advice and counseling. For the purpose of this chapter, the terms *gay* and *queer* will be used interchangeably. As self-identified lesbian and queer of color, the authors understand how using or labeling vulnerable communities might be risky and sometimes political. According to our experiences as former ESL instructors, some LGBTQ students, especially from communities of color, do not conform to the term *gay* or *lesbian*. Instead, they prefer to self-identify as queer of color, transgender, transsexual, pansexual, Latinx, and others.

In a study by Ríos Vega (2015), interviewee Juan (a pseudonym) and his relatives crossed the U.S.–Mexican border from rural Mexico when he was 5 years of age. Although Juan spoke more English than Spanish, it was obvious that his brown skin and stereotypical Latinx/Hispanic features made him the *Other*. As an effeminate and youngest son, Juan suffered rejection from his relatives, especially his oldest brother. Since Juan was living not with his parents but some friends, it was apparent that something deeper had happened to Juan to make him leave his relatives' home. Juan was a smart, sometimes opinionated teenager. He was involved in different school clubs and organizations. He also volunteered at the public library, since he loved computers and helping others. At school, most of his friends were English speaking and white females. Besides experiencing lack of support from relatives and feeling uncomfortable around other Latinx/Hispanic teenage boys, Juan lacked the appropriate immigration status to allow him to pursue college. Juan, like many Latin/Hispanic students in the United States, was undocumented.

During the final interview, Juan shared how after taking a lot of painkillers, he ended up in the hospital emergency room. Juan was clearly having some identity challenges, being a queer of color, living in this country. After Ríos Vega (2015) completed his book, being in touch on Facebook allowed him to mentor Juan in his higher education goals. Given his immigration status, Juan could not apply for federal support. Out-of-state tuition was triple the in-state tuition fees. Juan began using his Facebook account to come out as gay. Although he was able to apply for DACA and get a part-time job to support his education and personal expenses, he still experiences uncertainty because immigration policies keep changing, as a result of President Trump's hostile agenda against immigrants of color, especially Muslims and Mexicans, as terrorists and illegal aliens, respectively. This was a reminder to Juan of his double exile as an undocumented immigrant and a queer of color.

What Teachers Should Know and Why

A DREAMer activist (who wants to remain anonymous) explained what students need more than anything from the teachers they may turn to for help: information on legal questions and resources. If a teacher cannot give legal answers, he or she should be prepared to refer the student to an organization or to sympathetic providers of legal assistance. Thus, having those references ready so the student doesn't worry or get frustrated is essential. Many local organizations focus on helping queer immigrants. One example in Los Angeles, California, is Familia: Trans Queer Liberation Movement, which has a Facebook page. In the New York area, there is the Queer Detainee Empowerment Project, also with a Facebook page.

Besides referring students, the subject of homophobia can be problematic in the classroom. While teachers can make the classroom more comfortable for queer students, students should not feel pressured to identify as gay or lesbian, because it is dangerous for them to do so. Indeed the U.S. tradition of "being openly gay" actually has a very short history (25 years). Before that (and even still) people were afraid to lose their jobs, be driven out of their neighborhoods or homes, and be physically attacked. It would be important to understand some of what a gay immigrant student experiences.

DREAMers are young people who were brought to the United States as children and have not yet received legal documentation. How strange it must be to grow up in the United States and have so few rights! If their families reject them because they are gay, they have even less protection. Some may become homeless or resort to prostitution or gangs; they may hide in abusive relationships or dangerous living conditions. Survival for these DREAMers becomes a struggle for life on a daily basis. In short, LGBTQ DREAMers are treated as outcasts and criminals in our society because they are queer and therefore marginalized to begin with. Any number of survival coping strategies work for them. They live dangerous lives because of their status. Cisneros (2015) posits:

> LGBTQ undocumented immigrants face discrimination and exploitation because of their immigration status, in addition to discrimination based on sexual orientation, gender identity and expression. Though DACA has provided initial efforts to remediate the lack of formal employment opportunities available to DREAMers, the program is temporary and remains contingent upon restrictive eligibility criteria exclusive of the lived realities of being LGBTQ and undocumented within the context of the U.S. DACA requires that applicants not be convicted of a felony, significant misdemeanor, or three or more other misdemeanors. (p. 158)

For that reason, many LGBTQ and undocumented DREAMers cannot meet the guidelines to obtain DACA. In this chapter we will discuss several aspects of LGBTQ DREAMers' lives and struggles and suggest some ways that teachers can help.

DREAMers in Double Exile

As we try to piece together a picture of the difficulties for undocumented students who are DREAMers, also in the sense that they dream for a better, more secure life, we find a number of students "in exile" not only from their country of origin but also from their own families, who have rejected them for being lesbian, gay, bisexual, transgender, or queer. Juan's example at the beginning of this chapter clearly explains how many LGBTQ undocumented students experience double exile. Venezuelan filmmaker Irene Sosa (1999) some years ago released the film *Sexual Exiles*, which documents some of the reasons LGBTQ people have felt compelled to leave their families. One woman said how she missed her country but that she knew if she went back she would "have to hide significant parts of [herself] simply to prevent being killed." Today threats of deportation still torment some of those who left because of their sexual orientation and family rejection or those who self-identified as part of the LGBTQ community while living in the United States. Others who decided to remain in this country regardless of their undocumented status have to learn to live their own double exiles.

Laura (pseudonym), a student, came from Veracruz, Mexico, with her younger sister at age 16. While in ESL class, she and the author developed a very positive and strong relationship. Like Juan, Laura used Facebook to share her sexual orientation, mentioning a brand name (Duvalin) as her love and best friend. Suddenly, she started posting pictures of her partner, another Mexican woman. Laura and her partner invited author Ríos Vega over to their apartment for lunch. Reconnecting with Laura after 10 years, he learned that because of Laura's immigration status, she could not pursue college as she dreamed of doing in his classroom. Instead, Laura had worked in fast food restaurants and furniture factories and now in construction, where she had had two serious accidents. Laura also shared her family's reaction about her sexual orientation and that her parents, especially her mother, attended a Hispanic/Latin@ Christian church. Laura and her partner rented an apartment in a different city, away from Laura's parents, who sometimes visit her. Laura's double exile shows how as an undocumented immigrant from Mexico she could not pursue higher education and also how she had to move away from parents and relatives to live with her partner. Furthermore, Laura's current nontraditional job in construction (she is a roofer) makes her even more vulnerable to being lesbian baited and suspect within her own community.

It is important to understand how these undocumented youth may develop ways to resist rejection from their own communities and from mainstream society. Cruz (2011, 2012), in her studies with LGBTQ street youth (*testimonios*), suggests that as scholars, we need to analyze how intersections of power and oppression are "particularly illuminating," since they create the spaces to unpack how power works through issues of race, class, gender, and sexuality. Undocumented LGBTQ in schools experience double or triple layers of oppression and discrimination when compared with members of other communities of color. For instance, while most Latinx/Hispanic students are constantly oppressed through issues of race/ethnicity, gender, language, immigration status, and class by the mainstream culture, they also suffer rejection and oppression for being gays, lesbians, and queers by their own families and sometimes peers. In another study, Ríos Vega (2017) focuses on his own testimonio as a transnational queer of color and he unpacks how through his trips to his homeland and the development of a dual identity, gay and queer of color, he lives with physical and emotional borders, allowing him to develop what he has called a transnational *mariposa* (butterfly) consciousness.

Besides the complexities of identity and residency status in the United States, LGBTQ people suffer much marginalization and government repression within their own countries, whether Asian, Middle Eastern, African, or Latin American. In some countries (Russia, for example), gay men have been imprisoned and lesbians institutionalized for their sexuality. In Iran, after the 1978 revolution, gay sex was punishable by death and lesbian sex by 100 lashes, then death after the fourth offense (Rosenbloom, 1998). In Thailand, there is no explicitly antigay or antilesbian law but nonheterosexuals are thought of as abnormal and the transgender "kathoey" are associated with the sex industry. To have "gay pride" is a new and distinctly U.S. concept for many newcomers. Now with recent reactionary religious legislation in the United States, LGBTQs are not so easily accepted de spite the U.S. Supreme Court's positive decision on same-sex marriage in 2015. For example, under the guise of "religious freedom," Texas House Bill 3859 of 2017 allows discrimination against same-sex parents and youth according to the religious beliefs of child welfare agency employees.

A young lesbian from one of the former Soviet republics, who fears being found out by family members, has received asylum in this country as a lesbian. She did not come to the United States with her family but arrived to escape her patriarchal Muslim family's wrath for her lesbian identity and for being an independent woman, willing to speak up for herself. She emigrated not for economic reasons but to survive. Even though she has received asylum, she remains secretive because of potential violence and vengefulness from family members. In April 2017, news of the torture and disappearance of gay people in Chechnya had spread, and relatives there are being encouraged to take matters into their own hands. Threats have grown.

LGBTQ people have had difficulties sponsoring spouses from other countries, despite the new same-sex marriage equality laws. Besides losing the love and respect of family, many LGBTQ DREAMers and immigrants risk deportation, harassment, and humiliating detention center conditions. The complications of being LGBTQ and undocumented can create both physical and psychological hardships for these students. They prefer to hide their sexual orientation, since dealing with issues of racism, classism, English proficiency, and immigration status is overwhelming enough for them without adding another layer of marginalization and oppression.

According to the University of California, Los Angeles's Williams Institute, in 2013 there were an estimated 267,000 undocumented people identifying as LGBTQ; this huge number may have changed somewhat. The fact is that many people, especially young people, are reluctant to identify as queer because they risk possible rejection by family, societal marginalization, and even physical attacks, as well as imprisonment and deportation. These are life-threatening problems.

Costs of Rejection

Stories of young people being rejected and even thrown out of their homes abound. It is very important for all teachers to become aware of some of the problems of queer students. There are resources and films on the subject. Two support organizations with websites are GLSEN (glsen.org/educate/resources/guides) and Teaching Tolerance (www.tolerance.org/topics/gender-sexual-identity). The latter has a full issue of *Teaching Tolerance* magazine devoted to LGBTQ issues, published in the summer of 2015. In the film *Documented* (Vargas & Lupo, 2013), Jose Antonio Vargas, a Philippine-born and undocumented immigrant, tells his compelling and complex story as an "illegal" gay young person in the United States, in hiding while he built his career and searched for his mother. The film *Crossing Over* (Kramer & Marshall, 2009) portrays a range of different immigrants dealing with their status in Los Angeles. Another valuable resource is *El Canto del Colibrí* (Castro-Bojorquez, 2015), about Latinx/Hispanic fathers discussing their experiences with having gay and lesbian children. In the documentary, fathers and their children share how issues of gender expectations, religion, and family values and rejection, as well as family support, shape their experiences while living in the United States.

Bullying incidents offer teaching moments that can benefit all students. Trans students, as well as gay, lesbian, and queer students suffer a disproportionate rate of bullying. This is also dangerous for them if they are from other countries, because this is often unwanted attention that may get them into trouble with authorities. In looking at suicide statistics, suicide happens to be one of the leading causes of death for 15- to 25-year-olds, and queer youth have the highest rate comparatively. Note that the rate of suicide for Hispanic females is the highest, at 13.5%, yet it is not explicitly connected with homophobia. In addition to mental illness, bullying among teens is another factor that contributes to suicide attempts (Centers for Disease Control and Prevention, 2017b).

For immigrant youth who do not have any legal status, being openly gay is a huge risk to their being able to stay in the United States. Being openly gay makes them more vulnerable to being profiled by a homophobic and xenophobic mainstream society and rejected by their own kin. Witnessing how Latinx/Hispanic boys, especially from Mexico, tested each other's masculinity in high school by calling each other homophobic slurs in Spanish such as *puto* (faggot) or calling each other gay or engaging in "gay behavior" viewed as negative, Ríos Vega challenged their conduct. He urged them to reflect on the definition and connotation of the term *gay* and to consider how using the word in such a negative manner can offend many people.

The sociopolitical rejection of transgender people has a huge effect on undocumented transgender victims of deportation. According to *The New Yorker* magazine, one transgender immigrant imprisoned in an El Paso detention center was "repeatedly misgendered in the criminal complaint detailing her February 9th arrest" (Blitzer, 2017). These transgender prisoners are denied access to hormone therapy and are refused needed health care in general. Although there are reports of 200 cases of abuse from 2008 to 2013 in ICE facilities, these are not accurate figures of sexual assault and other abuse because detainees fear retaliation and exposure should they report the attacks (Blitzer, 2017). This is simply an unsafe situation for transgender undocumented detainees; they risk getting killed by other inmates or dying from improper drug use. A good source of more information about transgender issues is the National Center for Transgender Equality (transequality.org), which provides help on transgender issues to attorneys, government agencies, and activists.

The issue of immigration is extremely complex, and the situation is compounded for foreign students caught in their own countries' homophobic cultural assumptions. The Indian student at Rutgers accused of cyberbullying his gay roommate (Tyler Clementi), who then killed himself, had prejudices about gays and acted from homophobia. In schools, bullying is a huge problem for everyone who is LGBTQ but even more so for undocumented youth ("Suicide of Tyler Clementi," 2017).

Other problems not explicitly gay related also disproportionately affect queer youth. HIV has been rising at a greater rate among Latinx/Hispanics. At the age of 22 a man who had enlisted in the army was informed that he was HIV positive. Gutierrez decided to hide his HIV status from his family, who did not even know he was gay. "It was a sad situation. I thought the best thing to do was separate myself from my family and strike out on my own . . . and wait to die" (World AIDS Day, 2017). According to the organizations that help these HIV-positive Latinxs, many do not continue with treatment because of economic and social complications. One CDC study found that only 48% of Latinxs with HIV continue treatment (Centers for Disease Control and Prevention, 2017a).

Getting and Remaining Informed

Having conversations about any of these issues in the classroom can be a life-changing experience for homophobic students who have not had the opportunity to consider the issues. These students sometimes come from extremely patriarchal countries and societies, where gender (male/female) expectations are socially constructed. It is good for teachers to stay aware of what the situations are for LGBTQ people in these places. In an article on a website documenting LGBTQ rights in the world ("LGBT Rights by Country or Territory," 2017), it is astounding to note how many red Xs appear, indicating laws against LGBTQ rights. The widespread criminalization of queers is also explained on a BBC website ("Where Is It Illegal to Be Gay?" 2017), which states that in 5 countries and in parts of 2 others, homosexuality is punishable by death and in 70 other countries by imprisonment. DREAMers and other students are sometimes aware of these facts and statistics, so the classroom can be a safe place to discuss these problems.

Besides having conversations in classes and advocating for inclusive immigration reform that would help students, educators can facilitate a more successful experience in institutions for undocumented LGBTQ youth by being aware of the situation of undocumented LGBTQs; by referring students to helpful agencies, websites, and organizations; by preventing bullying; and by challenging institutionalized discrimination of both immigrants and LGBTQ people. One good resource for information is the Arizona Queer Undocumented Immigrant Project (www.facebook.com/pg/transqueerpueblo), a grassroots group that works for the liberation of trans/queer migrant communities in Phoenix, Arizona. This organization supports family members of LGBTQ immigrants to engage in migrant/social justice, through advocacy campaigns in order to free LGBTQ immigrants from detention. Immigrant parents speak out at school and community forums throughout the city. The pressures and psychological pain of the dual stigma of being LGBTQ and undocumented is enormous. Serrano (2014) explains,

> Unfortunately, the lack of a legal immigration status has prevented me and my community from being able to access safe spaces, for therapy, be it medical or psychological. Every single person that I have come across and built a relationship with on my journey as an activist has suffered from some type of bullying due to the color of their skin, nationality, immigration status, or for being queer. Sometimes, for some of us, it can be all of the above. Imagine living in a world where every single part of your identity is constantly under attack.

The last statement has such a profound impact: "when every single part of my identity is constantly under attack." We may find this hard to imagine, but experiencing it on a daily basis is quite beyond comprehension. As educators, how can we help these students? First, we can learn about their situations, learn about what it means to a person to be gay and undocumented, learn about LGBTQ issues and life. Three books that the authors recommend that are specifically geared to the educator are Lipkin (1999), Sears and Williams (1997), and Nelson (2009).

Although more and more scholars are trying to unveil LGBTQ issues in education, there is still an urgency to include how different intersectionalities shape LGBTQ students, especially undocumented ones. We realize that the American Educational Research Association (AERA) recently published an edited book titled *LGBTQ Issues in Education* (Wimberly, 2015); however, there is not a single chapter that talks in depth about the experiences of LGBTQ and undocumented students. Instead, the editor encourages scholars to document how multiple intersections of class, race, and other elements affect LGBTQ students' experiences, addressing only African American students. Again, there is a certain level of invisibility in academia about LGBTQ and undocumented students, usually representing the Latinx group.

Final Thoughts

Western influences have affected the way cultures treat gender. How does a Samoan transgender person (*fafafine*), who is recognized and accepted in his or her own country's culture, adjust to the marginalization he or she experiences in the United States? These are people who were born male but want to live their lives as female, and this is acceptable in several cultures (Herdt, 1993). When they are in American and European cultures they are forced to identify as one of the binary sexes. Educators are not educated about students' multiple issues and identities. A gay or lesbian student may have several identities to reconcile along with his or her language hurdles. Integrating sexual orientation and gender practices more decisively into teacher education programs would add this important cultural dimension to all programs. While this proposition will not be resolved over the short term, we cannot allow the prevailing right-wing, anti-LGBTQ, anti-immigrant sentiments to impede our progress.

Gendered practices in various countries can be quite complex and diverse. When one of the authors taught English to college students in Russia in 1993, two female students who were close friends often walked into class holding hands. They were not lesbian. The author noticed this kind of affection among Russian men as well. One friend in Moscow said that she didn't think these practices would continue because of "Western influences" and homophobia from the West. Same-sex affection and even sexual intimacy is common in many societies. The United States seems to be the least tolerant; any display of physical affection gets pigeonholed directly into homosexuality (Herdt, 1993). In Hong Kong, a movement of women (1865–1935) resisting marriage (*sou hei*) declared that sexual relations with a man were the worst transgression for a woman of their group (Blackwood, 1986). Because of the marginal status of LGBTQ people in society, ordinary U.S. citizens are often unfamiliar with LGBTQ lifestyles.

Despite the general openness regarding gender and sexuality concepts talked about publicly today, there are still people who have survived as gay, lesbian, bisexual, or transgender in some of the most repressive situations. Many have opted for traditional heterosexual marriages but had same-sex relationships outside marriage (Franeta, 2015). Describing a situation similar to what occurs in most Latin American countries, a Russian interviewee told one of the authors that an unmarried or childless women in Russia is seen as suspect, possibly lesbian. No one says anything explicitly, she said, but it is assumed that "there is something 'wrong.'" Nevertheless, every human being has the right to live with dignity.

The experiences and histories of people who have struggled with issues of gender and sexuality can be found in articles, in books, on websites, and in interviews with students themselves. The more teachers are encouraged to learn about practices in other countries and societies, the more they will be able to understand students' social behavior and use such information when the moment arises. Teachers need to develop a sense of trust and make their classroom nurturing spaces where diverse students can feel free to engage in critical dialogues about how issues of race/ethnicity, language, immigration, gender, class, and sexuality shape their everyday lives and well-being.

Imagine this: A person has made a great effort to leave home, move to a new place, and start a new life in San Francisco or New York and deal with all the other problems of being an immigrant. Day after day in the ESL classroom, he or she never hears the word *gay* or *lesbian*, except perhaps in a negative or joking context. The English textbook that is used portrays traditional families and heterosexual couples in conversations and grammar exercises. If there is a gay or lesbian family in a textbook, it is marginally represented, never modeled in a primary way. In the classroom, students may continue to hide their identity, a condition from which they hoped to escape, from which they hoped to be free, in the United States. ESL instructor and colleague Kappra (1999) makes some useful suggestions:

> First of all we must realize that though they are not visible, we do indeed have students who are lesbian or gay in our classrooms. We should be careful of activities which ask students to talk about romantic relationships, thus forcing them to come out against their will or lie about their sexual orientation. If the topic of homosexuality does come up, either as a planned discussion or accidentally, we need to ensure that negative comments about gays and lesbians are kept to an absolute minimum. We should never ask students what they think about gays, just as we would never ask them what they think about African Americans, Asians or any other minority group. (p. 19)

It matters what materials and textbooks teachers select for the classroom. We can promote respect for differences and for basic human rights in the classroom and advocate for social justice in education simultaneously. The instructor sets the tone in class by asking students to work with one another and by helping all students feel safe from negative comments. Inclusion of gay/lesbian/bisexual/transgender incidents, characters, and stories in discussions, in dialogues, even in grammar sentences are all very natural ways to make the student relax with his or her concept of family or lifestyle. It is up to teachers and school administrators to become more educated on the subject of sex and gender for the sake of the students. Educators of DREAMers can use a document on the website of Educators for Fair Consideration, a PDF file called *Top Ten Ways to Support Undocumented Students* (2017). It contains guidelines that are clearly stated, basic, and useful for addressing any undocumented student's concerns.

DREAMers have become inspiring activists as a result of their challenges. Advocating for these young people can save lives and create beautiful futures for all of us. Negotiating one's identity can take a toll. As authentic allies, teachers can help lift the burdens from these students by joining with them to fight for their human rights and the peace of mind of being considered legal. After all, as the great poet Maya Angelou (2015) wrote in her poem "Human Family," "We are more alike, my friends, than we are unalike" (p. 218).

References

Angelou, M. (2015). *Maya Angelou: The complete poetry.* New York, NY: Random House.

Blackwood, E. (1986). *The many faces of homosexuality.* New York, NY: Harrington Park Press.

Blitzer, J. (2017, February 23). The woman arrested by ICE in a courthouse speaks out. *The New Yorker.* Retrieved from www.newyorker.com/news/news-desk/the-woman -arrested-by-ice-in-a-courthouse-speaks-out

Castro-Bojorquez, M. (2015). *El canto del Colibrí* [Documentary]. Somos Familia & BAY-CAT (Baynew Hunters Point Center for Arts and Technology).

Centers for Disease Control and Prevention. (2017a). *HIV among Hispanics/Latinos.* Retrieved from cdc.gov/hiv/group/racialethnic/hispaniclatinos/index.html

Centers for Disease Control and Prevention. (2017b). *Lesbian, gay, bisexual, and transgender health.* Retrieved from www.cdc.gov/lgbthealth/youth.htm

Cisneros, J. (2015). *Undocuqueer: Interacting and working within intersection of LGBTQ and undocumented* (Doctoral dissertation). Arizona State University, Tempe, Arizona.

Cruz, C. (2011). LGBTQ street youth talk back: A meditation on resistance and witnessing. *International Journal of Qualitative Studies in Education, 24*(5), 547–558.

Cruz, C. (2012). Making curriculum from scratch: *Testimonio* in an urban classroom. *Equity and Excellence in Education, 45*(3), 460–471.

Franeta, S. (2015). *My pink road to Russia: Tales of amazons, peasants, and queers.* Oakland, CA: Dacha Books.

Herdt, G. (1993). *Third sex, third gender: Beyond sexual dimorphism in culture and history.* New York, NY: Zone Books.

Kappra, R. (1998–1999). Addressing heterosexism in the IEP classroom. *TESOL Matters, 8*(6), 19.

Kramer, W., & Marshall, F. (2009). *Crossing over* [Film]. United States: The Weinstein Company.

LGBT rights by country or territory. (2017). In *Wikipedia.* Retrieved from en.wikipedia.org /wiki/LGBT_rights_by_country_or_territory

Lipkin, A. (1999). *Understanding homosexuality, changing schools.* Boulder, CO: Westview Press.

Nelson, C. D. (2009). *Sexual identities in English language education: Classroom conversations.* New York, NY: Routledge.

Ríos Vega, J. A. (2015). *Counterstorytelling narratives of Latino teenage boys: From verguenza to echale ganas.* New York, NY: Peter Lang.

Ríos Vega, J. A. (2017). An unhealed wound: Growing up gay in Panama. *The Bilingual Review/La Revista Bilingue, 38*(4), 76–79.

Rosenbloom, R. (1998). *Unspoken rules: Sexual orientation and women's human rights.* New York, NY: Continuum International.

Sears, J. T., & Williams, W. L. (1997). *Overcoming heterosexism and homophobia: Strategies that work.* New York, NY: Columbia University Press.

Serrano, M. (2014, December 8). Op-ed: Undocumented queer and bullied. *The Advocate.* Retrieved from www.advocate.com/commentary/2014/12/08/op-ed-undocumented -queer-and-bullied

Sosa, I. (1999). *Sexual exiles* [Documentary]. Retrieved from www.irenesosa.com/Sexual _Exiles_2.html

Suicide of Tyler Clementi. (2017). In *Wikipedia.* Retrieved from en.wikipedia.org/wiki/Suicide _of_Tyler_Clementi

Top ten ways to support undocumented students. (2017). Retrieved from www.e4fc.org.

Vargas, J. A., & Lupo, A. R. (2013). *Documented* [Documentary]. United States: CNN Films.

Where is it illegal to be gay? (2017). Retrieved from www.bbc.com/news/world-25927595

Wimberly, G. L. (2015). *LGBTQ issues in education: Advancing a research agenda*. Washington, DC: American Educational Research Association.

World AIDS Day: Working to keep Latinos informed, healthy. (2017). Retrieved from www.nbcnews.com/news/latino/world-aids-day-working-keep-latinos-informed-healthy-n258801

Using Critical Narratives for Relationship Building Between a Chicana Feminist Educator and Her Students

Aurora Chang with Nancy Gutierrez

In this chapter, I recommend two main strategies for engaging DREAMers (and all students) in classroom learning. The first strategy is general but critically important—creating a "safe" classroom environment, defined as a place of risk where educators provide meaningful settings in which students are encouraged to experiment with their understanding of self and others through honest, fierce, and courageous dialogue and interactions. The second strategy is for students to write their own educational *testimonios*, that is, develop an autobiographical account of their educational histories. The rationale behind the use of these strategies lies in the belief that all students are experts in their own experiential knowledge and that authentic learning should occur in the context of risk taking and storytelling. I implemented these strategies by using culturally responsive pedagogical practices, drawing on my insights as an educator with 25 years of experience.

As an educator, I tend to pride myself on the following tenet—I will not ask my students to do anything that I wouldn't willingly do myself. I often repeat this phrase to show that I am truly committed to this principle and to my determination to walk a culturally responsive path (Gay, 2002). My rationale is that I enable students to disclose their *counterstories* and testimonios (Solórzano & Yosso, 2002) through sharing my own. I want to believe that this is true. If I ask students to share their educational autobiographies, I also develop one. If I ask students to divulge personal experiences about the impact of race and gender in their lives, I have no problem doing the same. For the most part, I want them to do as I do, not just as I say.

Once in a while, though, one comes across information that shakes one to the very core. The information is apparently commonplace, a regular interaction between teacher and student. What I learned about a student following a classroom assignment left me speechless. Let me explain. I required my Education, Identity

and Agency: Latin@ Issues in U.S. Educational Institutions class to read an article I had written. In it, I came out as a once undocumented immigrant, writing
about my *jornada* (journey) of protection, papers, and PhD status (Chang, 2011).
After class, Nancy, a bright, cheerful, and well-grounded student, approached me
respectfully and said, "*Doctora*, it's easy for you to write about this because you
have your papers now. I don't. What am I supposed to write about? Being undocumented is the major thing that impacts my educational story but I am afraid to
talk about it." Suddenly, my own story, my assignment, turned on me. Nancy was
right. How could I ask her to publicly share her immigration status, to implicate
herself, knowing that it could affect her in such a consequential way? After all,
there was no guarantee that, even though I felt that I had created a safe classroom
environment, her story would not leak and end up in the wrong hands, in the
hands of someone with malicious intentions. On the other hand, how could I stop
her from sharing this story if she chose to do so? Her situation became a teaching
nightmare for me.

As a Chicana feminist educator, I place great value on speaking the truth
about our experiences, but, as I was about to find out, such a philosophy is easier
to expound than to carry out. What are the pedagogical *riesgos* (risks) involved
in implementing teaching practices, such as testimonios or counternarratives,
that align with Chicana feminism? How do testimonios affect student and
teacher learning? How is it possible to create safe classroom environments without making personal and instructional trade-offs? To answer these questions
and to chronicle the interactions between Nancy and myself, I use Anzaldúa's
"La Conciencia de la Mestiza" framework. Our interactions included her struggle to decide whether to disclose her undocumented status to the class through
her academic work and my struggle to reconcile my responsibility for keeping
students safe while not censoring her ability to influence outcomes through her
critical analyses.

I maintain that there are real *riesgos* (risks) involved in trying to develop a
seemingly safe classroom culture when a teacher asks her students to explore
their personal and educational experiences. And when both student and *maestra*
(teacher) are people of color, an intensely delicate balance must be maintained between surviving academically and socially, and protecting oneself from the pain of
distressing situations, especially in a predominantly White, often unfamiliar and
hostile educational environment.

Testimonios are a powerful way to successfully unravel and document these
personal narratives. As Delgado Bernal, Burciaga, and Flores Carmona (2012)
state:

> Within the field of education, scholars are increasingly taking up testimonio as a
> pedagogical, methodological, and activist approach to social justice that transgresses
> traditional paradigms in academia. Unlike the more common training of research-
> ers to produce unbiased knowledge, testimonio challenges objectivity by situating the
> individual in communion with a collective experience marked by marginalization,

oppression, or resistance. These approaches have resulted in new understandings about how marginalized communities build solidarity and respond to and resist dominant culture, laws, and policies that perpetuate inequity. (p. 363)

In asking our young Chicanas/Latinas (and other students, specifically those of color) to develop their own testimonios, teachers as learners must be ready to make trade-offs in a struggle between their identity as *maestras* (teachers) and their identity as *estudiantes* (learners) in a *lucha de fronteras* (Anzaldúa, 1987), a struggle between two real identities that influence who we are.

Testimonios focus on individual experiences with oppressive conditions and on the actions of those suffering under these conditions. As such, testimonio is an instructional tool that enables critical discussions of sensitive, hot button issues. Whether in a formal classroom or in informal environments, such as the home, testimonios provide a way to examine and learn from personal experiences of oppression and resistance. (Delgado Bernal et al., 2012, p. 367)

In other words, if no risks are taken, there will be no reward. It is simply not enough to try to get our students to understand subject matter content. To effect change, educators must be change agents (Fullan, 1993), and that requires the kind of sacrifice that asks us to deeply question the underpinnings of our teaching practices. It will not be easy to examine our values and beliefs, and it will undoubtedly be a struggle, but it holds potential for nurturing who we truly are as we embrace the diversity of our cultural identities (Anzaldúa, 1987, p. 273). In other words, both maestra and estudiante must critically examine social and educational practices to expose the hidden assumptions and contradictions. Learning takes place by analyzing and reframing our evolving narratives.

I kept in touch with Nancy on a regular basis about her work in my education class. We discussed the content of her writing and the impact it was having on her and debated her decision to write about her undocumented status, a highly sensitive topic. At the center of this discussion was the complexity and power of Nancy's personal testimonio. A passage from Gutiérrez y Muhs, Flores Niemann, González, and Harris (2012) is relevant here:

As feminist scholars and those in critical race theory tradition have established, personal stories may bridge the epistemological gap that frequently appears between the lives of people with a particular privilege and those who lack that privilege (Delgado, 1989; Montoya, 1994). (p. 3)

As a faculty member in academia's ivory tower, I struggled with the gulf between my relatively privileged life and Nancy's lack of privilege as an undocumented undergraduate student of color. I knew that I was at a crossroads—how could I respectfully and purposefully weave our stories together and still relay the full story and protect Nancy's identity?

I start by focusing on the overlapping identities of a Chicana feminist educator and her undocumented Chicana activist student. I describe the simultaneously conflicting and intersecting identities of university life, immigrant status, young-and older-female feelings and opinions, and critical pedagogy. I discuss various avenues that I could have taken to address this dilemma and explain the process I used to seize the many possibilities that were opened to me once I decided to act (Anzaldúa, 1987, p. 271). In an academic climate that privileges Western thought and reasoning, I discuss my efforts to move away from the typical way of doing things by adopting a holistic, more inclusive approach (p. 272). Finally, I explore the ways in which my student and I developed a new awareness of ourselves by experiencing the power of our testimonios.

Relational Ethics—*Confianza y Prudencia*

Soliciting personal information from students and then writing about them in an ethnographic report has to do with relational ethics (Ellis, 2007) and is fraught with great responsibility and fear. A delicate balance must always be maintained between the acquisition and dissemination of information so that the testimonio remains true to the student's stories. For this reason, I asked Nancy to consider publishing her own narrative ("God's Soldier") so that her experiences could be appreciated. This understanding was part of our constant and time-intensive relationship. The word *trustworthiness* is often heard in discussions about establishing rapport with participants in the research process. What Nancy and I established was *confianza*, something that goes beyond trustworthiness. Not only does confianza foster trust but it also involves an ethic of mutually reciprocal caring (Valenzuela, 1999) that is a subtle, often unstated mixture of familiarity and trust. *Prudencia* involves being prudent and cautious in student–researcher interactions while the student's experiences are honored and respected. These two concepts were the centerpiece of our relationship and composed the ground rules that allowed us to tell our stories.

While the essence and meaning of the research story is more important than the precise recounting of detail (Bochner & Ellis, 2002), I continually attempted to stay mindful of how our interactions could influence the integrity of our narratives, as well as how my work was interpreted and understood. After all, after the chapter was written, Nancy and I had to be able to continue to live in the world of the relationship we had formed. The complex linkage of our relationship lays the foundation for my standpoint as a Chicana feminist educator. In the following section, I describe what it means to be culturally responsive through a Chicana feminist lens.

Cultural Responsiveness Through a Chicana Feminist Lens

What does it mean to engage in Chicana feminist pedagogical practices? For me, it means that I cannot separate the political self from the personal and academic self. What I learned as a Chicana feminist is that there is worth and potential in all women (Del Castillo, 1997); that Chicana feminism is a concept that refuses assimilation into the U.S. mainstream (Moraga, 1983); that we are hoarders of what is ours—"We hoard what our mothers, our *tías*, our *abuelitas* (aunts and grandmothers) hoarded: our values, our culture" (Mora, 1997, p. 292); that we strive to understand the political, social, and economic state of our people and actively develop personal awareness of the needs of women (Segura & Pesquera, 1996). Translating these beliefs into pedagogical practices means making them a part of the everyday interactions and different types of knowledge present in the classroom and beyond. By infusing these understandings into my curricular content and pedagogical approach, I hope to model culturally responsive practices.

Culturally responsive teaching "is based on the assumption that when academic knowledge and skills are situated within the lived experiences and frames of reference of our students, they are more personally meaningful, have higher interest appeal, and are learned more easily and thoroughly" (Gay, 2002, p. 106). When students' experiences are made an integral part of instruction, schooling becomes worthwhile, as it connects to their daily lives. A lack of interest in schooling is no longer an issue. This premise has been at the center of my work as a teacher and a scholar. In this process, I used "cultural scaffolding"—that is, I used "[the students'] own cultures and experiences to expand their intellectual horizons and academic achievement" (Gay, 2002, p. 109). I have used my own cultures and experiences to that end as well, so that when I use scaffolding I need to be careful to maintain a balancing act between my role as a teacher and as a learner. By sharing her own deeply ingrained stories of struggle, a teacher both models her expectations for her students and exercises caution and courage. She relies on her often distrusted instincts to invite students into her nonacademic, personal world, into her humanity. While there are very real risks in sharing, there are also great potential rewards.

Anytime we share part of personal lives with students, we become on permanent display. Once we tell our stories they cannot be taken back, and you can be certain that it will be repeated, possibly over and over again in situations where you have no control (assuming we believe we have control over our own classrooms). If a climate of authentic caring (Valenzuela, 1999) and trust has not been established within the classroom, it is almost guaranteed that the *cuentos* (stories) you reveal will be misunderstood and even exploited. This will happen because the appropriate conditions for communicating subtle shades of meaning are missing, potentially resulting in unintended consequences. In asking our students to create and share their own testimonios, we must strike a balance between our identities as teacher and student so that our work will be truly transformational. There are also relative levels of risk in sharing personal information that can never be taken back, in exposing one's feelings of vulnerability and intellectual weaknesses, and in being perceived by students and colleagues as crossing the proverbial line between the role of student and that of teacher.

Riesgos of Testimonios

As maestras, we must also understand our own privilege of age, occupation, and experience relative to that of our students. While our testimonios can be powerful and we want to encourage students to own their testimonios, I worry about the greater risk that our students will take in preparing a testimonio. They must deal with the borderlands, the area where their immigrant, undocumented, and Latina/o identities intersect to create dangerous personal and academic environments. I suppose we share that space, yet oftentimes there are significantly varying levels of stability in our lives. So, while there may be riesgo and reward involved for both maestra and estudiante, who has more to gain or lose and to what end?

It could be argued that an untenured professor, who should be treading lightly as she is initiated into academia, could set herself up for career failure by exposing her personal life and making it available for public criticism. An undocumented student, however, faces potential deportation should his or her information about his or her legal status reach a whistleblower. In an environment that is not risk free, teachers are in a position to guide these testimonios in different directions. A student's status exposes that student to risk in an environment meant to inspire and incite critical thinking, yet critical thinking does not carry the same weighty consequences for all involved. As a maestra, it is indeed my responsibility to ensure the safety of all of my estudiantes.

"Safe" Classroom Environments

How do we create safe classroom environments without making personal and pedagogical trade-offs? Is it truly possible to do so? As Leonardo and Porter (2010) note, a "safe classroom space is arguably more mythological than real because we must ask, safety for whom" (p 139). For the most part, when we talk about creating safe spaces, it is in reference to White students, rather than students of color. Leonardo and Porter (2010) emphasize that "a subtle but fundamental violence is enacted in safe discourses on race, which must be challenged through a pedagogy of disruption, itself a form of violence but a humanizing, rather than repressive, version" (p. 139). They posit that rather than encouraging White discomfort, it is more effective to redefine a classroom as "a place of risk" where "educators encourage students to experiment with their self-understanding, and to promote the audacious notion that they may change their minds by the end of the term" (p. 153). In many ways, I encouraged a place of risk with my own students and specifically with Nancy, given her particularly precarious context as an undocumented student.

By asking students to develop an autobiographical account of their educational histories, I provided an opportunity for them to highlight their different social identities, because social identities are central to the way we perceive, receive, and understand schooling. Furthermore, it "open[ed] up deeper engagements on race, both in the intellectual and practical sense as lived reality" (Leonardo & Porter,

2010, p.153). This assignment built on "the deep competencies that students of color have to offer" by drawing from their funds of knowledge (Moll, Amanti, Neff, & Gonzalez, 1992, p. 153). By choosing to reveal herself as an undocumented college student, Nancy engaged in a rigorous personal and academic exercise.

Disclosing Nancy's Undocumented Status: Pedagogical Riesgos

After reflecting on this pedagogical learning moment, I remain cautious about the way I approach the students in my classroom. This particular case had a positive outcome—Nancy's decision to share her narrative about her undocumented status was self-empowering and well received by the campus community (and coincidentally occurred within the context of the passage of the Deferred Action for Childhood Arrivals Act of 2012). However, trying to balance the critical need for student disclosure with the students' safety is still an extremely tenuous undertaking. Indeed, it is this tolerance for ambiguity that Anzaldúa (1987) insists upon that I must embrace. It does not mean that I will always make safe decisions, but it ensures that I am modeling the risk that I expect my students to take. The idea of risk in classroom practice becomes one of liability and necessity, both personally and pedagogically.

For female faculty of color who are already marginalized within academia's ivory tower, the idea of taking on additional risks seems unappealing at best and career damaging at worst. As Gutiérrez y Muhs et al. (2012) so astutely state in their groundbreaking book, *Presumed Incompetent: The Intersections of Race and Class for Women in Academia*, "Women of color must perform their social identities carefully and selectively to avoid being criticized, marginalized, dismissed or rejected by colleagues and students" (p. 8). Oftentimes, taking risks in classrooms is tantamount to professional suicide. Gutiérrez y Muhs et al. (2012) explain it this way: "When an academic woman of color's behavior thwarts expectations, the result may be what Peggy Davis calls micro-aggressions (Davis, 1989); subtle or blatant attempts at punishing the unexpected behavior" (p. 3). And yet there is constant internal strife that places professional "risk" and "safety" at odds with one another. Taking risks means defying White-stream expectations and being safe means paddling silently and unnoticed in turbulent academic waves. Because simply being a woman of color in academia is a risk in and of itself regardless of how one performs that role, choosing the path of safety becomes less and less a viable choice. This is not to say that some behaviors are not accompanied by negative consequences; nonetheless, it seems as though female faculty of color are damned if they do and damned if they don't. Thus, in our pursuit of academic success, the only "protection" we have against institutional privilege and subordination is our unapologetic embracing of our genuine testimonios.

There are real pedagogical riesgos involved in the ambiguity of developing a seemingly safe classroom culture, where a teacher (in this case, myself) explores and asks students to remain open about their personal educational experiences. I believe that without this risk, we close off spaces of transformation and becoming.

Indeed, "testimonio in academia disrupts silence, invites connection and entices collectivity—it is social justice scholarship in education" (Delgado Bernal et al., 2012, p. 370). Educators enter this work with the knowledge that to be effective and, perhaps most important, to fill that need in our soul we must inevitably deconstruct our teaching practices and our beliefs, and use our vulnerability to make the point that teaching, indeed, learning is a painful endeavor. True intellectual growth does not occur without the discomfort of relearning about ourselves. These discussions lead to powerful insights that allow healing and renewal to take place as together, teacher and student, we expose hidden internal assumptions and contradictions. "Our academic training insists that we work in solitude, yet the work of testimonio calls us back to reclaim solidarity with one another" (Delgado Bernal et al., 2012, pp. 370–371).

Working with and coauthoring this piece with Nancy nurtured my soul in ways that mutually encouraged and enriched our relationship with one another as intergenerational Chicana feminist scholars. And, perhaps more important, it cemented our dedication to promote social justice work. Ultimately, isn't this what risk taking in academia is all about?

God's Soldier

By Nancy N. Gutierrez

I was only 1 year old when my mother, a novice with barely 18 years of life experiences under her belt, guided my 7-month-old-sister and me through the inhospitable Sonoran Desert. She carried my baby sister in her arms as we walked through the desert with limited provisions and under extremely poor sanitary conditions. She risked her life, like any mother would, to ensure a better life for her children. My father enthusiastically awaited our arrival at the other side of the border. To them, "The Land of Opportunity" offered a chance at prosperity and success, an opportunity to live The American Dream, but they could never fathom the psychological disadvantages that my undocumented status would inflict on me.

I was not born in this country, but it is the only home I know. I learned the *Pledge of Allegiance*, and abided by American ideals. In high school I was enrolled in the Junior Reserve Officers' Training Corps (JROTC), a program designed to motivate young people to become better citizens. My high school's JROTC is among the top three largest and best in the nation and, ironically, I was commissioned to Cadet Colonel—the highest rank offered to only one student. My duty consisted of leading an entire regiment of over 500 students. While most were aware of my position, no one was aware of the ache I felt inside as we recited the cadet creed at the beginning of every class. No one knew how much I struggled with the line, "I will seek the mantle of leadership and stand prepared to uphold the Constitution and the American way of life," because deep in my heart I knew that I would not be given the chance to do so. I am not a legal citizen of this country and, in spite of my patriotism, being an upstanding citizen, and holding remarkable leadership abilities, I am still invisible to the rest of the world.

Not having an "official document" is both agonizing and unfair. I am deprived of numerous opportunities that citizens are privileged to enjoy. Such privileges, which many take for granted, include the opportunity to travel abroad and enjoy vacations. Meanwhile, my family and I could not attend my grandmother's burial in Mexico. If we left the country, we knew we would not be able to come back. Sadly, many doors remain locked to me, a reality that is unknown to others.

I had to work twice as hard as the ordinary individual if I wanted to attend a university. I studied rigorously and achieved academic success only to discover, as I reached the end of my high school career, that the doors of opportunity were inaccessible to me. My status prohibited me from enjoying an array of luxuries because I did not have a social security number. I never realized how nine small numbers could have such a huge impact. I could not apply to my "dream schools." I was restricted in every way, shape, and form. My status forbade me from receiving state aid and federal aid and, in many cases, decreased the number of scholarships available to me. Even though my aspirations were similar to those of other American children and I had excelled in school, I lived in the shadows of society simply because they had something for which I longed—proper documentation and legal status. It was intensely frustrating and overwhelming to acknowledge that my future was uncertain. I consistently questioned whether academic or other pursuits were even worthwhile.

A trip with the Schuler Scholar Program to visit colleges on the West Coast is an occasion that I will never forget. An airport security agent asked for my identification and, of course, I did not have one. My heart began to pound rapidly. I thought the worst. She looked at me suspiciously as I explained, "I'm with a school group. My counselor told me my school I.D. was fine." She looked at me again and let me board the plane. I was embarrassed, afraid, and angry. That day I experienced a variety of emotions but most of all, humiliation. This experience was yet another reminder of the unfairness of life. Luckily, I was allowed to board. If she had not let me pass, I am unsure of where I would be.

I am no different than immigrants of the past who came to this country in search of a better life, but instead we are dehumanized by society with the demeaning label of "alien." I was raised in this country and all that I do revolves around it. I do not understand why so many define students like me as criminals. It was not my decision to come to this country. I did not scream, "Mom, carry me through the hot desert so that others can destroy my dreams!" I cannot imagine that anyone tells his or her parents that. Instead, I envision how different my life would have been if I were born here. I do not blame my parents for bringing me into this country. It is not their fault that society cannot clearly define who constitutes an American. What is more American than an immigrant? As a land founded by immigrants, almost every American has an ancestor that was once an immigrant. Because of this, no individual deserves to be labeled a criminal when the only "crime" they committed was to search for a brighter future.

I wish to give back to the country that nurtures my dreams of becoming an immigration attorney and the professional my parents desire me to be. I yearn for my adopted country to open its doors to me and allow me to keep on dreaming. I live like an American, think like an American, and I want to *be considered* an American, yet America is destroying my dreams. Can I still call it home? I am unsure of where I belong. It troubles me to recognize that I am stuck in between two cultures. All my life I have been exposed to American ideals while constantly being reminded of my native culture. Choosing one is inconceivable because both have shaped me and have molded me into the individual that I have become. On the other hand, neither of these countries knows that I exist. Choosing between them is pointless and leaves me exactly where I am. Nowhere.

Life has not been a piece of cake, yet I have been blessed in many ways. The Schuler Scholar Program has been one of the biggest blessings, to date. From the moment they accepted me into the scholar program and awarded me a $20,000 scholarship, they were there to support me to the end through my struggles during the college admissions process. They never questioned my abilities or potential. It is because of them and my strong sense of conviction that I am now obtaining a degree in higher education at a private, liberal arts college. Unlike many colleges, Beloit College saw beyond my status. They valued me as an individual, valued my hard work and achievements; they valued my story. As a result, my family has witnessed my metamorphosis—from undocumented to unafraid to a successful Latina in college.

I am now a beneficiary of President Obama's Deferred Action and hold an employment authorization card, state I.D., and drivers' license. I can work, drive, travel, and be in this country legally, although I still lack a legal status. This new policy has provided me with endless opportunities and privileges that I never had before. I can drive my parents around and not be afraid to be stopped. It has definitely given me a sense of relief and safety, yet it has not given me the whole of my desires. I am still waiting for the day that will change my life—obtaining citizenship. Until that day comes, my current status will continue to empower me to make the best of life's conditions.

I am proud to be undocumented and I appreciate the struggles God placed on me. They have allowed me to become the determined and ambitious young woman that I am today—a young woman whose life goals have motivated her to always strive for excellence. From becoming the first one in my entire family to attend college, to being an active member in the community, I continue to push myself further so that I can always grow as a person. My journey has not and will not be tranquil, so long as I am challenged by the implications of my immigration status. Nonetheless, I will not create excuses. If I long for my dreams to come true, then I must make them come true. Not being a citizen of this country has only made me stronger. I may lack a piece of paper, but I make up for it in an abundance of faith and unyielding will. I am a believer that God gives his most difficult battles to his toughest soldiers and I happen to be a chosen one. That is something that, by no means, will alter. The sacrifices that my parents made will not be in vain. I know that one day God will bless us with El Sueño Americano—the American Dream.

References

Anzaldúa, G. (1987). *Borderlands: La frontera—the new mestiza*. San Francisco, CA: Aunt Lute Books.

Bochner, A., & Ellis, C. (2002). *Ethnographically speaking*. Lanham, MD: Altamira Press.

Chang, A. (2011). Undocumented to hyperdocumented: A "jornada" of protection, papers, and PhD status. *Harvard Educational Review, 8*(3), 508–521.

Davis, P. (1989). Law as microaggression. *Yale Law Journal, 98*, 1559–1577.

Del Castillo, A. 1997 [1974]. Malintzín Tenepal: A preliminary look into a new perspective. In Alma García (Ed.), *Chicana feminist thought: The basic historical writings* (pp. 122–126). New York, NY: Routledge.

Delgado, R. (1989). *Critical race theory* (2nd ed.). Philadelphia, PA: Temple University Press.

Delgado Bernal, D., Burciaga, R., & Flores Carmona, J. (2012). Chicana/Latina testimonios: Methodologies, pedagogies, and political urgency. *Equity and Excellence in Education, 45*(3) 363–372.

Ellis, C. (2007). Telling secrets, revealing lives: Relations ethics in research with intimate others. *Qualitative Inquiry, 13*(1), 3–29.

Fullan, M. (1993). *Change forces: Probing the depths of educational reform*. London, England: Falmer Press.

Gay, G. (2002). Preparing for culturally responsive teaching. *Journal of Teacher Education, 53*(2), 106–116.

Gutiérrez y Muhs, G., Flores Niemann, Y., González, C. G., & Harris, A. (Eds.). (2012). *Presumed incompetent: The intersections of race and class for women in academia*. Boulder, CO: University Press of Colorado.

Leonardo, Z., & Porter, R. K. (2010). Pedagogy of fear: Toward a Fanonian theory of "safety" in race dialogue. *Race, Ethnicity, and Education, 13*(2), 139–157.

Moll, L. C., Amanti, C., Neff, D., & González, N. (1992). Funds of knowledge: Using a qualitative approach to connect homes and classrooms. *Theory into Practice, XXXI*(2), 132–141.

Moll, L., Amanti, C., Neff, D., & Gonzalez, N. (2005). *Funds of knowledge: Theorizing practices in households, communities, and classrooms*. Mahwah: NJ: Lawrence Erlbaum Associates.

Montoya, M. (1994). Mascaras, trenzas, y grenas: Un/masking the self while un/braiding Latina stories and legal discourse. *Chicano-Latino Law Review, 15*, 1–37.

Mora, P. (1997). Nepantla: Essays from the land in the middle. In A. M. García (Ed.), *Chicana feminist thought: The basic historical writings* (pp. 292–294). New York, NY: Routledge.

Moraga, C. (1983). *Loving in the war years.* Cambridge, MA: South End Press.

Segura, D. A., & Pesquera, B. M. (1996). With quill and torch: A Chicana perspective on the American women's movement and feminist theories. In David Maciel and Isidro D Ortiz (Eds.), *Chicanas/Chicanos at the crossroads: Social, economic and political* (pp. 231–251). Phoenix, AZ: University of Arizona Press.

Solórzano, D. G., & Yosso, T. J. (2002). Critical race methodology: Counter-storytelling as an analytic framework for education research. *Journal of Qualitative Inquiry, 8*(1), 23–44.

Valenzuela, A. (1999). *Subtractive schooling: U.S. Mexican youth and the politics of caring.* New York, NY: State University of New York Press.

Part IV

FINDING, SHARING, AND TRANSFORMING IDENTITY THROUGH ART

DREAMers PERFORM

Carollyn James

CHAPTER 11

Using Music for Deconstructing Immigrant Discourses

A Critical Analytic Approach

Gertrude Tinker Sachs and Theresa Austin

In Hard Times for Critical Multiculturalism and Immigration

Our chapter addresses teachers' needs to educate both mainstream students and immigrant youth about their responsibilities and rights in a democratic society. True accountability for learning in the current political context includes teaching and learning about social and academic development. Teachers can support learners by drawing on the backgrounds of both (teachers and learners) in order for them to critically act together to contribute to their new communities by thinking through complex issues that are represented in diverse media forms. We strive to develop dispositions toward those who differ from them to show how a learning community can be built together. Teachers who believe in the importance of teaching all children recognize how neglecting any population will have significant consequences on the communities at large in terms of socioeconomics, justice, and politics. Most important, this includes preparing both dominant and immigrant youth to be critical of widely circulating anti-immigrant sentiment. Through an understanding of these messages, we believe that they may be able to develop adaptive and supportive behaviors to form alliances with immigrant communities in working toward social justice. We have a moral imperative to do so because we are designing "a better society for individuals and the collective" (Fullan, 2011 p. x).

As researchers in teacher education, we have evidence that teachers who conscientiously build on learners' background knowledge to introduce unknown material construct more meaningful knowledge together through these experiences (Lee, 2006; Morrell, 2000; Stoops Verplaetse & Migliacci, 2008; Turner, 2011). However, teachers often struggle when attempting to support students who have backgrounds different from their own and who fall outside their present knowledge of multicultural learners (Cochran-Smith, 2004; Delpit, 1995). In particular, immigrant and refugee children pose a significant challenge, not only because of the school's position on legal issues affecting their status as documented or un-documented but also because of distrust and fear felt by these newcomers. If the anti-immigrant trends, as represented by Arizona's State Bill 1070 and similar measures in other states, continue to restrict immigrants' entry and access to public services, building on learners' backgrounds will be highly problematic for both teachers and learners. What will this mean when the process of schooling denies immigrant children access to using knowledge from their backgrounds because of these students' fear of raising suspicions about their legal status? How can teachers prepare them to not only be successful with academic gatekeeping but also be successful sociopolitically in challenging injustice that threatens their family life and community?

A Proposal for Working with Complexity

We introduce a promising critical instructional approach to integrate music and various content areas while developing academic language and literacy. In particular, we see that mainstream teachers who teach social studies, government, economics, geography, and sociology in history can avail themselves of music that raises themes of immigration to further student engagement in the curriculum (Cummins, 2011). Many nationally used texts in social studies include chapters on the Industrial Age, immigrants, and empires, and most U.S. high school social studies curricula have units on immigrants and their role in the economic growth of the United States, in the Industrial Revolution of the past and in the information technology revolution of our day. However, even teachers who have immigrants in their own classrooms miss other curricular opportunities to draw productively on these students' resources without embarrassing or marginalizing them from their peers and, equally important, from the curriculum.

Why Music?

Currently, music has been placed on the endangered subjects list in the United States, where accountability in education has been narrowly focused on subjects monitored by local, state, and national high-stakes testing. Consequently, despite the high status music holds in the culture and the ubiquitous presence of music in everyday life, many schools have relegated music to the list of "specials" or extracurricular subject areas. Furthermore, numerous schools have drastically reduced budgets, which have eliminated music programs altogether. In August 2009, Arne Duncan, then secretary of education, issued a letter to school and community leaders in which he advocated for the role music and visual arts play in providing students with a well-rounded education. He discussed the 2008 National Assessment of Educational Progress (NAEP) Arts results that found that "only 57 percent of the 8th graders attended schools where music instruction was offered at least three or four times a week, and only 57 percent attended schools where visual arts were offered that often" (Duncan, 2009, p. 1). More recently, the NAEP's 2016 report states that "13% of U.S. students attend schools that offer music classes less than once a week." Our proposal also addresses the reinsertion of music into the curriculum for purposes of building critical consciousness (The Arts Education Partnership, 2016).

Although we focus on middle and high school, the analytic principles in our approach may be used in elementary school as well. The school and wider community stands to benefit from these efforts as they learn to appreciate the contributions made by each successive wave of immigrants and the community's issues of equity. We draw on Willis et al.'s (2008) notion of critical consciousness to show how scaffolding can accomplish a shift in perspectives. Willis et al. advocated "challenging the underlying assumptions that work in the internal and external worlds to privilege some while disprivileging others" (p. 5). In this manner, the analysis and appreciation of music may offer a space in which to consider deterring the historical replication of harsher treatment toward newcomers even by immigrants themselves. Many of these immigrants' collective short term memory conserves the legitimacy of exacting a "capitalist hazing" of sorts from each successive wave of newcomers. This suffering is obscured yet ironically also glorifies itself in the often cited Horatio Alger discourse of "My . . . (fill in the blank of a name of ancestor) . . . came here and worked hard to be successful without any government handout." Overcoming this "champion" discourse that elevates the past, erases racial privileges, ignores current local and global inequities, and ignores reduced availability of social resources requires a critical understanding of how multiple factors affect the context of immigration across time and in this context, an understanding of immigration as ecological and ultimately needed for the sustainability of our nation and our world (Franklin & Blyton, 2011).

To build a supportive instructional practice, we address the need for adequate scaffolding that builds teachers' ability to work on trust building through activities that empower students to interpret messages conveyed through music and then to create their own art projects (for example, slam poetry, music mash-ups, multimedia projects). We recognize that music has potential to provoke emotions, critical thinking, and actions.

The combination of lyrics and music encode messages that teachers can use in further developing their learners' critical consciousness. We show how analytic tools can be employed to interpret and construct new messages. This constructive process enables learners to critically interpret and construct messages in their environment and to act on these as savvy consumers and producers of music, reading between the lines and writing between the lines with music.

Music as a Medium for Building Critical Consciousness

Teachers play a very important role in helping learners appreciate how language and various discourse genres influence their thinking, emotions, and even actions both consciously and subconsciously (Juslin, 2008; Lane, Davis, & Devonport,

2011; Morris & Boone, 1998). Music is one important vehicle that can be explored to engage and empower students in critically interpreting how they and others are portrayed, how public opinion may be influenced, and how they read and, often subconsciously, buy into stereotypes. As both consumers and creators of music, young people can become more discerning through school-based projects using critical discourse analysis (CDA). Further institutional support can be found in the Common Core State Standards, which advocates for building higher-level thinking and creativity. The music standards call for "understanding relationships between music, the other arts and disciplines outside the arts" (Standard 8) and "understanding music in relation to history and culture" (Standard 9; National Standards for Music Education, n.d.).

In discussing the hip-hop music phenomenon, Seidel (2011) states, "Faced with racism, classism, ageism, and other forms of structural subjugation, many young people have developed the courage to break rules, the audacity to believe they can do things that have never been done and the creativity to imagine how" (p. 6). As facilitators, teachers in mainstream classrooms can empower students to seek new levels of school and civic engagement through applying CDA to something many learners invest time and attention in—music. Fairclough (2012) believes that CDA "allows one to incorporate elements of 'context' into the analysis of texts to show the relationship between concrete occasional events and more durable social practices, to show innovation and change in texts, and it has a mediating role in allowing one to connect detailed linguistic and semiotic features of texts with processes of social change on a broader scale" (p. 457).

CDA can be used in interdisciplinary and multimodal projects, as in the case of music, as it draws on different mediums to appeal to our senses. By drawing on the visual, the sound, instrumentation, the lyrics, and the rhythm, for example, artists are able to influence our senses and responses. According to Gee (1999), "Discourses are about being different 'kinds of people'" (p. 34)—about using socially accepted norms, or "big 'D' Discourses," and language-in-use norms, such as "little 'd' discourses" (Gee, 2015). As human beings, we express different kinds of discourses through our affiliations and upbringing. All our discourses are filtered and mediated through the lens of our historical, cultural, and linguistic experiences, for example. When we add the critical dimension to our discourses, we consider, for instance, issues of power, class, race, and gender and as Gee says, "the distribution of social goods and power" (1999, p. 68). Fairclough (2012) also includes the imaginaries in his understandings of discourse, a stance that is important for middle and high schoolers. He states that "discourses include representations of how things are and have been, as well as imaginaries—representations of how things might or could or should be" (p. 458).

In the following section, we discuss the procedures that we used to select and analyze two immigration songs on YouTube. These same procedures may serve to address both language and content standards for English language learners (ELLs) in middle and high school social studies units on immigration.

Applying Critical Discourse Analysis to Songs About Immigration

Background on Arizona Law. The passage of Arizona Senate Bill 1070 (SB 1070) in 2010 followed by a modification with House Bill 2162 (HB 2162) resulted in very strong reactions in the media from some of the major players in the music industry in the United States. These responses on the Internet ranged from giving interviews, posting comments on blogs, canceling participation in concerts, and singing about the immigration law. SB 1070 stated that "a law enforcement officer without warrant, may arrest a person if the officer has probable cause to believe that the person has committed any public offense that makes the person removable from the United States" (lines 37–39). The modification made with HB 2162 stated that "prosecutors would not investigate complaints based on race, color or national origin."

The Procedures for Selecting the Songs for Analyses. In a Google search, typing the words "songs about immigration" produced 13,100,000 hits in .76 seconds. A quick scan revealed collections of songs and references to songs about immigration that were composed as far back as 1868, such as "The Song of the Red Man," by Henry C. Wok, and as recently as this year, 2017, with Led Zeppelin's "Immigrant Song," originally released in 1970, featured on the soundtrack of the new movie *Thor: Ragnarok*. Given such a wealth of reference points, the research for this part of the chapter was limited to the key terms "Music on Arizona's immigration law." Google showed 5,040,000 hits in .88 seconds for this phrase. Following up on the music sites that came up indicated that the majority of the music could be located on YouTube. The search was thus narrowed to "YouTube songs on Arizona immigration law," which yielded 2,390,000 results in .96 seconds at the time of writing.

Browsing numerous sites evidenced that the same songs were recurring. Recognizing this saturation point, we decided that the selection would be narrowed to the top 10 songs, with the top five being used for our analyses. The ordering of the selected songs was based on the number of reported "views" on YouTube on September 27, 2010, and which we have updated, to be current. The ranking of the songs (Figure 11.1) indicates a breakdown by artist, song title, date posted, genre, duration, and number of views, with a link to the website. The final selection of the songs reflected different stances on immigration: pro-immigration, ambiguous, and anti-immigration.

Analytic Procedures

After repeated listening, the lyrics were transcribed verbatim and analyzed using Fairclough's (1989) critical analysis framework. The analyses included information on the artist and the sociocultural contexts and institutional influences. We also based our analyses on elements of music such as repetition, contrast, and rhythm and our natural emotional and imaginative responses. All the songs in our initial analyses are listed in Figure 11.1.

Figure 11.1. Pro- and Anti-immigration Songs

"Arizona" (Ambiguous)
Brian Haner
2.48 minutes
www.youtube.com/watch?v=GKFuYykPSxI
Date Posted: July 28, 2010
Genre: Comedy
Number of Views: 619,407

"God Save Arizona" (Anti-immigration)
Ray Stevens
4.13 minutes
www.youtube.com/watch?v=jWpOcZVnBrc
Date Posted: August 24, 2010
Genre: Country
Number of Views: 1,089,631

"Back to Arizona Rappers Protest Immigration Bill" (Pro-immigration)
DJ John Blaze, Tajji Sharp, Yung Face, Mr. Miranda, Ocean, Da'aron Anthony, Atllas,
Chino D, Nyhtee, Pennywise, Rich Rico, and Da Beast
8.12 minutes
www.youtube.com/watch?v=tfoTxZ_Thyc
Date Posted: May 6, 2010
Genre: Hip-hop
Number of Views: 47,165

"Arizona Song" (Anti-immigration)
Paul Shanklin
2.29 minutes
www.youtube.com/watch?v=vpxIp__9BIk
Date Posted: May 7, 2010
Genre: Parody
Number of Views: 22,300

"By the Time I Get to Arizona 2010" (Pro-immigration)
Toki Wright
4.43 minutes
vimeo.com/34348537
Date Posted: Not indicated
Genre: Rap
Number of Views: 19,957

It is important to note that while all these songs were posted as videos on YouTube, this analysis does not incorporate the words, actions, or graphics shown in the video and that because of copyright regulations and the difficulties we experienced in obtaining permission, we cannot report phrases or lines from the songs that were used in our initial analyses and report. We therefore refer to only the titles of the songs. The issue of copyright is a very important one for teachers to address in using the songs to spur discussion of critical issues.

In the following section, a summary of the analyses for our two top songs is given followed by a classification as pro-immigration, ambiguous, or anti-immigration categories for further discussion and elaboration.

The following two songs provide material to analyze and discuss the difficult topic of immigration. These procedures can help students compose their responses to these songs through their creative reappropriation of the elements in the songs for their own purposes.

Brian Haner—"Arizona" (2010). Brian Haner is known as a comical musician. In "Arizona" his music has an upbeat, happy, even rhythmic dance tempo and lasts for just under 3 minutes. The song's title signals a singular focus on the state of Arizona. Why is this state singled out? The male singer's voice reflects an accent from the southwestern area of the United States, aligned with the country-and-western genre. The opening stanza of the song orients the listener and provides justification for moving to Arizona. The repetition of the chorus implies the endorsement of Senate Bill 1070 (SB 1070; State of Arizona, 2010) because access to entering the United States from Mexico will be restricted and the song explicitly associates this action with the expectation that jobs will become available.

The lyrics make specific references to Hillary Clinton, as well as the president of Mexico, who are accused of being soft on immigration policy and indirectly responsible for arrival of immigrants. Harsh language is used for Hillary Clinton but no such language is used to describe the president of Mexico or any people in the U.S. administration. Accompanying the lyrics there is a joyful guitar strumming to give the impression that a political change will bring a positive outcome for those currently unemployed. Moreover, there is an underlying and implicit tone of respect for law and order provided that *those who are coming into the country* enter through the proper legal channels. This discourse of law and order assumes that the law is just and applicable to everyone and that preserving law and order equally benefits all. Often this is referred to as a hard line on crime, viewing as criminals those who do not follow this path.

Beyond both the implicit and explicit messages signaled through the lyrics, from a wider and societal/institutional level, the song could be interpreted as representing the interests of poor working-class Americans who are assumed to be willing to take even those low-paying bricklaying jobs, or the ones at Denny's and McDonald's. The tension in the sociocultural context is fueled by the current economic recession and the lack of jobs for many people without the skills that are demanded by global trade. The artist/voice suggests that some workers probably feel that the jobs that they can do now are being done by undocumented workers, thus conflating these immigrants' presence with the cause of suffering also brought about through voters' aligning themselves with the wrong political party. The singer, a male of European descent, leaves no doubt about his disillusionment with the current government, but the song conveys an inspiring message for people to take political action by voting. Brian Haner's (2010) "Arizona" can be classified as a tongue-in-cheek critique of those who hold anti-immigration positions. If interpreted as a parody, his anti-immigration stance can be called into question. What makes this a parody can be examined through the assumptions made about the actual attractiveness of low-paying jobs luring unemployed people to Arizona. For whom is this a compelling reason to move to Arizona? Looking closely at how the song's lyrics build this argument gives plenty of room for doubting the overt message; thus the parody.

Ray Stevens—"God Save Arizona." Stevens's song fits into the country music genre and begins with a strong, pulsating, quick beat that is representative of the music throughout the song. With a strong appeal to our sense of patriotism, the opening lyrics promote nationalistic pride, with references to the role that the battleship *Arizona* played in Japan's 1941 attack on Pearl Harbor. What was that role? This question would provide material for an inquiry into U.S. involvement in World War II and the important role that immigrant communities played, particularly Japanese American communities—despite internment.

Throughout, the song's lyrics convey a strong nationalistic message with a cadence carried out through drumming associated with marching infantry. The voiceover narration uses a deep, booming male voice telling a tale of great significance and breaking into song to convey the songwriter's intent to evoke a visceral response. The lyrics explicitly convey the songwriter's feelings. There are also explicit references to dissatisfaction with the administration.

At the institutional level this song supports those who are dissatisfied with "illegal aliens and immigration" to the United States, hence the appeals to patriotism. The imagery of the lyrics and music draw out the feelings of people who are dissatisfied with the pace of change in immigration policy and (in)action. At the sociocultural level, this male singer is a person of European descent who sings so lustily and hastens a call to action with the impassioned appeal for God to "save Arizona." We classified this song as anti-immigration.

Discussion and Implications for Our Classrooms

Despite the 2016 NAEP report that only "13% of students attend schools that offer music classes less than once a week" (The Arts Education Partnership, 2016), we know that children's and youth's lives are filled with music. As Campbell (2010) puts it, "Children's engagement in music frequently is paid minimal attention by teachers and parents, even when it may be the rich repository of children's intimate thoughts and sentiments. They have opinions about music, perspectives about where and when they listen to and 'do' music and for what reasons" (p. 5). We used a critical laungage awareness approach in this chapter to illustrate how teachers can use music that is readily available to engage students in communicating about difficult topics such as immigration. Through a critical approach we used informal music language to give a general description of the implicit and explicit messages in the selected lyrics, and we offer our perceptions of the sociocultural and institutional levels of analyses. We believe that teachers and students who have no formal training in music can use our approach as a model. We recommend the following procedures:

1. Based on the content units in your subject area, determine which issue(s) can be addressed (variation in songs about the same themes can be very productive in stimulating discussion, contrast, and stance taking).
   » Involve students in selecting the songs (conduct web searches or search their own collection) for themes you wish to include according to your criteria.
   » Determine grouping of students (may also work in groups on selecting music). If you do group work be sure to consider students who have varying backgrounds in music and whether you would like them to work together or not (e.g., formal or informal knowledge).
   » Model for students the procedures to analyze their songs. (Identify the genre and its elements, encourage personal connections, construct themes, identify structural elements in the composition, establish wider social connections, etc.). Draw on their emotions and their imaginations.
   » Let students create their own music and lyrics of a song of their choice. Encourage students to draw on their cultural resources to create their songs.
2. Make sure multiple perspectives on an issue are included in the selection of songs. Be sure to draw on students' rich cultural resources.
3. Consult with parents to prepare them for giving their consent and securing their participation (collect their resources, document their approval of a unit, respond to their concerns, involve them in evaluation/ assessment, and invite them to the final performances).

In developing the activities that we have described, teachers might draw on the selected standards and recommendations. The Teachers of English to Speakers of Other Languages International Association (TESOL) recommendations, based on Common Core Standards in Social Studies and Music, exemplify the multiple perspectives and higher-order thinking skills required of middle and high school students (Figure 11.2).

Figure 11.2. Recommendations and Standards

TESOL Recommendation (TESOL International Association, 2013)	Build on students' background and cultures; build background where necessary on using evidence from different types of text.
English Language Arts and Literacy in History/Social Studies Standards (National Governors Association Center for Best Practices and the Counsel of Chief State School Officers, 2010)	**Grade 6–8** Identify aspects of a text that reveal an author's point of view or purpose (e.g., loaded language, inclusion, or avoidance of particular facts). **Grade 9–10** Compare the point of view of two or more authors for how they treat the same or similar topics, including which details they include and emphasize in their respective accounts. **Grade 11–12** Evaluate authors' differing points of view on the same historical event or issue by assessing the authors' claims, reasoning, and evidence.
Music Standards (National Standards for Music Education, n.d.)	**Content Standard 4:** Composing and arranging music within specified guidelines <ul><li>Arrange a variety of traditional and nontraditional sound sources and electronic media when composing and arranging (Grades 5–8).</li><li>Compose music in several distinct styles, demonstrating creativity in using the elements of music for expressive effect (Grades 9–12).</li></ul> **Content Standard 7:** Evaluating music and music performances <ul><li>Evaluate the quality and effectiveness of their own and others' performances, compositions, arrangements, and improvisations by applying specific criteria appropriate for the style of music and offer constructive suggestions for improvement (Grades 5–8).</li><li>Evaluate a performance, composition, arrangement, or improvisation by comparing it to a similar model or exemplary models (Grades 9–12).</li></ul> **Content Standard 9:** Understanding relationships between music, the other arts, and disciplines outside the arts <ul><li>Describe distinguishing characteristics of representative music genres and styles from a variety of cultures (Grades 5–8).</li><li>Identify various roles that musicians perform, cite representative individuals who have functioned in each role, and describe their activities and achievements (grades 9–12).</li></ul>

The 2011 American Educational Research Association's 35th volume of the *Review of Research in Education* was devoted to youth cultures, language, and literacy. The editor, Stanton Wortham, notes that "almost all the chapters ask how educators could more productively relate to creative, global, and counterhegemonic youth practices. Instead of constructing youth as different and misguided, could educators learn from and work with youth culture?" (Wortham, 2011, p. x). Critical language awareness has provided us with a means for the analysis of music, a worldwide commodity that is dear to the hearts of young people. It also offers us a practical response to answer Wortham's urgent call as well as the authors' call to embrace immigrant and marginalized youth through the application of CDA to study and deconstruct hegemonic structures and discourses. CDA serves to empower disempowered and unengaged youth by developing their critical consciousness of dominant structures inherent in all genres of popular music. Through the preceding examples of the deconstruction of pro- and anti-immigration music using critical analytic tools, the underlying messages in the use of language, rhythm, and instrumentation can be interpreted on several levels. One could more deliberately or consciously reject or accept the messages in institutional structures such as music, rather than blindly accepting or being misled by them. With such tools, more young people may even be challenged to create their own countercultural responses (Alim, 2011).

Through the lens of multimodalities, CDA offers us many imaginaries and creative opportunities to examine music in the classroom. We did not analyze video in this chapter, but it too could be examined using the scaffolding that the critical lens of CDA affords us. There is no denying the challenges that the awareness of multilayering of discourses affords dominant, immigrant, and marginalized youth. Such approaches can indeed open doors for difficult conversations, spur many forms of humanistic and artistic expression, and invoke numerous forms of literacy experiences—all of which are needed if we are to draw on 21st-century critical thinking and multimodalities to promote a socially just agenda in our teaching.

References

Alim, H. S. (2011). Global ill-literacies: Hip hop cultures, youth identities, and the politics of literacy. *Review of Research in Education, 35*, 120–146.

The Arts Education Partnership. (2016). *The 2016 nation's report card (NAEP)*. National Center for Education Statistics, U.S. Department of Education. Retrieved from www.aep-arts.org/the-2016-nations-report-card-naep/

Blaze, DJ. J., Sharp, T., Yung Face, Mr. Miranda, Ocean, Da'aron, A., . . . Da Beast. (2010). Back to Arizona Rappers Protest Immigration Bill. Retrieved from www.youtube.com/watch?v=tfoTxZ_Thyc.

Campbell, P. S. (2010). *Songs in their heads: Music and its meaning in children's lives* (2nd ed.). Oxford, England: Oxford University Press.

Cochran-Smith, M. (2004). *Walking the road. Race, diversity, and social justice in teacher education*. New York, NY: Teachers College Press.

Cummins, J. (2011). Literacy engagement: Fueling academic growth for English learners. *The Reading Teacher, 65*(2), 142–146.

Delpit, L. (1995). *Other people's children: Cultural conflict in the classroom*. New York, NY: The New Press.

Duncan, A. (2009). Letter to school and community leaders. Retrieved from 2.ed.gov /policy/elsec/guid/secletter/090826.html

Fairclough, N. (1989). *Language and power*. London, England: Longman.

Fairclough, N. (2012). Critical discourse analysis. *International Advances in Engineering and Technology (IAET) ISSN: 2305-8285, 7*, 452–487. Retrieved from scholarism.net /FullText/2012071.pdf

Franklin, A., & Blyton, P. (Eds.). (2011). *Researching sustainability. A guide to social science methods, practice, and engagement*. New York, NY: Earthscan (Taylor and Francis Group).

Fullan, M. (2011). *The moral imperative realized*. Thousand Oaks, CA: Corwin.

Gee, J. P. (1999). *An introduction to discourse analysis: Theory and method*. New York, NY: Routledge.

Gee, J. P. (2015). Discourse, small d, big d. The International Encyclopedia of Language and social interaction, p. 1–5.

Haner, B. (2010). Arizona. Retrieved from www.youtube.com/watch?v=GKFuYykPSxI

Juslin, P. N. (2008). Emotional responses to music: The need to consider underlying mechanisms. *Behavioral and Brain Sciences, 31*, 559–621.

Lane, A. M., Davis, P. A., & Devonport, T. J. (2011). Effects of music interventions on emotional states and running performance. *Journal of Sports Science and Medicine, 10*, 400–440.

Lee, C. (2006). 'Every good-bye ain't gone': Analyzing the cultural underpinnings of classroom talk. *International Journal of Qualitative Studies in Education, 19*(3), 305–327.

Morrell, E. (2000). *Curriculum and popular culture: Building bridges and making waves*. Paper presented at the American Educational Research Association. (Eric Document 442720)

Morris, J. D., & Boone, M. A. (1998). The effects of music on emotional response, brand attitude, and purchase intent in an emotional advertising condition. *Advances in Consumer Research, 25*, 518–526.

National Governors Association Center for Best Practices & Council of Chief State School Officers. (2010). *Common Core State Standards for English language arts and literacy in history/social studies, science, and technical subjects*. Washington, DC: Authors.

National Standards for Music Education. (n.d.). Retrieved August 2, 2017, from www .musicstandfoundation.org/images/National_Standards_-_Music_Education.pdf

Seidel, S. (2011). *Hip hop genius: Remixing high school education*. Lanham, MD: Rowman & Littlefield.

State of Arizona. (2010). Senate Bill 1070. Retrieved from www.azleg.gov/legtext/49leg/2r /bills/sb1070s.pdf

Stoops Verplaetse, L., & Migliacci, N. (2008). *Inclusive pedagogy for English language learners: A handbook of research-informed practices*. New York, NY: Routledge.

TESOL International Association. (2013). Overview of the Common Core State Standards Initiatives for ELLs. Alexandria, VA: Author.

Turner, N. (2011). "Rap universal": Using multimodal media production to develop ICT literacies. *Journal of Adolescent and Adult Literacy, 54*(8), 613–623.

Willis, A. I., Montavon, M., Hunter, C., Hall, H., Burke, L., & Herrera, A. (2008). *Critically conscious research*. Language and Literacy Series. New York, NY: Teachers College Press.

Wortham, S. (2011). Introduction: Youth cultures and education. *Review of Research in Education, 35*, vii–xi.

CHAPTER 12

Interview Theatre

An Active Learning Pedagogy for Developing
Empathy and Allies for Immigrants in Our
Communities

Susan Harden and Robin Witt

In the classroom, it is often a challenge to raise student voices. Yet research indicates that the engaged pedagogies of embodied learning, active movement, and storytelling are impactful and empowering approaches toward creating inclusive and transformative classrooms for all types of students (Asher, 1969; Krashen & Terrell, 1983; Marsh, 1998; Ray & Seely, 1998). Empowering teaching strategies that raise student voice must also include community engagement (Cummins, 1986) and a reflection on social justice issues and policies (Wong, 1996). In this chapter, we explore how techniques involving interview theatre, community engagement, and social justice have been successfully used within an interdisciplinary theatre course at a university in Charlotte, North Carolina, to contest issues related to undocumented immigration, including the DREAM Act. For practitioners looking for engaged pedagogies that raise student voices and community awareness around issues of immigration, the process described is interdisciplinary and transferable to a variety of classrooms and educational settings.

The faculty in the Department of Theatre developed a new course, Theatre Collaboration, which students take early in the program of study for theatre majors and minors. Two instructors were recruited to coteach the course: an assistant professor of directing with an expertise in the Chicago Storefront Theater model of theatre and an assistant professor of education with an expertise in community-engaged scholarship. The coteaching of the course necessitated that the instructors take creative risks and trust the process (Fish, 1989), as we were completely uncertain of how our interdisciplinary relationship would evolve or what the final product of the curriculum would look like. We decided to embrace and be energized by the possibilities.

Course Design

The interdisciplinary nature of the course meant that we would have to model for our students the values of collaboration, listening, openness, creative risk taking, and caring. We designed course content that would combine storefront theatre, social justice, and community engagement pedagogies. The social justice issue explored during each offering of the course was designed to be selected based on a highly contested issue in the community. Our decision to choose the theme of immigration and the DREAM Act was influenced by a number of factors occurring at multiple scales and dramatically affecting the Charlotte community.

Local Demographic Growth and Change. Census studies from the Pew Charitable Trusts indicate that North Carolina is a Hispanic hypergrowth state, with the Hispanic population growing by over 200% since 1980. By 2011, North Carolina ranked 11th in the nation for total Hispanic population (Pew Research Center, 2011).

National DREAM Act Legislation. On the national level, DREAM Act legislation was under consideration. Young activists living in North Carolina had organized as a group, called the NC Dream Team. These activists were staging very public protests and hunger strikes to raise public awareness and with the aim of influencing the votes of North Carolina's U.S. senators, who ultimately voted against bringing forward the federal DREAM Act (Ovaska, 2010).

State-Level Anti-immigrant Legislation. The North Carolina State Legislature introduced several bills targeting immigrants, in alignment with anti-immigration policies adopted by other state legislatures like Arizona's SB 1070 law. These policies would require public school principals to verify citizenship (Fain, 2011), ban undocumented immigrants from state universities and community colleges, and mandate officers to determine immigration status of those arrested or detained (Ordonez, 2011).

Cultural Community Organizations Affirming Immigrants. The Levine Museum of the New South, an award-winning historical and cultural museum in Charlotte and an influential institution among the Charlotte elite, curated two exhibits designed to engage Charlotte residents around themes of immigration, education, and cultural change. The stated goals of the exhibits were to advance greater cultural awareness and acceptance.

University Efforts to Affirm Immigrants. The Theatre Department produced *Rowing to America*, a series of short plays exploring the immigrant experience in America. The post-performance talk-back included a panel of NC Dream Team participants as a way to engage the campus in a community dialogue about the DREAM Act.

It was clear to the instructors that the city of Charlotte and the state of North Carolina were at a crossroads in terms of their attitudes toward immigrants. Would our community be as welcoming and receptive as promoted in cultural institutions and campus performances, or would the city support exclusionary and unjust policies? We believed that the timeliness and intensity of the debate represented a critical juncture for the community and presented an opportunity for our students to listen and authentically mirror back to the community the debate in a meaningful, artistic, and impactful play devised by the students. We hoped that our students would learn about collaboration, theatre, social justice, undocumented immigration, and the DREAM Act and that this knowledge would create allies. We hoped that the broader community would learn about how constituents were engaging the issues of immigration and that the culminating class performance would point toward a more just future.

Interview Theatre Techniques and the Storefront Theatre Model

Interview Theatre (Paget, 1983), also known as verbatim or documentary theatre, is a technique that dovetails nicely with the pedagogical value of listening to the community. Interview theatre is a form of inquiry and qualitative research where the stories emerge from the interviews, privileging the voices of the interviewees over the social justice agendas of the instructors.

The Storefront Theatre Model is based on the idea of intimate productions in spaces not originally designed as theatres, such as retail buildings or storefronts (Bergman, 2010). Storefront theatre companies are typically innovative, resourceful, and efficient, as they are underfunded compared with larger, more traditional theatre organizations. Using a storefront theatre approach, university students collaboratively create all aspects of production, including script, design, production management, and advertising.

Social Justice and Community Engagement

We also decided that the content of the class should include subject matter grounded in social justice and community engagement theory and pedagogy. The concept of social justice is composed of two underlying claims: a desire for a just or fair society and the realization that the current social order falls short of that mark (Rawls, 1971). Pedagogically, this calls for the use of classroom activities that encourage critique of the status quo and reflection on how students might work to change the social order (Johnson, 2008). Policies that strengthen the social context for justice are those that encourage access, inclusion, equity, and trust (Bell, 2007; Putnam, 2000). Historically, the arts and arts education have been highly impactful avenues for addressing social justice issues (Greene, 1995). It is also important that social justice work be accomplished in partnership with the community (Boyer, 1996), making sure to prioritize the voice of community members (Stoecker, Tryon, & Hilgendorf, 2009).

Getting Started

As an introduction, students read a variety of plays from the interview theatre genre, including the Tectonic Theater's (Kaufman & Tectonic Theater, 2001) collaboratively written *The Laramie Project*, an exploration of the events surrounding the murder of Matthew Shepard, as well as Anna Deavere Smith's (1998) play *Fires in the Mirror*, an examination of the Crown Heights riots in 1991 involving the African American and Jewish communities. These examples of interview theater texts offered our students a powerful illumination of the intersections of social justice and community voice.

It was decided that students conduct their interviews in pairs. One student would interview the subject while the other took notes and completed a physical survey of the interview environment. Documents needed for the interview process included pre- and postinterview checklists, a consent form, interview instructions, and a physical survey. The authors will provide examples of these documents upon request.

A trusting relationship between interviewer and interviewee is key in generating a successful interview. Students learn that it is a leap of faith for interviewees to participate in this process. The interviewer has to assure the interviewee that the intentions of the project are to sincerely portray the person accurately, honestly, and verbatim. The performance of the interview is intended to honor the voice of the interviewee. The characters that students will perform are people living in their community. If the portrayal is inaccurate or insincere, the community may turn away from participating with the university. The university's community-engagement efforts could be permanently harmed. The consequences were also high stakes for NC Dream Team interviewees. Many risked arrest and deportation by stepping out of the shadows and allowing themselves to be interviewed.

Given the weight of the interview assignment, the classroom discussions leading up to the community interviews were critical. As a class, we needed to understand the essence of the undocumented-immigrant experience and gain clarity around definitions. Activities designed to support this learning included a detailed reading and discussion of the 14th Amendment to the United States Constitution, a review of academic research on recent immigration to Charlotte and patterns of settlement (Graves & Smith, 2010), a survey of local media to understand reporting about immigrants and media bias, a walking tour of an immigrant neighborhood in Charlotte led by an expert on immigration from a local cultural museum, a presentation by the executive director of the Latin American Coalition about the immigrant experience in Charlotte, participation in the local Chinese New Year festival, a viewing of the on-campus theatrical production of *Rowing to America*, and participation in a passionate and contested postproduction talk-back between the audience and the NC DREAM Team.

This research into the local immigrant experience provided a base of knowledge that students could use to more thoughtfully consider the selection of essential, yet indirect, questions that might reveal further insight into the immigrant experience in our community. Consequently, collectively as a class in dialogue, we decided on four interview questions:

1. What were the circumstances of your birth?
2. What is your biggest hope?
3. What is your worst nightmare?
4. What do you find compelling about the American Dream?

After the interview questions were selected, the next fundamental step in the process was teaching our students how to use their judgment to select a meaningful passage from the interview and then transcribing that excerpt verbatim into the script of a monologue that could be performed. The passage should be 2 to 3 minutes in length and the contents should be the most compelling or insightful sections relating to our theme of immigration and the DREAM Act. As a class, we would refer to this content-rich moment as the "gold" of the interview.

But the process of identifying when you hear something profound was a skill that needed to be developed through practicing close and careful listening to the interview. This required intellectual and creative discipline by the students. We wanted them to hear the words of the interview so that when the actor portrayed the interviewee on stage, he or she presented the authentic voice. To help develop listening skills, we required that students listen to the audio of their interview multiple times, regardless of how certain they were about the content. Some students listened to their interviews 50 to 100 times.

The students practiced their techniques with each other before we sent them out into the community. Once we were confident the students had acquired basic interview skills, we began our search for interview subjects. With our students, we put together a list of the types of community members we wanted to interview: undocumented college students, public school teachers, social workers involved with the immigrant community, law enforcement, and local politicians both for and against the DREAM Act legislation. The student's access to undocumented college students benefited from a postshow discussion following our Department of Theatre's production of *Rowing to America*, a series of short plays documenting the American immigrant experience, as mentioned earlier. Theatre Collaboration students met with student leaders of the NC DREAM Team after this performance and secured interviews.

Creating a Script

Although the semester-long devising activities were student generated and created by a dynamic cooperative, the instructors, with some input from the collective, were responsible for the compilation of the play script for performance. We had a variety of dramatic pieces that needed to be collated into a cohesive, compelling, and affecting performance script that included transcribed interviews, dramatic interpretation of extant texts, student reflections from journals, recordings of songs, and collages of photographs. Not all of the students' work was memorized, so we employed concert reading techniques using music stands, which allowed students to share work that they hadn't had the time to commit to memory. Because of the issues-based nature of this devised work, we attempted to alternate points of view sequentially, to vary dramatic forms. For example, we followed a large, whole-group, collective-voice, memorized piece from an extant script of the 14th Amendment with a small-group, unmemorized piece that highlighted anti-immigrant sentiment using music stands. The play text shifted in both form and content from section to section. We titled the text "Jumping Mountains: What Would YOU Do to Feed Your Family?" (youtu.be/AHruSZRGye4), based on a snippet of dialogue from one of the interviews.

The Performance

Indeed, as we began to prepare for our public performance, we found we had more than enough material to fill the target running time of 40 minutes. Because we were far more interested in our students' process in the collaborative creation of these pieces than we were in a polished production, we decided to present the work as an enhanced staged reading. We used black boxes to give us various levels; flashlights were used for dramatic lighting; and students sat on the floor, upstage of the action. In storefront theatre style, the students set up, stage-managed, choreographed, arranged harmonies, typed the script, designed the program, and selected and ran the sound.

Two sold-out community performances of the play were delivered free of charge in a 75-seat black box theatre on campus. The performances were attended by the local community and many of the interviewees attended as well. Students and audience members participated in talk-back conversations after the show. At the request of the university administration, the show was restaged twice for community audiences of specifically immigration and DREAM Act activists.

Becoming an Ally

The technique of interview theatre is very effective for engaging and building allies, as the phenomena is built into the process. Interview theatre is the experience of learning, listening, giving voice, and inhabiting that other person with honesty and authenticity. The essence of becoming an ally is when members of the dominant group, becoming aware of their privilege and power as a result of this group dominance, work to end the oppression of those in marginalized social groups (Broido, 2000). This course, and the community performance, raised the voices of the NC DREAM Team activists, oppressed by laws prohibiting access to citizenship. The curriculum presented opportunities for students and the audience to understand their own privilege as citizens. Also fundamental in the process of becoming an ally was coming to understand *Otherness*, an oppressed state of being marginalized by the mainstream or dominant group. Otherness can be understood from both the position of the dominant group and the positions of oppressed groups (Munin & Speight, 2010). The profound nature of interview theatre requires the student as actor to honor the perspective of the interviewee. The acting of this type of performance is an internal realization of otherness. The conventions of interview theatre required that the actor sincerely and authentically depict the interviewee voice and movement. The audience experience in the performance is also an awareness experience of otherness. The interviews captured untold stories of essential human concerns.

Empathy is also an important factor in becoming an ally (Munin & Speight, 2010). In the process of collecting interviews, our students spoke with community advocates. As captured in the monologues, the advocates spoke passionately and empathetically of the hardships of young, undocumented immigrants.

Implications for Teachers

Interview pedagogy integrates research, writing, critical thinking, current events, peer collaboration, public speaking, storytelling, field experiences, and performance, allowing for individual and group activities. Interview theatre can also be adapted for primary and secondary school classrooms by revising the steps (research, interview, and performance) so they are age appropriate. Interview theatre pedagogy is rich and adaptable as an educational method.

Furthermore, for teachers who want to respond to the extremely negative anti-immigrant messages bombarding students, interview theatre is an effective pedagogy that provides teachers with an empathy-building process for students, community interviewees, and community audience members. This embodied and intimate approach to understanding the perspectives of others is a powerful counternarrative to the anti-immigrant voices dominating the media and politics. It requires that students authentically listen, over and over again, to the interviews of immigrants and then for a student to actually become that interviewee and share the wisdom with the community. It tips the scales away from the constant and repetitive media and political messaging.

References

Asher, J. J. (1969). The total physical response approach to second language learning. *The Modern Language Journal, 53*(1), 3–17.

Bell, L. A. (2007). Theoretical foundations for social justice education. In M. Adams, L. A. Bell, & P. Grifn (Eds.), *Teaching for diversity and social justice* (pp. 3–15). New York, NY: Routledge.

Bergman, C. E. (2010). We do storefront theatre: Using Chicago's storefront theatre model as the foundation for a theatre curriculum. *Theatre Topics, 20*(1), 55–64.

Boyer, E. L. (1996). The scholarship of engagement. *Journal of Public Service and Outreach, 1*(1), 11–20.

Broido, E. M. (2000). The development of social justice allies during college: A phenomenological investigation. *Journal of College Student Development, 41*(1), 3–18.

Cummins, J. (1986). Empowering minority students: A framework for intervention. *Harvard Educational Review, 56*(1), 18–36.

Deavere Smith, A. (1998). *Fires in the mirror: Crown Heights, Brooklyn, and other identities.* New York, NY: Dramatists Plays Service.

Fain, T. (2011, June 8). Tensions flare over Folwell bill on illegal immigrants in schools. *The Winston-Salem Journal.* Retrieved from: journalnow.com/business/tensions-flare-over-folwell-bill-on-illegal-immigrants-in-schools/article_7b830e53-6f53-5f3b-a14d-cc17adcf0c06.html

Fish, S. (1989). Being interdisciplinary is so very hard to do. *Profession, 89*(1), 15–22.

Graves, W., & Smith, H. A. (2010). *Charlotte, NC: The global evolution of a New South city.* Athens, GA: University of Georgia Press.

Greene, M. (1995). *Releasing the imagination: Essays on education, the arts, and social change.* San Francisco, CA: Jossey-Bass.

Johnson, B. L., Jr. (2008). Exploring multiple meanings and pursuits of social justice: A reflection on modern, interpretive, and postmodern possibilities. *Teacher Development, 12*(4), 301–318.

Kaufman, M., & Tectonic Theater Project (2001). *The Laramie Project.* New York, NY: Vintage Books.

Krashen, S. D., & Terrell, T. D. (1983). *The natural approach: Language acquisition in the classroom.* Oxford, England: Pergamon Press.

Marsh, V. (1998). Total physical response storytelling: A communicative approach to language learning. *Learning Languages, 4*(1), 24–28.

Munin, A., & Speight, S. (2010). Factors influencing the ally development of college students. *Equity and Excellence in Education, 43*(2), 249–264.

Ordonez, F. (2011, March 30). Immigrant students march in Uptown against new bill. *The Charlotte Observer.*

Ovaska, S. (2010, June 28). One of three on hunger strike for Dream Act hospitalized. *The Raleigh News and Observer.*

Paget, D. (1983). Verbatim theatre: Oral history and documentary techniques. *New Theatre Quarterly, 3*(12), 317–336.

Pew Research Center. (2011). *Demographic profiles of Hispanics in North Carolina.* Retrieved from www.pewhispanic.org/states/state/nc/

Putnam, R. D. (2000). *Bowling alone: The collapse and revival of American community.* New York, NY: Simon & Schuster.

Rawls, J. (1971). *A theory of justice.* Cambridge, MA: Belknap Press of Harvard University Press.

Ray, B., & Seely, C. (1998). *Fluency through TPR storytelling: Achieving real language acquisition in school.* Berkeley, CA: Command Performance Language Institute.

Stoecker, R., Tryon, E. A., & Hilgendorf, A. (2009). *The unheard voices: Community organizations and service learning.* Philadelphia, PA: Temple University Press.

Wong, S. D. (1996). Institutional policies and language minority students in the U.S. *TESOL Quarterly, 30*(3), 583–586.

BECOMING AN ALLY

Carollyn James

CHAPTER 13

Teachers as Allies

A Call to Action

Anne Marie Foerster Luu and Lori Dodson
with Hareth Andrade-Ayala and María Verónica Cevallos Rodríguez

> When will we deploy our greatest strengths? When will we work with one another, instead of against one another? When will we fix these issues permanently? He. She. They. You. Me. We can all chip in, so when the crisis erupts, don't ride the easy route. Take the road less traveled and assume responsibility.
>
> —Kiera Luu, Grade 11, 2017

The U.S. Supreme Court, in *Plyler v. Doe* (1982), recognized that "the deprivation of education takes an inestimable toll on the social, economic, intellectual, and psychological well-being of the individual, and poses an obstacle to individual achievement." Regarding undocumented students, in *Americans by Heart*, William Pérez (2012) noted, "The school system . . . shelters them from the constraints and effects of 'illegality.' . . . The better and longer the buffer that suspends the effects of their 'illegality' is preserved, the stronger the opportunity to successfully compete in school, develop a positive self-image, and prepare themselves for full and active participation in the legal world" (p. 113). Pérez points out that educators are key to creating safe environments in which students of undocumented status can thrive. This safe space could begin to erode once a student learns of his or her undocumented status. "Negative feelings of not belonging create disengagement from the life the student knew and therefore disinterest in wanting to achieve success at that time and in the future" (María Verónica Cevallos Rodríguez, personal communication, September 21, 2017). Despite a harsh and uncertain political climate that is at the crossroads of xenophobia and misguided nostalgia, undocumented students are affected daily by forces that need to be recognized and addressed in order to create a buffer where students can reach their full potential. Cristina Igoa (1995), a Philippines-born immigrant from Colombia, informs teachers about the importance of establishing a safe and nurturing classroom environment where children are expected to achieve high academic standards. As María Verónica Cevallos Rodríguez explains, "Undocumented students are expected to be as much and achieve as much as peers who may or may not be in the same position" (personal communication, September 21, 2017).

As teachers, we can anticipate that we will have undocumented students in our classrooms whom we are preparing for a life that requires continuous learning through college or career training programs. Teachers need to understand their students and the realities of their lives from multiple perspectives to create emotionally and physically safe learning environments, use and create resources that support students inside and outside the classroom, and actively engage as advocates in undoing the dehumanizing forces of our times: the vitriolic rhetoric that is seeping into our classrooms and the overall policy direction that can be characterized as "anti-immigrant."

Our Students' Realities

The realities of living undocumented in the United States present numerous challenges, as noted throughout our book, that become apparent in the educational pursuits of students at all ages. The numbers to consider are sobering. There are an estimated 11 million undocumented immigrants living in the United States. Of 3.2 million public high school graduates in 2017, 65,000 were estimated to be undocumented. Of those students, only 5–10% make it to college (U.S. Department of Education, 2015). The journey to high school graduation is fraught with challenges that school systems, school leadership, and individual educators can begin to address to increase the number of undocumented students who make it to college. An educator's responsibility is to recognize that these challenges pose dilemmas, because there is often a disconnect between the culture of school and the challenges faced by undocumented students and students from mixed-status families. This tension is depicted in the documentary *East of Salinas*, in which elementary-age student Jose is unable to fully participate in important family events, such as traveling with siblings to visit his grandmother, because he is unable to leave the country—a circumstance of being undocumented (Mow & Pacheco, 2015). The culture of schooling may be to solely focus on the content of the class rather than also examining the pedagogical choices made to engage students in that content. The chapters of this book have outlined dynamic pedagogies that have the potential to transform the experience of schooling for students like Jose and their families. Without understanding the benefits of the dilemmas approach presented in Chapter 2 by Thorp, Sánchez, and Sánchez Gosnell, the danger would be to see the lives of our DREAMers and undocumented students from a deficit perspective rather than one that would compel us to be creative in our responses to challenges. Teachers need to stay informed by learning the stories of their students and focus on student potential, student rights, and a strong sense of social justice. These are the teachers who will develop transformative practices to challenge the status quo.

In order to challenge the status quo, educators need to be well informed about the obstacles presented by having an undocumented status. Although some people nostalgically note that their great-grandparents arrived in the United States with little more than a bundle of clothes, the challenges today are significantly different. In Chapter 1, Wong orients us to the sociopolitical and historical contexts of immigration and the anti-immigrant language used today (Getzels P, & López E., 2012). The language and the issues are complex. The roads were never paved with gold, and success in the United States means more than just "standing in line" and "working harder and longer than everyone else." Immigration policies have changed over time, making it more difficult to move to the United States with documented status and providing little recognition of the humanitarian crises abroad, some of which are directly related to U.S. foreign policy, natural disasters, and political uprisings. Compulsory education has changed the lives of children with graduation requirements based on higher academic standards than at the time our grandparents immigrated. The opportunities to earn a living wage have changed, resulting in the need to work more than 80 hours per week at a minimum wage job just to subsist. In fact, to provide for their families, undocumented parents may be working in jobs that pay significantly lower than minimum wage and that require long hours without providing benefits or sick leave.

Immigration status presents challenges for families and older students to provide basic human needs such as food, shelter, restful sleep, and clothing. We may find that some students begin to miss school as they work at night to help provide food and shelter for their families. Younger siblings may come to school to share breakfast or lunch. Some students may present challenges related to being home alone while other family members work multiple shifts. Ultimately some students who are left alone for extended periods of time are susceptible to those who might take advantage of lack of adult supervision. There are also families that have to share accommodations in order to make ends meet, resulting in restless sleep and little space and quiet to do homework. Income-related challenges can also prevent families from having technology, such as the Internet, computers, and printers, that is needed to complete and extend study at home.

There are families and students who are challenged with issues of safety—physical, economic, and emotional—that can be interpreted as behavior concerns at school, as noted by Thorp in Chapter 3. The undocumented status of some of our students and family members may cause them to avoid seeking the help of police out of fear of revealing their undocumented status. Young students may express a fear of police when learning about community helpers in school. This fear isolates them and makes the undocumented families vulnerable to nefarious elements of the neighborhood. Children may not be learning and growing through play on playgrounds and in parks. A student might raise his or her fears in class as the student talks about how he or she can't open the door or walk to the neighbor's apartment for fear of ICE (Immigration and Customs Enforcement) raids. The resulting stress could keep students from fully participating in school, sports, and social activities.

A distressing and compelling aspect of the realities of being an undocumented student comes to life in the voices of the students who share the mental health impact of needing to live in the shadows. The sense of fear, the anxiety over change, the immoveable obstacle of belonging and not belonging at the same time are all challenges that educators can come to understand and begin to mitigate. A 19-year-old DREAMer from a small town in Washington describes the experience of learning about her status as "Nothing was the same anymore. Everything I thought I was going to be, everything I did, totally different. It was like I was living some other person's life. But it wasn't. This was me. It was my life" (Gonzales, Suárez-Orozco, & Dedios-Sanguineti, 2013, p. 1186). It is not enough to simply recognize that this happens to our students; we can be ready to be an open and nonjudgmental resource and a source of encouragement. It could take only one strong relationship with a caring adult to make a difference. Gonzales introduces us to another high school student who said about her friend and one of her teachers, "I don't know what I would have done without their help. I was scared and gave up on going to college. They had to shake me out of it, you know like 'snap out of it, okay? You're going to do it.' I really owe them for that" (Gonzales, Suárez-Orozco, & Dedios-Sanguineti, 2013, p. 1188). Beyond the personal connection between students and educators, educators can systemically create supportive school environments through developing mentoring programs, encouraging students to participate in extracurricular activities, creating safe spaces to share personal struggles and celebrate achievements, and establishing student support groups for applying to college (Gonzales, 2016).

Part of reversing the impact of undocumented status on the mental health of students is supporting them in their search for ways to have control over their lives and the decisions that come with adulthood. Most people in the United States take their mobility—the freedom to move for employment, family, and social opportunities—for granted, but undocumented students and families may have an inability to apply for jobs without a social security card, to acquire college loans and financial aid to cover tuition, and to get a driver's license.

In-state tuition rates are a critical factor in access to higher education for many undocumented students who have earned a high school diploma. As noted by Pérez (2012) in *Americans by Heart*, "The United States was founded upon the notion that achievement should trump status. These students have worked hard to overcome the hardship of poverty to become valedictorians, athletes, artists, and academic champions" (p. 152). Spinney, in Chapter 7, and Violand-Sánchez and Price, in Chapter 8, clearly describe the challenges and ways in which students can advocate for themselves and develop an extended support network. Nevertheless, it is vital for DREAMers, mentors, teachers, and counselors to stay current on policies for admission and tuition, as without federal immigration reform, these policies are determined state by state. As this book went to press, California, Minnesota, New Mexico, Oregon, Texas, and Washington allowed both in-state tuition rates and state financial aid. These are the states that value the strengths and potential contributions of our DREAMer population.

In addition, the driver's license hurdle alone is a huge problem for undocumented students and family members across all grade levels. Currently only 16 states and the District of Columbia allow people without documentation to obtain a driver's license. The inability to get a license could impede family participation in school meetings and events where they could become part of the fabric of the community rather than being seen as "visitors" or uninvolved; dynamic school communities thrive on the participation of all families. When older students cannot get a driver's license, they are less likely to participate in internships, after-school activities such as sports and theater, and college visits. They may come to view their opportunities as only what is available to them by public transportation or walking, a significant challenge outside economically vibrant urban districts.

Despite all these challenges, there are undocumented students who may show no sign of distress or fear. We can't know about the needs of our students until we have developed trusting relationships. All teachers of immigrant children can openly engage with students through casual conversation, greeting family members warmly, checking in frequently, and predicting roadblocks. While reflecting on Gladwell (2013) and her own personal immigration experience, Sandra Duval notes:

> For many immigrant youth, they compare their lives to other immigrant youth and families. Some of their struggles become the norm, so they move through it embracing pain *and* joy. They reach for their full potential or search for their rightful place. They search for a sense of belonging. Teachers can help augment the joy and make the pain less intense, diminish isolation, and help students celebrate who they are. All this as they remind students to keep forging forward. They can bring so much to the U.S. tapestry if we do not allow their immigration status to engulf their worth, dream, and potential. (personal communication, October 1, 2017)

Creative Responses Made by Allies

That which compels us to respond creatively to these and the many other challenges is what will make educator allies to undocumented students and students of mixed-status families. The dispositions that will foster that creativity are a belief in student potential, a sense of social justice for family and student rights, and a belief that teachers can partner with students and families to improve their lives. Forming our responses is best done while listening to the stories and perspectives of the students and families involved, as no two stories are exactly the same (Adichie, 2009). Duval, in Chapter 4; Bright and Kasun, in Chapter 6; Franeta and Ríos Vega, in Chapter 9; Chang, in Chapter 10; and Harden and Witt, in Chapter 12, passionately urge us to seek out and learn from the unique stories of our DREAMers and undocumented students. In so doing, we can creatively personalize our responses to their realities (Table. 13.1).We can partner with them and cheer them on.

Table 13.1. Realities and Responses

Goals	Realities	Responses	Examples
Well-rested students Adequate nutrition Healthy bodies	Frequent absences Sleepiness Irritability Frequent illnesses Frequent headaches	Recognize that if there is a need, families may not ask for help. Make resources available without judgment and without undue or multiple steps for access.	Partner with local food banks, coat drives, furniture redistribution centers, or free clinics to position them to bring their resources within reach of the community in need. Making the resources available and encouraging participation will give students and families the opportunity to self-advocate.
Students and families feel safe at school	News that demonizes immigrants/ Prevalence of myths regarding immigrants Schools that require a narrow set of documents to register students Word-of-mouth warnings about probable raids Bullying and anti-immigrant bias within the staff and among peers	Do not ask immigration status. Provide translated materials on school safety policies. Engage bilingual counselors and parent outreach. Remain judgment free. Confront bias in the school and the community.	Convene informational meetings with translators that address current issues in the community (raids, deportations). Develop legal custody plans. Develop a broad list of ways to establish residency and proof of age to register students. Hire parent/community coordinators. Develop a corps of bilingual liaisons for large school events and student liaisons to help newcomers transition.
Healthy relationships with peers and adults	Low participation in school events such as concerts, sports, meetings, advisory councils, curriculum nights Disconnect from or discomfort with adults and/or peers in the school	Build trust through predictability and consistency. Check in frequently. Provide time and space to hear student and family stories. Partner students for group projects and lunch buddies. Recognize when transportation is needed.	Offer flexible meeting schedules/home visits, transportation/carpools for school events, specific and personal invitations, translation services, welcoming/bilingual front office staff, homework clubs, and peer tutoring/mentoring. Making the resources available and encouraging participation will give students and families the opportunity to self-advocate.

Strong self-esteem Resilience Confidence Drive to achieve Respect for and from others	Frequent moves, gaps in learning for children and family members, basic level of commitment Not seeing positive cultural images and role models in the resources chosen for the classroom and mentoring programs Not knowing the contributions of immigrants to the story of the United States Marginalization of racial and economic groups within the planning process of school activities, programs, and celebrations Not discussing or providing for student realities in the classroom Silencing student stories/testimonios	Use assessment that leads to advocacy. Develop ways to document student needs and progress so that families have access to current information when registering at a new school. Enact direct-intervention plans to address learning gaps. Partner with mentors within the community and hire diverse staff/ Encourage college and high school students to mentor youth and children. Get students involved in school activities such as plays, musical groups, art projects, sports, and clubs. Learn about students' cultures beyond stereotypes, heroes, holidays, and food. Explore resources for anti-bias education through Jim Cummins, Lisa Delpit, Alma Flor Ada, Paulo Freire, Geneva Gay, Henry Giroux, Gary Howard, Sonia Nieto, Glenn Singleton, Angela Valenzuela, Joan Wink, Shelley Wong, Howard Zinn, and others.	Utilize the Dilemmas Approach (featured in Chapter 2). Create a community organization such as The Dream Project (featured in Chapter 8). Engage with community organizations such as Identity Inc. (featured in Chapters 13 and 14). Plan with the Roots and Wings Transformative Model (featured in Chapter 4).

Pedagogy and Relationships

The projects allies choose can encourage students to envision themselves in the spaces of their dreams. Our choices matter for them to envision college to become doctors, business owners, scientists, politicians, and teachers. We can plant the seed in their mind to stand strong for their dreams and find ways to seek resources for support. We can develop allies and advocates among classmates and colleagues by bringing the issues into schoolhouse conversations.

As teachers, we continuously learn about our students, their interests, and their lives with the goal of making their assignments relevant. The pedagogies we choose can incorporate dialogic practices and incorporate choice in topics to explore ways of demonstrating mastery of objectives. Duval, in Chapter 4, passionately encourages us to use counterstories to foreground student histories and complex identities. She explains the importance of continuously learning about students as individuals and as members of cultures of strength. Mitchell and Burnham, in Chapter 5, use project-based, experiential learning to teach students about the U.S. political system and engage learners in contemporary issues of political advocacy. These are dynamic strategies that not only address curricular requirements but also build positive teacher-to-student and peer-to-peer relationships—a critical aspect of identity development and nurturing self-esteem.

As teachers, we have the opportunity to plan dynamic and transformative academic experiences with and for our students by carefully planning for critical topics, language forms, and language functions (see Table 13.2). These academic experiences can be specifically designed to engage all students in learning about issues of social justice, particularly immigration issues and the DREAM movement. The realities of living in the United States as undocumented students will be understood by a broader audience, undocumented students will be affirmed, and peers will become allies of their neighbors and friends.

In order to achieve this transformative goal, teachers would consider what is required of them in the curriculum and enhance it with critical topics. A student of Mexican heritage might learn how the geographic changes of the southern border caused family members who once lived in Mexico to now live in America. In this example, the critical topic is U.S. expansion; the language form could be to write a research paper on how U.S. expansion affected populations living near the southern border, the population of native peoples, and those who were supported by the U.S. government to move west and claim land. And the language function could be to analyze using first-person narratives of the people affected. Another example would be to explore the critical topic of immigration. The language form could have students develop role-plays for presentation in class. In this example the language function could be to synthesize information learned by researching groups of immigrants (Chinese), histories (migration to work on U.S. railroad construction), first-person narratives (letters home requesting marriage arrangements), and U.S. policy of the relevant period of history (Chinese Exclusion Act of

1882). Think of the stories that would be lost if immigration was taught from only a Eurocentric Ellis Island perspective.

Elementary school students are taught to make self-to-text connections with what they read. However, younger undocumented children do not always see their heritage reflected in what is taught. During a unit on the civil rights era many Latino/a students and Asian students might wonder how they fit into American history. During segregation, what school would they attend? Where on the bus would they have to sit? To find the answers to these questions, educators have to look beyond the textbook. The website Colorín Colorado (www.colorincolorado.org) has a book list to help teachers find resources. The critical topic is the history of the civil rights movement in the United States. The language form could be developing a role-play with the language function of explaining the effect of the changes in law on different populations. Colorín Colorado highlights the book *Separate Is Never Equal*, by Duncan Tonatiuh (2014), which tells the story of Sylvia Mendez's family's court case—a case that led to the desegregation of California schools and set the precedent for *Brown v. Board of Education*.

During a unit on families, the critical topic, children might create a class museum of artifacts important to their family. The language form could be an interview of family members to write about the significance of their artifact. As children explain why they chose an artifact, the function of the language, educators and peers could see beyond the surface level of the student's culture. In Takoma Park, Maryland, immigrant students worked with a local artist to create mosaic tiles about artifacts from their home country. Their artwork now hangs above the inner door of their neighborhood's community center. Their ESOL teacher Rachna Rikhye turned the experience into a book, *The Mosaic Community* (Rikhye, Stepp, Livio, & DiCurcio, 2012), that featured not only the artifacts students chose but also their hopes and dreams for their new community.

Hope is a major factor in student success. The research done by Identity, Inc., of Montgomery County, Maryland, notes that "there is a phenomenon known as the 'toxic mirror' that greatly influences how immigrant children see themselves. These immigrant children confront discrimination and stereotyping in many areas of their lives. This may be one factor contributing to young people not feeling good or positive about their futures" (The Community Foundation & Identity, Inc., 2014). Teachers can address this in part by inviting college students to speak to their class, work with their after-school programs, and partner with students on community projects. The transformative curricular choices and pedagogies we use in the classroom and the relationships we build will make a difference in processing the public messages faced by our students, as exemplified by Tinker Sachs and Austin in Chapter 11.

Fostering a sense of hope for the future is a significant contribution that teachers can make. This can be done through writing, as writing provides immigrant children an opportunity to take pride in their communities and their dreams and share their pride with others. In *Authors in the Classroom*, children's book authors Alma

Flor Ada and F. Isabel Campoy (2004) note that "writing and publishing books in the classroom can be a helpful tool for honoring the communities to which the children belong, for portraying the life experience of children's families, and for recognizing the accumulated wisdom of parents and relatives" (p. 33). This sense of pride was clear in Dario's description of his family and his dream of being an engineer.

Becoming Politically Active

In addition to helping students find themselves within the curricula, there are ways to speak out and speak up with our students. The recent rhetoric about immigration has led to confusion about what teachers can do to support the needs of their students. Many teachers have been advised not to discuss immigration status. In fact, as we are reminded in the Dear Colleague Letter sent on May 8, 2014, by the U.S. Department of Education and Department of Justice, it is illegal for schools to request a student's immigration status (Department of Education & Department

Table 13.2. Topic, Form, and Function: Lessons for Developing Allies and Advocates in the Classroom

Critical Topic	
Family Varieties	Racism, Civil Rights Movement
Friendship, Interpersonal Relationships	Current Events
Academic Success, Effort and Persistence	Critical Language Analysis
History, Recognizing Marginalized Groups	College Application Process
Political Process	Wellness
Rights and Responsibilities, Civil Engagement	

Language Form	
Poetry	Public Service Announcement
Art	Role-Play
Research	Essay
Friendly Letter	Article
Music	

Language Function	
Critique	Synthesize
Compare and Contrast	Problem and Solution
Analyze	Inform
Describe	Infer
Explain	Persuade
Request	Cause and Effect

of Justice, 2014). The Family Educational Rights and Privacy Act (FERPA) restricts student files to intentional educational use only except in the case of a health or safety threat. We might feel that we cannot have true knowledge of the challenges being faced by our young and vulnerable students.

Contrast an "I can't ask" approach (ignore the issues) with an approach that involves opening our eyes to the endless possibilities for problem solving (no situation is hopeless). Can a teacher face negative consequences for openly supporting undocumented children and youth? The public vitriol may influence teachers more than the law; however, the recommendation is clear. When engaging in the issues teachers have an at-work responsibility that has workplace restrictions based on the culture of the school and local expectations. However, the First Amendment rights of freedom of speech and assembly are not forfeited simply by one's choosing to be an educator. William Moreno of the National Education Association notes that we have political power and the right to use it (personal communication, April 6, 2016). In 2007, teachers in Tulsa, Oklahoma, scrambled to assure families, who fearfully kept their children away from schools in response to rumors about raids, that there would be no immigration enforcement action on the school playgrounds. It is a workplace responsibility to make sure students are in school. Former National Education Association general counsel Michael D. Simpson stated that teachers cannot be conscripted into the ranks of the Immigration and Customs Enforcement (ICE) police and forced to verify the documented status of students who seek to enroll in school, as stated in one of the rulings resulting from California Proposition 187 in 1994 (Walker, n.d.).

Outside the school building or formal functions of the school, educators can use their freedom of speech to write articles in support of immigration reform that includes pathways to legal status, petition legislators, hold informational house parties, present at conferences, and more. In 2012, the state of Maryland passed a version of the DREAM Act with the support of individual teachers and the union (Foerster Luu, 2013). Learn your rights and responsibilities as outlined in the National Education Association's (2015) publication *ALL IN! How Educators Can Advocate for English Language Learners* and develop an advocacy day where you open the conversation to more colleagues who are looking for advice and camaraderie within the local context. Learn more about your local, state, and federal laws so that you can extend those conversations to lawmakers, policymakers, and school board members.

Educators can follow grassroots organizations like United We Dream in order to stay current and find ways to get involved outside of school such as their National Educators Coming Out Day in the fall and National Institutions Coming Out Day in the spring—days designed with educators in mind, to publicly support undocumented students. They publish a toolkit to guide educators through the process of becoming allies (Richards & Bohorquez, 2015). Educators can partner with organizations like the Dream Project, profiled by Violand-Sánchez and Price in Chapter 8, and IDEAS (Improving Dreams, Equality, Access, and Success) at the University of California, Los Angeles. In addition to this, there are supportive voices and political action opportunities in organizations such as TESOL (Teachers of English to Speakers of Other Languages), with their policy briefs and position statements (TESOL, 2011; Cutler, 2017) and annual advocacy summit.

The possibilities are endless when you open your mind to the clues, address the dilemmas that you note, and respond within the curricula and beyond. The responsibility is for educators to do everything we can to make these students strong enough, confident enough, and defiant enough to fight for immigration law changes in the future. We cannot solve the problem alone, but we can be part of the solution with the choices we make in our pedagogy (encouragement, relationships, believing in our students, judgment-free decisionmaking), our use of community resources, and our political action. Chapter 14 is a great place to begin looking for resources. We can do this for and with Danna, Dario, Hareth, and Natalia. There is hope, as eloquently shared by Sandra Duval in this stanza of one of her poems:

> Out of my desire to hear the echo of my voice in America
> and see my footprints in its landscape,
> my songs extol the cherished memories of there
> while my feet respond to the fluid rhythms of here.
> And in between a new configuration emerges
> which is neither Here nor There.
> This novel form was born of my struggle
> to unearth who I was there and to assert who I am here.
> The delicate co-mingling of these two worlds,
> each richer because of the other
> has produced a new place for me.
> This world that is in-between that I inhabit
> has transformed me.
> I do not just remember the past or ponder the future.
> My vision is a horizon without demarcations
> that transcends what I have known and what I know now.
>
> —Sandra Duval

References

Adichie, C. N. (2009, October 7). *The danger of a single story.* Retrieved from www.ted.com/talks/chimamanda_adichie_the_danger_of_a_single_story

The Community Foundation for the National Capital Region, & Identity, Inc. (2014). *Connecting youth to opportunity: How Latino youth perspectives can inform a blueprint for improving opportunity in Montgomery County, Maryland.* Retrieved from identity-youth.org/wp-content/uploads/2016/06/hs-cyo-latinoyouth_report_pdf-final.pdf

Cutler, D. (2017, September 6). TESOL denounces decision to end DACA, calls on U.S. Congress to act. Retrieved from tesol.org/news-landing-page/2017/09/06/tesol-denounces-decision-to-end-daca-calls-on-u.s.-congress-to-act

Flor Ada, A. & Campoy, F. I. (2004). *Authors in the classroom: A transformative education process*. Boston, MA: Pearson.

Foerster Luu, A. (2013, February 13). In the pursuit of happiness, Maryland voters said it matters [Blog post]. Retrieved June 30, 2017, from blog.tesol.org /in-the-pursuit-of-happiness-maryland-voters-said-it-matters/

Getzels P., & López E. (Directors). (2012). *Harvest of empire: A history of Latinos in America*. Thompson-Marquez, W.; López, E.; Getzels, P.; Goron Getzels, H.; & Orr, J. (Producers). United States: Onyx Films.

Gladwell, M. (2013). *David and Goliath: Underdogs, misfits and the art of battling giants*. London, England: Penguin.

Gonzales, R. G. (2016). *Lives in limbo: Undocumented and coming of age in America*. Oakland, CA: University of California Press.

Gonzales, R. G., Suárez-Orozco, C., & Dedios-Sanguineti, M. C. (2013). No place to belong. *American Behavioral Scientist, 57*(8), 1174–1199. doi:10.1177/0002764213487349

Igoa, C. (1995). *The inner world of the immigrant child*. New York, NY: Routledge.

Mow, J., & Pacheco L. (Directors). (2015, December 28). *East of Salinas*. In Sally Jo Fifer & Sandie Viquez Pedlow (Executive Producers), *Independent Lens*. San Francisco, CA: Rock Salt Creative, LLC and Independent Television Service in association with Latino Public Broadcasting.

National Education Association. (2015, March). *ALL IN! How educators can advocate for English language learners*. Retrieved from www.colorincolorado.org/sites/default/files /ELL_AdvocacyGuide2015.pdf

Pérez, W. (2012). *Americans by heart: Undocumented Latino students and the promise of higher education*. New York, NY: Teachers College Press.

Plyler v. Doe, 457 U.S. 202 (1982). Retrieved from supreme.justia.com/cases/federal/us/457 /202/case.html

Richards, J., & Bohorquez, L. M. (2015). *National institutions coming out day: Institutional policies and programs with and for undocumented students toolkit*. United We Dream. Retrieved from unitedwedream.org/wp-content/uploads/2015/01/UWDN _InstitutionalToolKit_final-1.pdf

Rikhye, R. (2012). *The mosaic community*. Silver Spring, MD: Diversity International.

TESOL. (2011, December 20). Statement on the re-introduction of the DREAM Act in the US Congress (May 2011). Retrieved from www.tesol.org/news-landing -page/2011/12/20/tesol-statement-on-the-re-introduction-of-the-dream-act-in-the -us-congress-(may-2011)

Tonatiuh, D. (2014). *Separate is never equal: Sylvia Mendez and her family's fight for desegregation*. New York, NY: Abrams Books for Young Readers.

U.S. Department of Education. (2015, October 20). *Resource guide: Supporting undocumented youth*. Retrieved from 2.ed.gov/about/overview/focus/supporting -undocumented-youth.pdf

U.S. Department of Education, & U.S. Department of Justice. (2014, May 8). *Dear colleague letter: School enrollment procedures*. Retrieved from justice.gov/sites/default/files /crt/legacy/2014/05/08/plylerletter.pdf

Walker, T. (n.d.). *Caught in the crossfire*. Retrieved from nea.org/home/7855.htm

Resources for Allies, Activists, and Advocates for Immigrant Children and Their Families

Elaisa Sánchez Gosnell, Janna Mattson,
Doug Hernandez, and Maryam Saroughi

This chapter lists resources to support advocates and allies who are seeking social and educational justice for undocumented immigrant children and their families. Recommended community and national organizations, scholarly academic books, first-person narrative works, and scholarly journal articles offer an examination of the DREAM Act and aspects of immigration from various perspectives, including educational, social-emotional, and legal perspectives. The top national and local DREAM organizations are representative of the types of groups that are making a difference in the lives of undocumented immigrants (see Table 14.1). The web pages in this chapter should be checked on a regular basis, as many of them update and add new information.

Although these resources will help you advocate for social justice and equity in a highly charged political environment, please keep in mind that there are many more resources available that are specific to your communities.

The following questions will guide you as you become an ally and advocate for and with your students.

1. What are the focus and rationale of the book, article, study, report, or fact sheet?
2. How does this information help me to address the needs of the immigrant children and families I work with?
3. How can I adapt the essence of these materials into useful guidelines for my situation?
4. What steps do I need to take to implement these recommendations at my site? Will creating a team help to carry them out?
5. How can I share this information with others in similar situations?

Table 14.1. Top National and Local DREAM Organizations

Name	Type	Location
Top National Dream Organizations		
United We Dream (UWD)	Activism, Young People, Deportation Support	DC, TX, NY
Mexican American Legal Defense and Educational Fund (MALDEF)	Policy, Attorney Support	DC, CA
UCLA Labor Center	Leadership Building, Community Support	CA
National Immigration Law Center (NILC)	Policy, Research	DC, CA
FWD.US (Facebook)	Social Media, College Outreach	DC, CA
Generation Progress	Research, Organizing	DC
UnidosUS (formerly NCLR)	Research, Policy	DC
UndocuMedia	Social Media, Community Outreach	CA
Top Local DREAM Organizations		
Dream Act Coalition	Community Organizing, Communications	AZ
Virginia Organizing	VA Policy, Community	VA
Make the Road NY	Community, Activism	NY
CT Students for a Dream	Activism	CT
New Mexico Dream Team	Activism	NM

DREAMer and Immigrant Youth Organizations

10,000 Degrees (www.10000degrees.org/)

10,000 Degrees is a California-based organization providing a list of private scholarships for undocumented students, including both national and California-based scholarships.

Callahan, R. (2013). *Coming of political age: American schools and the civic development of immigrant youth.* New York: Russell Sage Foundation.

This book outlines the importance of immigrant youth involvement in the political process through empirical data. The author proposes that the educational system and course offerings specific to civics and political mechanisms are the linchpin of shaping political engagement.

Dominguez, N, Duarte, Y., Espinosa, P., Martinez, L., Nygreen, K., Perez, R., Ramirez, I., & Saba, M. (2009). Constructing a counternarrative: Students Informing Now (S.I.N.) reframes immigration and education in the United States. *Journal of Adolescent and Adult Literacy, 52*(5), 439–442.

> Written by students at the University of California, Santa Cruz, this journal article challenges the reader to reframe traditional thinking of undocumented immigrants, changing the view of them from objects of pity to contributing and valuable members of American society and members of the human race—not illegal aliens.

Dream Project (www.dreamproject-va.org)

> The Dream Project is an organization in Arlington, Virginia, that provides mentoring, scholarships, and internships to undocumented students in the area. (See Chapter 8.)

Educators for Fair Consideration (E4FC) (www.e4fc.org)

> Educators for Fair Consideration is an organization dedicated to empowering undocumented students to pursue college, a career, and citizenship in the United States. It also provides lists of scholarships and fellowships and other guidance directly to undocumented students—at both the undergraduate and the graduate level.

Latin American Coalition (La Coalición) (www.latinamericancoalition.org)

> The Latin American Coalition is a community that promotes full and equal participation of all people in the civic, economic, and cultural life of North Carolina through education, celebration, and advocacy.

Golden Door Scholars (www.goldendoorscholars.org)

> Golden Door Scholars is a nonprofit dedicated to increasing educational opportunity for undocumented students. The organization provides undocumented students with both scholarships and internship opportunities along with tips related to the college application process.

Nicholls, W. (2013). *The DREAMers: How the undocumented youth movement transformed the immigrant rights debate.* Stanford, CA: Stanford University Press.

> This investigative book begins with two historical chapters: one on the United States political landscape before the DREAM Act was first introduced and another a history of how the DREAM Act movement began. The remaining chapters outline the mobilization of movement through various grassroots organizations, interviews of DREAMers and activists, and social media.

Community and Religious Organizations

Catholic Charities USA (catholiccharitiesusa.org)

> Catholic Charities is the second-largest provider of social services in the United States, behind only the federal government, serving more than 10 million people per year regardless of their religious, social, or economic backgrounds. It provides medical, dental, educational, vocational, and legal services for low-income immigrants and refugees.

Identity, Inc. (identity-youth.org)

This organization is working with youth and families in Montgomery County, Maryland. It is a strong example of how persistent dedication to understanding the needs of youth and families can lead to program and policy development to foster stronger communities and student success.

League of United Latin American Citizens (LULAC) (www.lulac.org)

LULAC is the oldest Hispanic civil rights organization in the United States. Since 1929 it has fought to obtain full access for Hispanic Americans to the U.S. political process and to improve economic, educational, health, and housing conditions for Latinos by advocating for their civil rights. It provides current research on issues important to the Hispanic community to inform advocates. They include information on the economic benefits of comprehensive immigration reform.

Make the Road New York (www.maketheroadny.org)

This organization is embedded in the community and highly visible to passersby. They want to be seen as they work to build the power of Latino and working-class communities. They are focused on social justice through organizing, policy, transformative education, and more. They are a great model of a community organization with extensive services for immigrants.

Mexican American Legal Defense and Educational Fund (MALDEF) (www.maldef.org)

MALDEF is a national nonprofit legal organization that employs litigation, policy, advocacy, and community education programs to protect and promote the civil rights of the Latino community. MALDEF works with parents, community members, activists, educators, and school authorities to promote social change that brings Latinos into the mainstream of American political and socioeconomic life. The website includes many resources with up-to-date information on issues affecting Hispanics and the immigrant community.

United We Dream (unitedwedream.org)

United We Dream is the largest immigrant youth–led organization in the nation. This organization is made up of over 100,000 immigrant youth and allies and 55 affiliate organizations in 26 states. The purpose of United We Dream is to organize and advocate on behalf of immigrant youth and families, regardless of immigration status. It has resources to support undocumented youth pursuing higher education.

Education and Curricular Resources

Association for Library Service to Children (dia.ala.org)

This website is a division of the American Library Association's Diversity in Action. It showcases an extensive list of books for teaching about cultural diversity and the immigrant experience.

Bigelow, B. (2006). *The line between us: Teaching about the border and Mexican immigration*. Milwaukee, WI: Rethinking Schools.

This book is a compelling exploration of the history between the United States and Mexico and how the global economy has influenced immigration, communities, and personhood. The author offers teachers and students a deeper understanding of the many lines between countries and within countries and those that separate the rich and the poor. Ultimately, this book offers teachers creative tools, a sizable list of classroom-appropriate films, and powerful classroom activities that give students opportunities to engage in discussions about inequality.

Children of Immigrant Families [Special issue]. (2004). *The Future of Children, 14*(2). (jstor.org/stable/i273916)

This journal issue addresses a broad range of topics related to the life circumstance of immigrant families and their children, from birth to adolescence. The articles provide analyses of the strengths and challenges facing children growing up in immigrant families, and information on the types of resources and supports they need today to become engaged citizens of tomorrow.

Cull, N. J., & Carrasco, D. (2004). *Alambrista and the U.S.-Mexico border: Film, music, and stories of undocumented immigrants.* Albuquerque, NM: University of New Mexico Press.

This book tells the story of creating the acclaimed 1977 film *Alambrista*. It is an example of the challenges and the joys faced by a young Mexican as he crosses the border to find employment to support his family back home.

First Book (www.firstbook.org)

First Book is an organization where allies can obtain free books for their school or community program serving children from low-income families. It also provides high-quality books on college preparation; healthy eating and exercise; antibullying; science, technology, engineering, and math (STEM); diversity; and many other topics, as well as bilingual titles and resources. First Book partners with Latino Education and Advocacy Days (LEAD) to add a Latino Interest Titles category. This section includes books written in Spanish, bilingual (dual-language) titles, books that feature Latino characters, and books by Latino authors and illustrators that reflect Hispanic culture and heritage. Anyone who works at a Title I school or in a community program that serves at least 70% children from low-income families is eligible to participate in the First Book program.

Immersion (www.immersionfilm.com)

This 2009 video from Media That Matters focuses on an elementary student who has strong mathematics skills, but is a beginning English language learner. The film depicts a family that supports their child with their best resources and a teacher who struggles to understand his needs.

Immigrant children [Special issue]. (2011). *The Future of Children, 21*(1). (www.futureofchildren.org/resource-links/children-immigrant-families)

This journal issue includes background information on immigrant children and families as well as special articles focusing on early care and education, K–12 educational outcomes, and access to higher education for children of immigrants.

Kugler, E. G. (Ed.). (2012). *Innovative voices in education: Engaging diverse communities.* Lanham, MD: Rowman & Littlefield.

This book provides narratives from teachers, administrators, and community leaders who offer unique perspectives on fostering the engagement of diverse populations.

The authors discuss the intersectionality of issues faced by marginalized students, who are often segregated and disenfranchised.

Olsen, L. (2008). *Made in America: Immigrant students in our public schools.* New York, NY: New Press.

This book is the outcome of Laurie Olsen's 2 years of research in a southern California high school in the early 1990s. Using this high school as a societal microcosm, Olsen explores the challenges of being an immigrant in the United States through class, race, and racial relations. Olsen points out the problems with how immigrant children are educated in the United States and offers solutions to the barriers these children experience.

Patel, L. (2013). *Youth held at the border: Immigration, education, and the politics of inclusion.* New York, NY: Teachers College Press.

Patel uses the voices of seven immigrant students at Franklin High School in Boston. The first seven chapters include student narratives and author analyses of their education and how their outside responsibilities, documentation status, and socioeconomic factors have shaped it. The last four chapters are broader examinations of these issues.

Pérez, W. (2012). *Americans by heart: Undocumented Latino students and the promise of higher education.* New York, NY: Teachers College Press.

Pérez begins the book with a discussion of the historical, educational, and legal challenges faced by undocumented students. He also uses statistics and personal interviews to disprove the common perception that students who are undocumented are criminals, showing that they are, in fact, rather engaged both in civics and academics. Pérez discusses the central role community colleges play in putting a student who is undocumented on the path to higher education and the additional challenges students face post-college. He concludes with a proposal of new educational and immigration policy framework.

Rethinking Schools (rethinkingschools.org)

Rethinking Schools is a magazine with a consistent social justice voice advocating for immigrant rights and the relationship to education. Teachers can find countless articles and issues dedicated to these topics.

Saavedra, C. M. (2011). Language and literacy in the Borderlands: Acting upon the world through *testimonios. Language Arts, 88*(4), 261–269.

This article is a testimonio about a Nicaraguan refugee fleeing civil war in the 1980s. It suggests curricular connections for the classroom.

Staehr Fenner, D. (2014). *Advocating for English learners: A guide for educators.* Thousand Oaks, CA: SAGE.

This book helps educators position themselves as allies of and advocates for pre-K–16 English learners and immigrant children and families and includes information on career training. It is a great complementary resource to the dilemmas process discussed in this book.

Suárez-Orozco, C. (2008). *Learning a new land: Immigrant students in American society* (1st ed.). Cambridge, MA: Belknap Press of Harvard University Press.

With the goal of studying the immigration experience from a developmental perspective, the author conducted a 5-year study of 407 Boston-area immigrant students between the ages of 9 and 14 from Mexico, Central America, China, Haiti, and the Dominican Republic. Both qualitative and quantitative research methods are used as chapter focuses include academic performance and engagement, relationships, learning English, and portraits of varying levels of student achievement.

Swope, S. (2004). *I am a pencil: A teacher, his kids, and their world of stories*. New York, NY: H. Holt.

Sam Swope, an author of children's books initially hired by the Teachers & Writers Collaborative to teach a 10-day writing workshop to a 3rd-grade class in Queens, New York, has chronicled his 3 years with these students, who all either are immigrants or have parents who are immigrants. Organized chronologically by grade and by projects he worked on with the students, this narrative provides honest reflections on his triumphs and struggles as a teacher working with a diverse group of students.

Teaching Tolerance: Immigration (www.tolerance.org)

Teaching Tolerance is a project of the Southern Poverty Law Center. It provides teachers with free resources to help reduce prejudice, improve intergroup relations, and support equitable school experience for school-age children. Classroom lessons designed to develop sensitivity to immigration and undocumented families and to explore common myths about immigrants are available for grades K–12.

The College Board (professionals.collegeboard.com/guidance/financial-aid/undocumented -students)

Accurately advising undocumented students is a critical aspect of working with undocumented students. The College Board provides information about higher education policies related to undocumented high school graduates.

Immigrant History and Narratives of Undocumented People

Chang, I. (2004). *The Chinese in America: A narrative history*. New York, NY: Penguin.

Iris Chang's *The Chinese in America* offers an easy-to-read narrative of what Chang describes as two stories: The first explains why at certain times over the course of history the Chinese decided to emigrate to the United States and the second explores the challenges they experienced upon arrival. Chang strives to break down Chinese stereotypes and misconceptions about Chinese contributions to American society.

Hutchinson, G. (2009). LIMBO: Marie Gonzalez & the DREAM Act. *Reflections: A Journal of Writing, Service-Learning and Community Service, 8*(2), 62–93.

This journal article embodies the power of art and narrative to connect people and give voice to those whose stories are untold. Dr. Glenn Hutchinson outlines his playwriting effort in "LIMBO: Marie Gonzalez & the DREAM Act," based on interviews with an undocumented student, Marie Gonzalez.

Immigrant Learning Center, Inc. (2012). *Immigrant struggles, immigrant gifts.* (D. Portnoy, B. M. Portnoy, C. E. Riggs, & W. A. Cornelius, Eds.). Fairfax, VA: GMU Press.

A project of The Immigrant Learning Center, this book contains chapters written by anthropologists, historians, and sociologists on the history of various immigrant groups in the United States and the development of and obstacles to their achievements and contributions. It dispels myths about Mexican immigrants, both documented and undocumented. Other immigrant groups in this book include Black West Indian Americans, Chinese Americans, and Muslim Americans.

Igoa, C. (2009). *The inner world of the immigrant child.* New York, NY: Routledge.

This book presents a teacher's effort to understand and reveal the inner world of immigrant children. Hearts and minds of children are revealed through powerful, personal stories, which offer a qualitative and ethnographic report of their hopes, dreams, and fears. The author gives readers classroom practices that facilitate belonging and self-empowerment and support immigrant children through often traumatic and unknown transitions.

Madera, G. (2008). *Underground undergrads: UCLA undocumented immigrant students speak out.* Los Angeles, CA: UCLA Center for Labor Research and Education. (books. labor.ucla.edu/p/55/undergroundundergrads)

This work highlights the struggles of potential DREAMers. It provides first-person accounts of young adults who passionately want to continue their educational experiences, but who face obstacles because of their immigration status.

Nazario, S. (2007). *Enrique's journey.* New York, NY: Random House.

Inspired by her housekeeper, a Guatemalan woman who was separated from her children for 12 years, Nazario retraces the journey of Enrique, who travels by train top from Tegucigalpa, Honduras, to Nuevo Laredo, Mexico, in order to find his mother in the United States. Nazario faces dangerous and brutal conditions that are, as she describes, only an "iota" of what these children, as young as 7 years old, face in search of their parents.

Orner, P. (Ed.). (2008). *Underground America: Narratives of undocumented lives.* San Francisco, CA: McSweeneys Books.

Containing first-person narratives of 24 undocumented immigrants living in the United States, this book is part of Dave Eggers and Lola Vollen's Voice of Witness project (voiceofwitness.org/), whose mission is to use oral history to bring human rights issues to national attention.

Pérez, W. (2009). *We are Americans: Undocumented students pursuing the American dream.* Sterling, VA: Stylus.

Pérez's work includes personal narratives of undocumented students along with the author's own observations and informal interview of their teachers and peers. Special features of this book are the author's introduction, which includes an in-depth look at the myths surrounding undocumented persons and a history of the DREAM Act as well as a reading group guide.

Valdés, G. (2005). *Con respeto: Bridging the distances between culturally diverse families and schools: An ethnographic portrait.* New York, NY: Teachers College Press.

> This book can help educators understand the challenges faced by immigrant families as they prepare their children for success, the values they teach, and the resilience they engender.

Welcome to USA.gov (www.welcometousa.gov/)

> This website is dedicated to providing immigrants and the organizations that serve them with basic settlement information, increasing awareness of federal government resources available to immigrants, and supporting the needs of receiving communities and immigrant-serving organizations.

Wong, K., Shadduck-Hernandez, J., Inzunza, F., Monroe, J., Narro, V., & Valenzuela, A. (Eds.). (2012). *Undocumented and unafraid: Tam Tran, Cinthya Felix, and the immigrant youth movement.* Los Angeles, CA: UCLA Center for Labor Research and Education.

> This book is a tribute to two DREAM student activists, Tam Tran and Cinthya Felix, who died tragically, in a car accident. The first part of the book contains student and faculty narratives reflecting on Tran and Felix's advocacy work. The second part includes student and faculty essays on the immigrant youth movement from different perspectives, including those of gay and lesbian youth, and different countries such as Iran, Mexico, and the Philippines.

Legal Information, Policy Analysis, and Immigrant Rights Organizations

American Immigration Council (AIC) (www.americanimmigrationcouncil.org)

> The Council's goal is to help shape a 21st-century vision of American immigration through research and policy advocacy, legal education and litigation, educational outreach, and international exchange. Its Education Center sponsors an annual Celebrate America creative writing contest for 5th-grade students to explore the effects of immigration on their lives, other projects for various grade levels, and mini-grants for educators. The AIC publishes the *Educators' Immigration Resource Guide*, which offers K–12 lesson plans, book and film reviews, and other resources that value the contributions of immigrants. The website includes current state-by-state information on the economic and political power of immigrants.

AYUDA (ayuda.com)

> AYUDA advocates for low-income immigrants through direct legal, social, and language services; training; and outreach in the Washington, DC, metropolitan area. They work to address the illegal efforts of individuals misrepresenting themselves as licensed attorneys who offer legal services to immigrants. In partnership with Georgetown University Law Center's Community Justice Project, AYUDA published a report titled *To Protect and Serve: Accessing Justice for Victims of Notario Fraud in the Nation's Capital.* There is also a manual, *Notario Fraud Remedies: A Practical Manual for Immigration Practitioners.*

Brickman, J. (2006). Educating undocumented children in the United States: Codification of *Plyler v. Doe* through federal legislation. *Georgetown Immigration Law Journal, 20*(337), 385–405.

The author proposes that because of repeated attempts by Congress to overturn *Plyler v. Doe* (1982), it should be codified by federal legislation, as the benefits outweigh the cost of educating children who are undocumented. He further argues that public schools should request federal reimbursement for their education. This article also includes an extensive history of the case.

Chomsky, A. (2014). *Undocumented: How immigration became illegal.* Boston, MA: Beacon Press.

This book explores the history of U.S. immigration policies and how policies are created to exclude and exploit groups of people, especially immigrants from Mexico and Central America.

Chomsky, A. (2007). *They take our jobs! And 20 other myths about immigration.* Boston, MA: Beacon Press.

This book dismantles 20 common myths about education, including "Immigrants take American jobs," "Immigrants don't pay taxes," and "The rules apply to everyone, so new immigrants need to follow them just as immigrants in the past did." Chomsky describes how race, ethnicity, and gender are used to marginalize immigrants.

Chuang, S., & Moreno, R. (Eds.). (2011). *Immigrant children: Change, adaptation, and cultural transformation.* Lanham, MD: Lexington Books.

This book offers a discussion of the increasing immigrant populations of Canada and the United States. The book will inform teachers and policymakers of the unique characteristics and challenges facing immigrant children and their families.

Golash-Boza, T. M. (2012). *Immigration nation: Raids, detentions, and deportations in post-9/11 America.* Boulder, CO: Paradigm.

This book provides a critical analysis of the role of the "immigration industrial complex," the Department of Homeland Security, and U.S. immigration policies from the perspective of their effect on family separations and the denial of human rights to mixed-status immigrant families in the wake of 9/11.

Kids in Need of Defense (KIND) (www.supportkind.org/en/)

KIND provides quality and compassionate legal counsel to unaccompanied refugee and immigrant children in the United States. To this end it created a pro bono movement of law firms, corporations, nongovernmental organizations (NGOs), universities, and volunteers to ensure that no such child appears in immigration court without representation. Its pro bono attorneys provide mentorship until a case is completed. KIND also works to change law, policy, and practice to improve the treatment and protection of unaccompanied children in the United States by advocating before Congress and the federal government and through public outreach and trainings, including Know Your Rights presentations.

Kohli, A. (2008). Educating undocumented students: The legacy of *Plyler v. Doe. Northwestern Journal of Law and Social Policy, 3*(2), 185.

This article provides sociological and demographic information in order to support better-informed decisions for students who are immigrants. Kohli provides facts to dispel myths about undocumented students. He outlines the contributions of undocumented workers to the economy.

Migration Policy Institute (MPI) (www.migrationpolicy.org)

MPI is dedicated to the analysis of migration and immigration worldwide. It provides U.S. immigration reform resources with up-to-date information on the debate under way in Washington, DC, including updates about DACA. Its ELL Information Center addresses the growth of pre-K–12 English language learners across the United States; how they are faring in schools; and the policies affecting them through demographic maps, fact sheets, and state-level data resources.

My Undocumented Life (mydocumentedlife.org/tag/lgbtq/)

This blog is written by an immigrant who successfully navigated the educational system as an undocumented student. The resources here are extensive and inclusive of LGBTQ immigrants in double exile.

National Immigration Law Center (www.nilc.org)

This resource covers current immigration policies and litigation. It engages in court cases to ensure that due process rights of immigrants are protected.

The Pew Research Center's Hispanic Trends Project (www.pewhispanic.org)

The Pew Research Center launched the Hispanic Trends Project in 2001 to improve understanding of the Hispanic population's diversity and to chronicle Latinos' growing impact on the United States. It publishes demographic studies and research on Latino identity, education and immigration trends among other Latino social matters, and materials that can be used by educators and activists wishing to inform colleagues, administrators, community organizations and legislators.

The Southern Poverty Law Center (SPLC) (www.splcenter.org)

The Southern Poverty Law Center is dedicated to fighting hate and bigotry and seeking justice for the most vulnerable members of our society. It is internationally known for tracking and exposing the activities of hate groups. It works to achieve the ideals of equal justice and equal opportunity through litigation, education, and other forms of advocacy. Through its Teaching Tolerance project, it provides free resources that teach school children to reject hate, embrace diversity, and respect differences. Its Immigrant Justice page (www.splcenter.org/what-we-do/immigrant-justice) provides up-to-date information on events affecting undocumented children and their families.

UnidosUS (www.unidosus.org)

Formerly the National Council of La Raza (NCLR), UnidosUS conducts applied research, policy analysis, and advocacy to increase policymaker and public understanding of Hispanic needs and to encourage the adoption of programs and policies that equitably serve Hispanics. They publish facts on issues affecting minority, limited-English-proficient, and low-income Hispanics from infancy through adulthood. The website has an education link with information and materials on early childhood, K–12, and higher education. Their report *Buenos Principios: Latino Children in the Earliest Years of Life* addresses health care and education concerns for Latino infants and toddlers (publications.unidosus.org/bitstream/handle/123456789/1212/Buenos_Principios.pdf).

Urban Institute (www.urban.org)

The Urban Institute engages in open-minded, evidence-based research to diagnose social, economic, and governance problems facing the United States. They include resources on immigrant children and their families. Of special interest is a paper by Golden and Fortuny titled *Young Children of Immigrants and the Path to Educational Success* and *Five Questions for Ajay Chaudry on Children of Immigrants.*

Professional Organizations, Unions, and Professional Development

American Federation of Teachers (AFT): Immigration Resources (www.aft.org/our-community/immigration)

The AFT is a union that provides educators with resources in English and Spanish about protecting students. Topics covered include immigrant rights, immigration raid, dos and don'ts if ICE comes to your house, and steps for families to create an emergency plan.

Colorín Colorado! (www.colorincolorado.org)

This bilingual (Spanish and English) website has extensive resources for educators and families. It has book lists for crossing-the-border and immigration stories where teachers and teacher educators can find materials appropriate for their students. It also has extensive links to helpful videos, articles, and professionals in advocacy.

National Education Association (NEA): Immigration (www.nea.org/home/immigration.html)

The National Education Association is a union that provides educators with resources, including a "DREAMers Welcome" poster featuring butterfly artwork and information about what educators can do when communities are threatened by immigration raids. The collective voice of union members was able to stop the deportation of a North Carolina student.

TESOL Advocacy and Policy Summit (www.tesol.org/advance-the-field/advocacy-resources/tesol-advocacy-policy-summit)

Educators from across the United States gather to learn about the latest federal education policies and how to advocate for English language learners at the federal level. On the last day of the summit participants meet with their state's representatives and senators to advocate for their students.

Social, Emotional, and Physical Well-Being

American Psychological Association, Presidential Task Force on Immigration. (2012). *Crossroads: The psychology of immigration in the new century.* (apa.org/topics/immigration/report.aspx)

This document explains the traumatic experience encountered by undocumented youth, including racial profiling, ongoing discrimination, immigration raids, random checks of family member's immigration status, separation from deported family members, and placement in detention camps. It concludes with the importance of forming trusting relationships between undocumented youth and caring teachers.

Brion-Meisels, L., Brion-Meisels, S., & Hoffman, C. (2007). Creating and sustaining peaceable school communities. *Harvard Educational Review, 77,* 1–6.

The Peaceable Schools and Communities framework connects the personal, professional, and political aspects of peace and justice while promoting school and community unity. It provides a set of guiding principles for educators and community members, positive definitions of the self at the individual level, and the promotion of social justice.

Cavazoz-Rehg, P. A., Zayas, L. H., & Spitznagal, E. L. (2007). Legal status, emotional well-being, and subjective health status of Latino immigrants. *Journal of the National-Medical Association, 99,* 1126–1131.

The authors explain that many Latino immigrant youth are at risk of low health quality as a result of trauma, prejudice, discrimination, separation from family members, poverty, low levels of education, unsafe work environments, and low English proficiency. Undocumented youth are at a higher risk of mental and physical health problems, because of the exposure to anxieties and worries about legal status and possibility of deportation.

Child Welfare Information Gateway (www.childwelfare.gov/topics/systemwide/diverse-populations/immigration/wellbeing)

This website offers documents about challenges and traumatic experiences faced by immigrant youth, such as the consequences of having a parent deported. Teacher allies can use the immigrant service directory to find resources available in their state.

García Coll, C. T. (2009). *Immigrant stories: Ethnicity and academics in middle childhood.* Child Development in Cultural Context. New York, NY: Oxford University Press.

The purpose of this book is to expand the comprehension and understanding of the "immigrant paradox," meaning that children in their middle childhood from immigrant families often do better academically and behaviorally and have more resilience than their native-born peers. This book challenges the stereotype of low-performing immigrant children.

GLAAD: Resources for Immigrants (www.glaad.org/blog/resources-immigrantsrecursos-para-inmigrantes)

This website has resources for LGBTQ educators and immigrants that address their unique needs and discuss the issues from their unique perspectives.

Gonzales, R. G. (2016). *Lives in limbo: Undocumented and coming of age in America.* Oakland, CA: University of California Press.

This book covers the lives of 150 undocumented young adults as they reflect on the challenges of growing up undocumented in the Los Angeles area. The author addresses the mental health impact that status has on youth transitioning into adulthood.

Health Behavior in School-Aged Children (HBSC) (www.hbsc.org)

The HBSC research network conducts cross-national research in 45 countries and regions across Europe and North America. HBSC research focuses on areas such as clinical medicine, epidemiology, human biology, pediatrics, pedagogy, psychology, public health, public policy, and sociology.

Illinois Coalition for Immigrant and Refugee Rights (ICIRR) (www.icirr.org)

ICIRR works with organizations and programs to empower the immigrant community in Illinois. Its website provides health care resources for immigrants and refugees. It also introduces fact sheets to make documented and undocumented immigrants aware of health options, including Medicaid and Medicare, in different languages.

Illinois Refugee Mental Health Task Force (ILRMH) (www.ilrmh.org)

ILRMH is a volunteer task force working to raise awareness about the negative impact of current political policies toward immigrants and their detrimental effects on the health and well-being of immigrant youth and their families. The organization also calls attention to immigrants' mental health needs and offers information on available services. ILRMH provides resources about the health and well-being of trauma-exposed immigrant populations. It offers a series of projects, resource lists, and trainings for teachers.

Kennedy Forum Illinois Resources & Hotlines to Support Youth (thekennedyforumillinois. org/resources-to-support-youth)

This website provides a list of crisis hotlines, centers, and associations that help individuals with mental disorders. These resource centers can help Illinois educators support undocumented youths who need mental health assistance.

Morrison, S., Walley, C., Perez, C., Rodriquez, S., Halladeen, I., & Burdier, V. (2016). School counselors working with undocumented students. *VISTAS online*. Retrieved from counseling.org/docs/default-source/vistas/article_4383fd25f16116603abcacff-0000bee5e7.pdf?sfvrsn=4

This article explores academic, college, career, and socioemotional challenges and obstacles faced by undocumented students. It suggests strategies for teachers to use when teaching this population of students.

National School Climate Center (NSCC) (www.schoolclimate.org)

The NSCC promotes a positive school climate that fosters social, emotional, and academic skills. Its goal is to help schools to integrate crucial social and emotional learning with academic instruction to prevent dropout, reduce physical violence and bullying, and to develop healthy and positively engaged adults.

About the Contributors

Hareth Andrade-Ayala is passionate about social change, working with policy, communities, and organizations to help immigrant families through education. She is the founder of Dreamers of Virginia and cofounder of the Dream Project. She is a poet and frequent speaker. The combination of her immigrant background and advocacy experience gives her a unique ability to bridge issues of immigration and education. Hareth has a BA from Trinity Washington University in Washington, DC.

Theresa Austin, PhD, is a daughter of an Okinawan immigrant mother and African American father, raised and educated to cross national, racial, linguistic, and religious borders. Her dream is to see that such rich education be continuous across borders and not a privilege reserved for elites. She is a professor at UMASS–Amherst.

Anita Bright, PhD, is a professor in the Graduate School of Education at Portland State University. A National Board–certified teacher with over 20 years of experience as a K–12 educator, Anita is the ESOL program supervisor and teaches courses in ESOL, social justice, and mathematics education.

Brett Burnham, PhD, is a health educator and researcher who focuses on ameliorating health disparities within underserved and minority communities and has accumulated over 8 years of interdisciplinary experience in the fields of secondary and postsecondary education, community organizing, global health and development, community health education, and peacebuilding.

Aurora Chang, PhD, is an assistant professor at Loyola University Chicago School of Education, where she teaches coursework on social justice education. Her research focuses on undocumented students' paths of educational survival, resistance, and persistence and what educators can do to support them.

María Verónica Cevallos Rodríguez came to the United States from Quito, Ecuador, at age 10. Currently in Gaithersburg, Maryland, she works for a local nonprofit serving at-risk youth. She earned a BA in Communication from the University of Maryland.

Danna Chávez Calvi is a Bolivian native and a former external president of Mason DREAMers, a student organization at George Mason University that aims to create a more inclusive environment for undocumented students through education and advocacy. After earning her BA in communication with a minor in Spanish, she has continued working with first-generation immigrant students at Manassas City Public Schools through the Advancement Via Individual Determination (AVID) program.

Jennifer Crewalk has served on the Mason DREAMers advisory board since 2011 and helps students with liminal statuses to access educational, financial, and emotional support through advocacy efforts on campus and in the community. Jennifer earned a BA in psychology from Rutgers University and an MSEd in intercultural communications from the University of Pennsylvania. She is currently a PhD candidate in educational psychology at George Mason University.

Lori Dodson has taught in PK–5 for 13 years. She currently serves as an ELL national professional training instructor for the National Education Association (NEA). She has also served as a board member of her local TESOL affiliate.

Sandra Duval, PhD, works in PK–12 classrooms, leadership, and curriculum development, and she is a teacher education professor in university and school district settings. Her BA is in sociology and secondary education. Her MA from Teacher's College, Columbia University, is in bilingual education. Her doctorate from the George Washington University is in special education with an emphasis on bilingual education.

Anne Marie Foerster Luu, NBCT, has taught in PK–12 settings for 19 years. She is an adjunct faculty member (focused on assessment as an advocacy tool) of McDaniel College's TESOL program. She was honored by TESOL International as their Teacher of the Year 2013.

Sonja Franeta is a writer, educator, and activist. She has a BA in English and an MA in Russian literature and studied comparative literature at UC Berkeley. She was a teacher, a machinist, and a union/political activist. She has two books of interviews and stories showcasing the LGBTQ community.

Nancy Gutierrez was born in México and raised in Illinois. She became the first in her family to earn a college degree, in 2015 from Beloit College in Wisconsin in health and society. She is an academic coach/mentor to underrepresented minority, low-income, and first-generation college-bound youth.

Susan Harden, PhD, is an assistant professor of education at UNC Charlotte and the director for the civic minor in Urban Youth and Communities and the Charlotte Community Scholars undergraduate research program. Her expertise is in understanding community engagement at cultural institutions and developing engaged scholarship in higher education.

Doug Hernandez is an educator who has taught children from infancy to adolescence. He is the associate director of George Mason University's Early Identification Program, providing holistic supports for first-generation college-bound students. Doug is currently a doctoral student in Mason's School for Conflict Analysis and Resolution.

Carollyn James is a figurative artist and educator who serves a diverse community of English learners in Maryland. Her art is a reflection of the souls she encounters in her community as evidenced by the sincerity and warmth revealed in their portraits. Her art is in galleries as well as in the private collections of both individuals and corporations. She has received several awards for her works, including the 2013 Individual Artist Award in Visual Arts: Painting from the Maryland State Arts Council. She is also being included in a national art collection tour of Asia for the U.S. Department of State.

G. Sue Kasun, PhD, is an assistant professor of language education at Georgia State University. Her research focuses on English learners, transnationalism, ways of knowing, and teacher education, all through critical lenses. She is a former ESOL teacher and administrator in both U.S. and Mexican schools.

Janna Mattson is the instruction and social sciences librarian at George Mason University Libraries, where she supports first-generation college students. She has her BA in music from Virginia Commonwealth University, an MLS from Queens College, and a graduate certificate in eLearning from George Mason University, where she is pursuing a master's in education.

Dario Lopez, originally from Tapachula, Chiapas, Mexico, is a first-generation high school graduate and came to the United States in 2001. He is working toward his undergraduate degree in electrical engineering in Portland, Oregon, and serves as a volunteer tutor in mathematics, physics, chemistry, Spanish, and engineering.

Tiffany Mitchell, PhD, is a social justice educator and advocate for children, with over 8 years of experience. She has a BS in political science and communications from Old Dominion University, a master of arts in teaching from American University, and a PhD in multilingual/multicultural education and education policy from George Mason University.

Natalia arrived in Virginia at the age of 4. She was an honor roll student throughout her schooling and is pursuing a degree in arts education. She was awarded a National Silver Medal Award from the Art and Writing Scholastics Awards and nominated as a Certificate of Merit recipient for the National Society of Arts and Letters at the Kennedy Center.

Maria Gabriela ("Gaby") Pacheco is a nationally recognized immigrant rights leader. In 2010, with three other undocumented students, she led the Trail of Dreams, a four-month walk from Miami to Washington, DC, to call attention to the plight of immigrant families under the threat of deportation. In 2012, as political director for United We Dream, she spearheaded the efforts that led to the Deferred Action for Childhood Arrivals (DACA) program. Gaby holds an AA degree in music education, an AS degree in early childhood education, and a BA in special education K–12 from Miami Dade College.

Marie Price, PhD, is a professor of geography and international affairs at the George Washington University. She is a nonresident fellow of the Migration Policy Institute and serves on the board of the Dream Project. Her current research is on spatial dynamics of immigrant inclusion and exclusion and issues of the undocumented.

Juan A. Ríos Vega, PhD, is an assistant professor at Bradley University, Department of Teacher Education. He has a BA in English and education from the University of Panama; an MA in curriculum and teaching with an emphasis in ESL; a women's and gender studies certificate; and a PhD in philosophy in educational studies, cultural studies concentration, from the University of North Carolina at Greensboro.

Sylvia Y. Sánchez, PhD, is an emerita faculty member of early childhood education at George Mason University. She is known for her research in early bilingualism, integrated early childhood teacher education programs, and the use of family stories to prepare teachers to work with culturally, linguistically, and ability-diverse children and their families.

Elaisa Sánchez Gosnell, PhD, is a retired educator in the field of bilingual/multicultural education focusing on young children whose home language is not English in ECE and ECSE settings. She has provided staff development and training for educators working with culturally, linguistically, and ability-diverse young children and their families at the local, state, and national levels. She taught at George Mason University and in public schools in the Washington, DC, metropolitan area.

Maryam Saroughi is a graduate research assistant and a PhD candidate at George Mason University with a specialization in educational psychology. Her research interests include intercultural communication; social justice for all students, including immigrants with different generational status; and students' success, with a focus on students' academic self-regulation, self-efficacy, and well-being.

Samantha Spinney, PhD, has 15 years of experience working in education, research and evaluation, and policy analysis. She has spent her career teaching and evaluating programs that serve students from marginalized communities, including immigrant youth. She currently works as an education researcher at ICF and an adjunct professor at the George Washington University.

Gertrude Tinker Sachs, PhD, is an associate professor of ESOL, language, and literacy at Georgia State University. She is the chair of the Department of Middle and Secondary Education. Her research interests include reading/literacy in English as a first or second language, culturally responsive teacher professional development, and fostering the development of dialogic learning environments.

Eva K. Thorp, PhD, is an emerita faculty member of early childhood special education at George Mason University. Her research, publications, and grants have focused on family professional partnerships and infusing culturally responsive practices in education. She consults with institutions of higher education to better include these practices in courses and field experiences.

Rodrigo Velasquez-Soto is a community leader and advocate based in Northern Virginia. He is a past president of Mason DREAMers and currently serves on the advisory board. Having previously lived as an undocumented immigrant, his passions center around education, public policy, and social justice.

Emma Violand-Sánchez, PhD, is the founder and president of the board of the Dream Project. She was a member of the Arlington Public Schools Board and adjunct faculty at Georgetown University; she retired as the supervisor of the English for Speakers of Other Languages/High Intensity Language Training Office. Dr. Violand has received numerous community leadership awards and has several publications on learning styles and family engagement.

Robin Witt is a theater director and associate professor of theater at the University of North Carolina–Charlotte. She is a member of Chicago's Steep and Griffin Theatres. Her productions of *Men Should Weep* and *London Wall* were awarded 2015 and 2016 Jeff Awards for Best Production and Best Director.

Shelley Wong, EdD, is an associate professor at George Mason University in teaching culturally and linguistically diverse and exceptional learners and multilingual multicultural education. A former president of TESOL International, she is author of *Dialogic Approaches to TESOL: Where the Ginkgo Tree Grows* and coeditor with I. Nasser and L. Berlin of *Examining Education, Media, and Dialogue Under Occupation: The Case of Palestine/Israel.*

Index

Authors

Subjects